Bond
No.1 for exam success

SATs Skills

Grammar and Punctuation Workbook

10–11 years

OXFORD
UNIVERSITY PRESS

OXFORD
UNIVERSITY PRESS

Great Clarendon Street, Oxford, OX2 6DP, United Kingdom

Oxford University Press is a department of the University of Oxford.
It furthers the University's objective of excellence in research, scholarship,
and education by publishing worldwide. Oxford is a registered trade mark
of Oxford University Press in the UK and in certain other countries

British Library Cataloguing in Publication Data
Data available

978-0-19-274561-3

10 9 8 7 6 5

Paper used in the production of this book is a natural, recyclable product
made from wood grown in sustainable forests. The manufacturing process
conforms to the environmental regulations of the country of origin.

Printed in China

Acknowledgements

Cover illustrations: Lo Cole

Illustration: **p43** Tanja Jovicic/Shutterstock

Although we have made every effort to trace and contact all copyright
holders before publication this has not been possible in all cases. If notified,
the publisher will rectify any errors or omissions at the earliest opportunity.

Links to third party websites are provided by Oxford in good faith and for
information only. Oxford disclaims any responsibility for the materials
contained in any third party website referenced in this work.

(A) Underline the most appropriate modal verb each time so that the sentences make sense. [6]

Example: (Can/Should/Shall) you make it to the match on Sunday?

1 I am so tired I (can/could/shall) fall asleep right now.

2 I am going to the dentist today so I (could/may/must) brush my teeth after breakfast.

3 (May/Will/Would) I ask a question?

4 We (could/must/would) go to the park but it depends upon the weather.

5 (Can/Should/Would) I open the door for you?

6 I (may/might/should) do my homework but I want to play outside.

> **Modal verbs** are 'helper' **verbs** that change the meaning of other **verbs**. **Modal verbs** can suggest how likely something is to happen. **Modal verbs** include 'can', 'could', 'may', 'might', 'must', 'shall', 'ought', 'should', 'will' and 'would'.
>
> **Example:** She may go to the cricket match.

(B) Turn these past tense sentences into the present progressive form using 'is', 'are' or 'am' and the 'ing' ending of the verb. [5]

Example: I watched a film. *I am watching a film.*

1 We shouted out loud.

_____

2 I jumped high.

_____

3 Rose cried with joy.

_____

4 They fought over the computer game.

_____

5 He tidied his bedroom.

_____

> **Verbs** can be used in the past or the present tense. In the present tense, the progressive form of a **verb** describes events that are in progress: an action that is happening. The **present progressive** form uses 'is', 'are' and 'am' and the 'ing' ending of the **verb**.
>
> **Example:** I am learning the guitar.

 Helpful Hint

Remember that a **verb** is a doing or being word and can be used in different tenses: past, present and future.

11

(c) Add the correct pronoun in each space so that the paragraph makes sense. One has been done as an example. [5]

1–5   Mo and Dev were pond dipping at the butterfly park.

They had been at the park for an hour and were feeling very

proud of _____. Mo had identified lots of little

creatures, while Dev had found a newt, _____

was really amazing as _____ are so shy.

Mo's dad was picking the boys up in his taxi so they packed up

_____ pond-dipping nets and waited outside for

_____.

💡 **Helpful Hint**

Remember that **personal pronouns** are used instead of the name of a person, place or object (such as 'I', 'you', 'he', 'she' and 'them') and that **possessive pronouns** show who or what the **noun** belongs to (such as 'his', 'hers', 'its', 'ours' and 'theirs').

Pronouns are used in place of **nouns**. **Relative pronouns** are used to introduce a **relative clause** (which can give more information about the **main clause**). **Example**: This is the match that we want to see. **Reflexive pronouns** end in 'self' or 'selves' and refer back to the **subject** (the **noun** or **pronoun** that the sentence is about) of the sentence or clause. **Example**: She saw herself in the photo.

Relative pronouns: that, when, where, which, who, whom, whose.

Reflexive pronouns: myself, yourself, himself, herself, itself, ourselves, yourselves, themselves.

(d) Add a relative pronoun in each space so that each relative clause makes sense. [5]

Example: *Have you seen the pencil* that *was on the table?*

1   They visited Tom, _____ lived in Wales.

2   Caleb, _____ is 9, is the eldest child.

3   _____ we went camping, our tent leaked.

4   Where is the book _____ I was reading?

5   Jade, _____ birthday is today, is 11.

A **relative clause** either identifies the **noun** or it gives extra information about the **main clause**. It begins with a **relative pronoun**: that, when, where, which, who, whom, whose.

💡 **Helpful Hint**

Essential information can be linked to the clause using either 'that' or 'which'. This is called a **restrictive clause**. **Example**: We are staying in a villa that/which is near the coast. To provide inessential information to the sentence, a **comma** is added first and it is followed by 'which'. This is a **non-restrictive clause**. **Example**: She loves the villa, which is just as well!

10

E) Write out these sentences, adding a dash before and after the parenthesis in each sentence. [5]

Example: *Mrs Jackson everyone's favourite postwoman sorted the mail.*

Mrs Jackson — everyone's favourite postwoman — sorted the mail.

1 Copper with the chemical symbol Cu is a soft, orange-red metal.

_____

2 Lady Jane Grey the nine-day queen was imprisoned in the Tower of London.

_____

3 Silk a fabric first developed in China is created by silkworms.

_____

4 William also known as the Conqueror was England's first Norman king.

_____

5 Jess began to write as she did each morning in her diary.

_____

A **parenthesis** is a word or a short phrase that gives extra information in a sentence. The plural is '**parentheses**'. **Parentheses** can be marked in three ways: dashes show importance or urgency by drawing attention to the words; brackets show less importance and enclose the parenthesis; **commas** show the least level of importance and don't make the information stand apart from the text as much. **Example**: Sam – Mrs Wood's son – is coming to stay.

Yes, I should love to come and stay with you (in Devon) next July.

The suspect, Mr Moss, will attend court on Friday 17th October.

F) Underline the modal verbs and negative modal verbs, and circle the conjunctions in this paragraph. One has been done as an example. [6]

1–6 (When) you finish your breakfast, we <u>could</u> go to the shops,"

Dad said. He looked at the sky thoughtfully. "If it starts to rain though, we might need to take our coats," he added.

Rav said, "Dad, if it is sunny, can we go to the park afterwards?"

Dad looked at his watch. "Unless you hurry up with your breakfast, we won't be going anywhere!"

A **conditional sentence** has two clauses and the **main clause** is dependent, or conditional, on the other clause. **Conditional sentences** often use modal and negative **modal verbs** (such as 'ought' or wouldn't') and the **conjunctions** 'if', 'when' or 'unless'. **Example**: I may go if Mum takes me.

11

(G) Write whether the use of ellipsis in these sentences shows suspense, omission or stopping. [7]

Example: *She said she was going out … but didn't say where.* omission

1   We had a great time at the party then, well …

_____

2   The car rounded the corner at breakneck speed and into the path of the oncoming lorry … _____

3   I was halfway through the field … I saw the bull heading towards me. _____

4   We thought about doing it, but decided not to.

_____

5   Driving on the motorway will be easier. _____

6   "Well," hesitated Mrs Piper, "I wonder ..." _____

7   Just as he thought he was safe, Miss Fu span round furiously … _____

> **Ellipsis** is where an expected word has been missed out (omission).
>
> **Example:** 'I love sweets so I went to the shop to buy some sweets.' can be written as 'I love sweets so I went to the shop to buy some.' The word 'sweets' has not been repeated at the end of the sentence.
>
> In writing, **ellipsis** can show suspense using three dots (…).
>
> **Example:** He stared up in horror …
>
> It can also be used to show that someone is stopping their thoughts or speech.
>
> **Example:** Now, what was I doing …

(H) Underline the preposition phrases. There are two in each sentence. [6]

Example: *The book <u>from the library</u> had been borrowed <u>by my brother</u>.*

1   The tall, thin man beside the street light is watching the house over the road.

2   The woman peered through the window as the police car pulled up at the kerb.

3   The young shepherd appeared over the hill with his flock of sheep.

4   The boy from next door came to the quiz.

5   "The tennis racquet over there is mine," she said, pointing at the bench.

6   She believed an ogre lived under the bridge but she had never been down to see it.

> **Prepositions** often describe the location of a **noun**.
>
> **Example:** The picture is on the wall.
>
> A **preposition phrase** begins with the **preposition** and is followed by a **noun**, **pronoun** or **noun phrase**.
>
> **Example:** 'inside the box'. A **preposition phrase** helps to give more detail to a sentence.

13

Ⓐ Use words from the following sentences to complete the table. [12]

It was a fabulous idea for the fleet of ships to sail into Southampton all at once before they sailed to Asia.

I have an interest in visiting Japan where troops of monkeys play and the forests of trees grow. My enthusiasm for travel is great!

Common nouns	Proper nouns	Collective nouns	Abstract nouns

> A **common noun** is the general name for a person, place or thing. **Proper nouns** always have a capital letter and are used for names of people, places, days, months and organisations. **Collective nouns** are used for groups of people or things. **Abstract nouns** refer to ideas or feelings. **Example**: skill, beauty.

Ⓑ Write whether these sentences are written using the active or passive voice. [8]

Example: *Elena is eating a sandwich.*   *active*

1   Mum ate the last slice of birthday cake. _____

2   The children's toys were tidied up by the nursery staff.

_____

3   Annie's teeth were cleaned every six months. _____

4   Dad baked an apple pie for dessert. _____

5   Julien broke his phone on holiday. _____

6   The biscuits were all eaten by the night staff. _____

7   Raj put his birthday money in the bank. _____

8   The children were given a lift home from school.

_____

> In the **active voice**, the action is being done by the **subject** (the person or thing in the sentence).
>
> **Example**: Squirrels hide the acorns.
>
> In the **passive voice**, the subject has the action done to them.
>
> **Example**: The acorns were hidden by the squirrels.

 Helpful Hint

Remember, the **passive voice** focuses on what happens, rather than who does it, while the **active voice** usually includes this information.

20

(c) Turn these present perfect sentences into the past progressive form using 'was' or 'were' and the 'ing' ending of the verb. [5]

Example: *Molly has opened the letter.*   *Molly was opening the letter.*

1   I have listened to the exciting match on the radio.

   _____

2   She has driven way above the legal speed limit.

   _____

3   Alice has slid wildly down the bank towards the path at the bottom.

   _____

4   Moses has cycled quickly to his friend's house.

   _____

5   He has eaten toast and honey for breakfast before school.

   _____

Helpful Hint

Remember that the past tense has already happened and the present tense is happening now. The **past progressive** tense describes events that happened in the past where the action was ongoing.

(d) Use each word once to complete the sentences. [4]

> surely   maybe   definitely   probably

Some **adverbs** tell us how likely something is.

Example: "Surely he sent his mum a birthday card," said Gina.

"Perhaps he forgot," said Jake.

1   It has been so cold lately, we will _____ have some snow soon.

2   I'm at the end of your road now, so I will _____ be there within the next five minutes.

3   _____ you want to eat dinner first, before you eat that pudding?

4   _____ I'll have soup for lunch today, I'm not sure.

Helpful Hint

Remember, some **adverbs** such as, 'maybe' and 'perhaps', can come at the beginning of the clause. Other **adverbs** that indicate possibility usually come in front of the main **verb**.

9

(E) Underline the formal phrases so that this letter is written in a formal style. One has been done as an example. [7]

Dear Mr Morgan

(I'm made up/I am delighted to hear) that building work will (be beginning/commence) next Monday. (I am inclined to agree/Yeah, you're right) that a design such as this is (spot on/most suitable) for the village and I am sure that you will be (extremely happy/ well chuffed) with the outcome.

Please do (give me a bell/get in touch) if (you need any info/I can be of further assistance).

(All the best mate/Yours sincerely)

Ian Goodall

> **Informal (personal) writing** is used when writing for ourselves, our family and friends. **Informal writing** uses **personal pronouns** (such as I, me, you), contractions (such as I'm, don't, can't), incomplete sentences and common phrases. **Formal (impersonal) writing** does not use contractions and often uses the third-person word 'it' instead of personal pronouns.

(F) Write out these sentences, using commas in the correct places. [6]

Example: *My cats Fred and Ginger are very friendly.*

> *My cats, Fred and Ginger, are very friendly.*

1   My hobbies include riding my pet parrot and swimming.

   _____

2   The newsagent I forget his name orders my magazine for me each week.

   _____

3   Dana invited Meera Amelia Jodie and Beth to her party.

   _____

4   Next month before I go on holiday I must remember to ask Jamie to look after the cats.

   _____

5   I put the paper drinks bottles and cans in the recycling bin.

   _____

6   Al enjoyed running the countryside and all outdoor pursuits.

   _____

> **Commas** are used to separate items in a list, to separate the extra information (**parenthesis**) from the **main clause** and to avoid ambiguity so that the meaning of a sentence is clear.

13

(G) Place a colon in the correct places in the following text. [3]

Example: *He pondered before replying "What he said is true."*

He pondered before replying: "What he said is true."

The explorer Edward Wilson
- came from Cheltenham
- was a superb artist from a very early age
- was chosen to accompany Scott on his expedition to the South Pole.

Edward Wilson said "I will accompany Scott on his expedition as his artist, regardless of the dangers to my life."

He had several responsibilities to record the ice shelf, ice caves, penguins and other wildlife. Sadly, Wilson died with Scott on their expedition, but he provided us with a great deal more information about the South Pole.

> A **colon** (:) can be used before **bullet points**, before an explanation, before a list that follows a **main clause**, after a character's name in a playscript and before introducing a quotation.

(H) Write the following out using bullet points using the correct punctuation. [2]

1   To do   tidy room   return library book   call Grandma

_____

_____

_____

_____

2   My reasons for choosing this book are   I like the picture on the cover   the main character is similar to me   it is set in the 1960s

_____

_____

_____

> **Bullet points** are used to list key information. There are different ways to punctuate **bullet points**.
>
> If the text following a **bullet point** is not a proper sentence, it does not need to begin with capital letter and end with a full stop.
>
> If the text following the **bullet point** is a full sentence, it should begin with a capital letter and end with a full stop. Remember to always introduce bullet points with a colon.

5

(F) Write out these sentences, changing the subject for subjective personal pronouns and changing the object for objective personal pronouns. [3]

Example: *Jeff and Jackie visited the castle.* *They visited it.*

1 Mr Singh enjoyed his visit to the museum.

_____

2 Juliet and Ruby acted in the school play

_____

3 Toby was reading to Amelia and Grace.

_____

There are two types of **personal pronouns**: **subjective** and **objective**. The **subject** in a sentence comes before the **verb** and the **subjective personal pronouns** that replace the **subject** are: I, you, he, she, it, we, they. The **object** comes after the **verb** and the objective **personal pronouns** that replace the **object** are: me, you, him, her, it, us, them.

(G) Put a hyphen in the correct place so that each sentence makes sense. [5]

Example: *Where is the second hand bookshop?* *second-hand*

1 My aunt has a part time job at the hospital.

2 There are no smoking signs at the cinema.

3 My mum does twenty four hour shifts at work each month.

4 We are proud to sell sugar free sweets and drinks.

5 We watched the man eating shark carefully from the shore.

A **hyphen** can link words together to make the meaning clear. **Example:** The twenty five year olds all enjoyed the party.

Hyphens can make the meaning clear: The twenty five-year-olds all enjoyed the party.

(H) Underline the informal phrases so that this letter is written in a personal style. One has been done as an example. [7]

Hi Grandpa

(<u>How are you</u>?/I trust that you are well.) Have you heard that (Father has resigned from his position?/Dad has quit his job?) Mum says it's time for him to (rise to the challenge/sort himself out) and find something else. She says that they (are broke/do not have sufficient funds) and she is (most unhappy/in a right mood). I hope that (the situation will soon resolve itself/it'll soon be OK). Can't wait to see you on Sunday.

(Yours sincerely/Lots of love and kisses)

(Jess xxx/Miss Jessica Hastings)

15

Quick quiz

1   **Choose a modal verb so the sentence makes sense.**

Jakub asked if he (shall/could/would) ride his bike to the park.

2   **Turn this past tense sentence into the present progressive form.**

She cleaned her scooter. _____

3–6 **Add a pronoun in each space so that the paragraph makes sense.**

"Help _____" Mum said to everyone and _____ all tucked into the

feast. There was loads of food. _____ knew how to feed _____!

7   **Add a relative pronoun in the space so that the relative clause makes sense.**

We travelled to Egypt _____ we sailed along the Nile.

8   **Write out this sentence, adding a comma before and after the parenthesis.**

The work of Henry Moore the famous sculptor can be seen at the Yorkshire
Sculpture Park.

9–10 **Underline the modal verb and circle the conjunction in this sentence.**

If I get a guitar for my birthday, I could join a band.

11   **Decide how the ellipsis is used in this sentence.**

I need to get some yellow paint because I don't have any. _____

12–13 **Underline the two preposition phrases in this sentence.**

Under the tree we found the dormouse sleeping in his nest.

14   **Decide whether this sentence uses a personal or impersonal style.**

It is advisable that our customers register their computer with us. _____

15   **Underline the conditional phrase in this sentence.**

When I get home I am going to make a smoothie.

16–17 **Write these words with hyphens in the correct place.**

lefthanded _____ reenter _____

17

Ⓐ Underline the most appropriate modal verb each time so that the sentences make sense. [5]

Modal verbs ⓘ
help to show how likely something is to happen. These can include the negative form: can't, couldn't, may not, might not, mustn't, shan't, shouldn't, won't, wouldn't.

Example: *We (couldn't/wouldn't/shouldn't) make too much noise as my sister is asleep.*

1 It was so light, I (mustn't/won't/couldn't) get to sleep.

2 You (can't/won't/may) believe what I have just heard!

3 It is important to remember that you (wouldn't/won't/mustn't) touch a firework after it has been lit.

4 I used to love peanut butter but now I (shan't/can't/won't) stand it!

5 (Mustn't/Wouldn't/Can't) you prefer to do something else?

Ⓑ Write out these sentences, adding a comma before and after the parenthesis in each sentence. [5]

Example: *The smoke detector with its new battery worked perfectly.*

The smoke detector, with its new battery, worked perfectly.

1 Babbacombe model village set in award-winning gardens is my favourite place to visit.

_____

2 The life span for a dog is on average 10–14 years.

_____

3 Kanchenjunga India's highest mountain is nearly 8,600 metres tall.

_____

4 In winter when it is cold I wear a woolly hat.

_____

5 The pond teeming with wildlife is in the centre of the garden.

_____

💡 **Helpful Hint**

Remember that **parentheses** are additional words or short phrases that add new or unconnected information to the sentence. Dashes, brackets or **commas** can be used to show **parentheses**.

10

c Add the correct pronoun in each space so that the paragraph makes sense.
One has been done as an example. [7]

"Would *you* like to come round to my house?" _____ asked Jasmine and Jaimee.

The twins, _____ new house had been empty for nearly a year, had just moved in

across the road and _____ were delighted that people were now living there. I was

even happier as the girls were the same age as _____. Happily, _____

were able to come over, so _____ all played games in the garden and enjoyed

_____ very much.

Helpful Hint

Remember that there are four different types of **pronoun**: personal,
possessive, relative and reflexive. **Pronouns** are used to replace the **noun**.

D Underline the conditional phrases in these sentences. [9]

Example: *I won't go <u>unless you do</u>.*

1   Unless you brush your hair, you will look scruffy on your school photograph.

2   The roses will bloom until November as long as we don't have a sharp frost.

3   If you have finished your homework, we could play rounders with the others on
the playing field.

4   I'd like to be the goalkeeper, if Ahmed doesn't mind.

5   We're going to the theatre in London, providing we can get tickets.

6   As long as Mrs Tang agrees, I will arrange a coach for the journey.

7   Providing the doctor says he is well enough, Matthew will come out of hospital
on Tuesday.

8   I should arrive before the performance begins unless the bus is running late.

9   I'll put my name down for the competition if you do too.

16

Ⓔ Place a different time adverbial from the list at the beginning of each sentence to show the sequence of events. One has been done as an example. [4]

| Finally | First | Meanwhile | Next | Second |

First, cream together 100 g each of butter and sugar.

1 _____, add two beaten eggs, 200 g of self-raising flour and two teaspoons of cocoa, stirring until the mixture is light and fluffy.

2 _____, put the batter into two 18 cm tins and bake for 25 minutes at 180°C in a pre-heated oven.

3 _____, whip 300 ml of double cream, adding 2 teaspoons of icing sugar.

4 _____, remove the cake from the oven, allow it to cool, then fill it with the cream mixture.

> **Time adverbials** such as 'next', 'after that' and 'finally' help to link ideas together and show the order in which something happened. When they are placed at the start of a sentence they are described as fronted adverbials. **Example**: After the thunderstorm, the sun began to shine.

Ⓕ Turn these words into verbs by adding a suffix: 'ate', 'en', 'ify' or 'ise'. [10]

Example: *sad*   *sadden*

1 captive   _____

2 equal   _____

3 light   _____

4 solid   _____

5 loose   _____

6 pressure   _____

7 pure   _____

8 donation   _____

9 electric   _____

10 fright   _____

> A **suffix** is a group of letters that can be added to the end of a **root word** to turn it into another word. A **root word** is a word that can have a **prefix** or **suffix** added to it. A **noun** or **adjective** can be turned into a **verb** by using the **suffixes** 'ate', 'en', 'ify' or 'ise'. The **root word** may need to be changed before the **suffix** is added, using the spelling rules you already know.

14

Ⓖ Underline the main clauses in this paragraph. One has been done as an example. [5]

<u>He quickly finished painting the bench</u> as he was keen to get the job done before the football match. On his way out, he ran into Grandma who was visiting for the afternoon. She went for a wander in the garden, with no idea that he had painted the bench. The sun was warm and Grandma closed her eyes and slept.

Ⓗ Underline the six spelling or grammar mistakes in the following text. Then write the original word and the correct word below. One has been done as an example. [6]

The painting had been <u>hang</u> on the drawing room wall for decades. The watercolour was a pale, pastel-coloured seascape of a lady lucking out to sea. Although the hint of a smile played at the corners of her mouths, her eyes looked heavy with sorrow. Who was the lady? Who had painted her? Who did she look so sad? The painting had long been forgotted by everyone. The sun had bleached the wallpaper around it from primrose yelow to sickly cream, yet the painting lay untouched by the sun, shielded by it's protective glass.

Example: *hang*   *hanging*

1 _____   _____

2 _____   _____

3 _____   _____

4 _____   _____

5 _____   _____

6 _____   _____

11

A Underline the formal phrases so that this report is written in an impersonal style. One has been done as an example. [5]

<u>(On Wednesday 27th September at 17:42</u>/Last Wednesday at about a quarter to six), the duty officers (entered the property/went into the house) after a call was made to the station. (Going in/Upon entering the property), PC Jackson saw the suspect carrying a large holdall in his left hand and a games console in his right hand. PC Jackson (asked the suspect to remain in the kitchen/told the man to stay in the kitchen) while the house was searched by PC Khan. A number of mobile phones and DVDs were (recovered from the suspect's holdall/found in his bag). The suspect was arrested (on suspicion of theft/for stealing things).

Signed: PC Jackson

B Turn these past tense sentences into the present progressive form using 'is', 'are' or 'am' and the 'ing' ending of the verb. [5]

Example: *I called Danielle.*   I am calling Danielle.

1 We spoke to the head teacher about traffic outside the school.

_____

2 They swam across the English Channel to raise money for charity.

_____

3 Our friend came first in the pancake-tossing competition.

_____

4 Those girls were playing netball after school.

_____

5 Mr Nash built a shed for his tools in the garden.

_____

💡 **Helpful Hint**

Remember that the past tense has already happened and the present tense is happening now. The **present progressive** means that the action or event is in progress.

10

Ⓒ Write the following sentences formally, in the subjunctive form. [5]

Example: *If I was you, I'd definitely go on the trip to Spain.*

If I were you, I would definitely go on the trip to Spain.

1   I wish it was Christmas already!

_____

2   He could go to the beach if the weather was nicer.

_____

3   I would eat the cake if it was lemon and poppy seed flavour.

_____

4   She would make it to the concert if the train was on time.

_____

5   I would answer my phone if I was sure it was you.

_____

> The **subjunctive mood** is usually used for formal speech and writing. It is sometimes used to express a wish, a suggestion or to talk about something that has not happened (or might not happen).
>
> We use the subjunctive form 'were' instead of 'was' with 'I', 'he', 'she' and 'it'.

Ⓓ Underline the conditional phrases in these sentences. [8]

Example: *If you tidy your bedroom, you can go out with your friends.*

1   Providing the weather is fine, we will hold the summer fair on the playing field.

2   I would like to have a dog if it was already house trained.

3   We may go to Spain for our holiday this year, unless we have to buy a new car.

4   When the school bell has rung, we can all go out into the playground for break.

5   You can go to football as long as Dad is back in time to take you.

6   Unless there is a problem, I will meet you outside the cinema on Saturday afternoon.

7   We're going to the beach at the weekend, providing it's not raining heavily.

8   "Would you like to come to see the band with me, if I can get tickets?"

> Remember, a **conditional sentence** is when one part of the sentence is dependent on another part.

(E) Turn these words into verbs by adding a suffix: 'ate', 'en', 'ify' or 'ise'. [12]

Example: *operation*   *operate*

1   agony   _____

2   beauty   _____

3   damp   _____

4   class   _____

5   concentration   _____

6   glory   _____

7   category   _____

8   wide   _____

9   tight   _____

10   separation   _____

11   horror   _____

12   inflation   _____

 Helpful Hint

Remember that a **noun** or **adjective** can be turned into a **verb** by using a
suffix. The **root word** may need to be changed before adding the **suffix**.

(F) Underline the main clauses in this paragraph. One has been done as an example. [5]

<u>The two boys and the girl stood at the doorstep</u>, their faces expectant. The girl was fed
up with wearing the pointed hat and she didn't like carrying the broom. The older boy had
chosen a ghost costume while his younger brother was dressed all in red, with a huge pair
of horns. The girl crossed her fingers, hoping for sweets or some stickers.

 Helpful Hint

Remember that a **main clause** is one that can stand alone as a
simple sentence.

17

(G) Use words from the following sentences to complete the table. [6]

The family snuggled under warm blankets as they settled into the seats. The ponies had bells attached to their reins and, as the sleigh gently moved, the bells tinkled prettily. The snow reflected the moonlight — what a magical night!

Adverb	Adjective	Pronoun

(H) Underline the six spelling or grammar mistakes in the following text. Then write the original word and the correct word below. One has been done as an example. [6]

The Georgian period was a <u>fascinate</u> period of history in the 18th and 19th centuries. The Georgians resigned from 1714 to 1830 and, during this era, the first four kings were all called George! Although previous rulers all shaping our lives, the Georgians had the gratest influence on how we live today; they're impact was enormous. Wear would the edwardians or the Victorians be if it were not for the Georgians?

Example: *fascinate*   *fascinating*

1 _____   _____

2 _____   _____

3 _____   _____

4 _____   _____

5 _____   _____

6 _____   _____

Answers

Unit 1

(A) **1–6** could, must, May, could, Can, should

(B) **1** We are shouting out loud.
  2 I am jumping high.
  3 Rose is crying with joy.
  4 They are fighting over the computer game.
  5 He is tidying his bedroom.

(C) **1–5** themselves, which, they, their, him

(D) **1–5** who, who, When, that, whose

(E) **1** – with the chemical symbol Cu –
  2 – the nine-day queen =
  3 – a fabric first developed in China =
  4 also known as the Conqueror
  5 – as she did each morning –

(F) **1–6** "When you finish your breakfast, we could go to the shops," Dad said. He looked at the sky thoughtfully. "If it starts to rain, though, we might need to take our coats," he added.
  Rav said, "Dad, if it is sunny, can we go to the park afterwards?"
  Dad looked at his watch. "Unless you hurry up with your breakfast, we won't be going anywhere!"

(G) **1–7** stopping, suspense, suspense, omission, omission, stopping, suspense

(H) **1** beside the street light, over the road.
  2 through the window, at the kerb.
  3 over the hill, with his flock of sheep.
  4 from next door, to the quiz.
  5 over there, at the bench.
  6 under the bridge, down to see it.

Unit 2

(A) **1–12**
Common: ships, monkeys, trees
Proper: Southampton, Asia, Japan
Collective: fleet, troops, forests
Abstract: idea, interest, enthusiasm

(B) **1–8** active, passive, passive, active, active, passive, active, passive

(C) **1** I was listening to the exciting match on the radio.
  2 She was driving way above the legal speed limit.
  3 Alice was sliding wildly down the bank towards the path at the bottom.

  4 Moses was cycling quickly to his friend's house.
  5 He was eating toast and honey for breakfast before school.

(D) **1–4** probably, definitely, Surely, Maybe

(E) **1–7** I am delighted to hear, commence, I am inclined to agree, most suitable, extremely happy, get in touch, I can be of further assistance, Yours sincerely

(F) **1** My hobbies include riding, my pet parrot and swimming.
  2 The newsagent, I forget his name, orders my magazine for me each week.
  3 Dana invited Meera, Amelia, Jodie and Beth to her party.
  4 Next month, before I go on holiday, I must remember to ask Jamie to look after the cats.
  5 I put the paper, drinks bottles and cans in the recycling bin.
  6 Al enjoyed running, the countryside and all outdoor pursuits.

(G) **1–3** The explorer Edward Wilson: Edward Wilson said: He had several responsibilities:

(H) **1** To do:
  • tidy room
  • return library book
  • call Grandma
  2 My reasons for choosing this book are:
  • I like the picture on the cover.
  • The main character is similar to me.
  • It is set in the 1960s.

Unit 3

(A) **1–4** definitely, perhaps, clearly, possibly

(B) **1** (the Marybelle Rose)
  2 (who lived to be 90)
  3 (born just a few weeks ago)
  4 (the largest island in the Caribbean)
  5 (on Saturday)

(C) **1–6** she, their, her, yours, mine, ourselves

(D) **1** underneath the shed, with her seven cubs
  2 in his trawler, out to the ocean
  3 through the woods, between the tree branches
  4 in the oven, on the kitchen table

(E) **1–6 Determiner:** the, some **Pronoun:** herself, they **Preposition:** into, across

(F) 1 He enjoyed his visit to it.   3 He was reading to them.
    2 They acted in it.

(G) **1–5** part-time, no-smoking, four-hour, sugar-free, man-eating

(H) **1–7** How are you?, Dad has quit his job?, sort himself out, are broke, in a right mood, it'll soon be OK, Lots of love and kisses, Jess xxx

Quick quiz

1 could   2 She is cleaning her scooter.
3 yourselves   4 we/they   5 She
6 us/them   7 where
8 The work of Henry Moore, the famous sculptor, can be seen at the Yorkshire Sculpture Park.
9–10 (If) could
11 Omission
12–13 Under the tree, in his nest.
14 Impersonal   15 When I get home
16 left-handed   17 re-enter

Unit 4

(A) **1–5** couldn't, won't, mustn't, can't, Wouldn't

(B) 1 Babbacombe model village, set in award-winning gardens, is my favourite place to visit.
    2 The life span for a dog is, on average, 10–14 years.
    3 Kanchenjunga, India's highest mountain, is nearly 8,600 metres tall.
    4 In winter, when it is cold, I wear a woolly hat.
    5 The pond, teeming with wildlife, is in the centre of the garden.

(C) **1–7** you, I, whose, we, me, they, we, ourselves

(D) 1 Unless you brush your hair
    2 as long as we don't have a sharp frost
    3 If you have finished your homework
    4 if Ahmed doesn't mind
    5 providing we can get tickets
    6 As long as Mrs Tang agrees
    7 Providing the doctor says he is well enough
    8 unless the bus is running late
    9 if you do too

(E) 1 Second 2 Next 3 Meanwhile 4 Finally

(F) **1–10** captivate, equalise, lighten, solidify, loosen, pressurise, purify, donate, electrify, frighten

(G) **1–5** he was keen to get the job done before the football match, he ran into Grandma who was visiting for the afternoon, She went for a wander in the garden, The sun was warm, Grandma closed her eyes and slept.

(H) 1 lucking, looking   4 forgotted, forgotten
    2 mouths, mouth   5 yelow, yellow
    3 Who, Why   6 it's, its

Unit 5

(A) **1–5** entered the property, Upon entering the property, asked the suspect to remain in the kitchen, recovered from the suspect's holdall, on suspicion of theft.

(B) 1 We are speaking to the head teacher about traffic outside the school.
    2 They are swimming across the English Channel to raise money for charity.
    3 Our friend is coming first in the pancake-tossing competition.
    4 Those girls are playing netball after school.
    5 Mr Nash is building a shed for his tools in the garden.

(C) 1 I wish it were Christmas already!
    2 He could go to the beach if the weather were nicer.
    3 I'd eat the cake if it were lemon and poppy seed flavour.
    4 She would make it to the concert if the train were on time.
    5 I would answer my phone if I were sure it were you.

(D) 1 Providing the weather is fine
    2 if it was already house trained
    3 unless we have to buy a new car
    4 When the school bell has rung
    5 as long as Dad is back in time to take you.
    6 Unless there is a problem
    7 providing it's not raining heavily
    8 if I can get tickets

(E) **1–12** agonise, beautify, dampen, classify, concentrate, glorify, categorise, widen, tighten, separate, horrify, inflate

(F) **1–5** The girl was fed up with wearing the pointed hat, she didn't like carrying the broom, The older boy had chosen a ghost costume, his younger brother was dressed all in red, The girl crossed her fingers.

(G) **1–6 Adverb:** gently, prettily **Adjective:** warm, magical **Pronoun:** they, their

(H) 1 resigned, reigned   4 they're, their
    2 shaping, shaped   5 Wear, Where
    3 gratest, greatest   6 edwardians, Edwardians

Unit 6

(A) **1–6** re-press, co-worker, pre-recorded, co-star, pre-existed, co-own

(B) **1–8** active, passive, active, active, active, passive, passive, passive

(C) **1** It was rung by her. **2** We went to see him.
3 They climbed steadily up it.

(D) **1–7** Can't remember, I don't care – it's all good, I don't have to go to, do the same old thing, truly HORRENDOUS!

(E) **1–6** formulate, signify, patronise, strengthen, simplify, visualise

(F) **1–5** huge, quiet, warm, wet, narrow

(G) **1–4** Second, After that, Meanwhile, Finally

Quick quiz

1–3 Second, Next, Finally
4 falsify
5 realise
6 identify

7–10 It is not possible to, road congestion, it is hoped that, the estimated time of arrival will be

11 I wash my hands of you. Remain quiet.
12 It's nice and toasty. I want nothing more to do with you.
13 Shut up! It's lovely and warm.

14 surounded/surrounded
15 inhabat/inhabit
16 has/have
17 know/knows
18 their/there
19 observe/observed
20 feet/feat

Unit 7

(A) **1–5** wouldn't, Won't, can't, don't, mustn't

(B) **1** (who gurgled happily)
2 (in North-East Africa)
3 (who signed the Magna Carta)
4 (usually a mountain)
5 (a breed of British pig)

(C) **1** outside the window, against his body
2 across the grass, to its nest
3 around the Christmas tree, on the top
4 from Dad's desk, beside the notepad
5 from the bakery, up Ben Nevis

(D) **1–4** himself, We, it, who

(E) **1** invasive, steadily **3** vividly, beautiful
2 prehistoric, stealthily **4** hurtful, spitefully

(F) **1–6** complex, simple, compound, complex, compound, complex

(G) **1–4** when the land lies under thick snow, Although the winter is long and hard, When the seasons change, once the ice melts.

(H) **1** eratic, erratic **5** here, hear
2 wipped, whipped **6** breaked, broke
3 walking, walked **7** persisting, persisted
4 chanced, changed

(I) **1–4** interaction, irresponsible, untested, enchantment

Unit 8

(A) **1** Pip bought the ingredients for a fish pie.
2 Jon taught Michael how to play the piano.
3 The ice cream melted in the sunshine.
4 Ishmael thought about his friend who is on holiday in Australia.
5 Abdullah and Talal visited their brother in hospital.

(B) **1–2** He, it **5–9** He, himself, His, he, it
3–4 her, them **10–11** Which, it

(C) **1** clothes; the chest, empty; her shoes
2 beautiful; the flower
3 dancer; she appeared
4 *Private Peaceful;* David Walliams, *The Demon Dentist;* Anthony Horowitz, *Stormbreaker;* Michelle Magorian
5 packed; the audience
6 park; they
7 Herefordshire; Attingham, Shropshire; Kenliworth

(D) **1** As long as, can **5** ought, if
2 Unless, will **6** Providing, should
3 If, would **7** may, as long as
4 might, if **8** If, must

(E) **1–6** semi-industrial, ex-teacher, co-pilot, anti-poverty, pre-owned, Pre-Roman

(F) **1–7** done you the world of good, got the hang of landscape pictures!, tickled pink, What d'you mean, are you good enough?, bet that's popular, Anyhow, must dash, See you Sunday!

(G) **1–6** it was too dangerous not to wear a hard hat and protective gear, safety had to come first, The lift raised the men back to ground level, the smell of fresh air was truly wonderful, The man wiped the thick film of black dust from his face, he set off towards home

(H) **Conjunction:** yet, and, but **Pronoun:** they, Their, themselves **Modal verb:** should, must, might

(I) **1** If I were tired enough, I might be able to fall asleep.

2 If ballet were easier, everyone could do it.

3 I would find out interesting things if I were someone's pen pal.

4 I wish I were playing football this weekend, if only I didn't have a broken leg.

Unit 9

(A) **1** fantastic **2** difficult **3** sad **4** scared

(B) **1–3** suspense, omission, omission

(C) **1** at the postman, up the path

2 at the information centre, next to the church

3 outside Dudley, in the West Midlands

4 beneath the big top, through the crowds

5 around the pool, off the diving board

6 around the table, from huge plates

7 After music practice, outside the hall

8 over the ocean, through the clouds

(D) **1–5** Secondly, Thirdly, Meanwhile, Then, Finally

(E) **1** Seeing the ice cream van

2 because I was still hungry

3 where I work on Saturdays

4 After the play

5 because of the rain

6 ordered the day before

7 Before she could save her work

8 at its best in the spring

(F) **1–7** reformed, enjoyment, imposing, inactive, disagreeable, unavoidable, imperfection

(G) **1–7** simple, compound, complex, simple, complex, compound, complex

(H) **1** Dr Delaney was seeing her patients at the surgery.

2 The chef was preparing the food in the kitchen.

3 Our friend was completing the crossword during his morning break.

4 The elephants were walking around the enclosure.

5 The receptionist was printing out the information for the customer.

(I) **1** cue, queue **4** it's, its

2 easily, easy **5** activitiies, activities

3 We'all, We all **6** hole, whole

Unit 10

1 wouldn't **2** won't

3 It was now July and, coming from the west, the storm looked foreboding.

4 I looked up, shielding my eyes against the sun, and saw the aeroplane.

5 The summer fete has, with regret, been postponed until further notice.

6 From base camp, by huskies

7 at the archives, with local history records

8–11 Happy Birthday!, have a super fun day, Hugs and kisses, Aunty Mimi

12–14 complex, simple, compound

15–17 presenting, unfriendly, recovering

18 foolishly, broken

19 initial, carefully

20 successfully, beautiful

21 slender, skilfully

22 Joan is joking with her old friend Derek.

23 Anders is carrying the boxes from the car.

24–29 their, herself, whose, yourselves, He, yours

30 When, can

31 If, could

32 Providing, will

33 may not, unless

34 ought, may

35–39 auto-immune, twenty-odd, re-sign, re-sort, hard-working

40–45 the horses were in their stables, we tramped along the road, The ducks and geese were all settled down, the chickens just needed rounding up and securing in their hen house, The final stage of the nightly ritual was to feed the cat, then we went to bed

46–48 suspense, stopping, omission

49 watching the mouse **53** dorset, Dorset

50 when the sun is shining **54** shunning, shunned

51 know, knowledge **55** theres, there's

52 cost, coast

(A4)

Ⓐ Put a hyphen in the correct place so that each sentence makes sense. [6]

Example: *It was so cold I had to deice the car windscreen.* de-ice

1   Connor needed to repress his trousers before his interview.

_____

2   Rachel is my coworker; we work well together.

_____

3   My brother prerecorded the programme before we went on

holiday. _____

4   The actor and his costar both won an Academy Award.

_____

5   The dinosaurs preexisted human beings.

_____

6   Philip and his sister, Christine, coown a caravan in the Lake

District. _____

> A **prefix** is a group of letters that can be added to the start of a word to turn it into another word. A **hyphen** can join a **prefix** (for example, 'anti', 'ex' and 'co') to a word to help make the meaning clear, especially if a word has a different meaning without the **hyphen**. **Example**: One meaning of 'recover' is 'regain', but 're-cover' (where the **prefix** 're' means 'again' or 'do again') means to cover again: 'We re-covered our books.'
>
> The **hyphen** can also be added if the last letter of the **prefix** is the same vowel that begins the word. **Example**: 're-elect'.

Ⓑ Write whether these sentences are written using the active or passive voice. [8]

Example: *Elena is eating a sandwich.* active

1   Joe walked all the dogs in the neighbourhood.   _____

2   The jelly was made by a famous chef.   _____

3   I answered two questions in class today.   _____

4   Miss Hill wrote on the board with a permanent pen!   _____

5   The librarian put the books away.   _____

6   The match was attended by hundreds of people.   _____

7   The mystery was left unsolved by the detectives.   _____

8   The water was knocked over.   _____

14

C Write out these sentences, changing the subject for subjective personal pronouns and changing the object for objective personal pronouns. [3]

Example: *Aleksander played the piano.* He played it.

1 The doorbell was rung by the girl.

_____

2 Myself and my friend went to see Mr Choudry.

_____

3 Jack and Harry climbed steadily up the ladder.

_____

Helpful Hint

Remember that the **subject** in a sentence comes before the **verb** and the **object** comes after the **verb**.

D Underline the informal phrases so that this diary entry is written in a personal style. One has been done as an example. [5]

Friday afternoon.

Well, today was amazing! I called Emily and (this evening I have been invited to a social event/I'm off to a party later)! (I cannot recall/Can't remember) whether it was her cousin's birthday or whatever, but (I don't care – it's all good/I am happy regardless of the reason)! It means that (I do not have to attend/I don't have to go to) the rugby match with Matt. It's bad enough that I can't be left alone but to have to sit for hours watching my brother (do the same old thing/play in the team) is (truly HORRENDOUS!/less than enjoyable). Instead, I'm going to dance, eat and talk to Emily all night! Xxx

E Turn these words into verbs by adding a suffix: 'ate', 'en', 'ify' or 'ise'. [6]

Example: *length* lengthen

1 formula _____

2 sign _____

3 patron _____

4 strength _____

5 simple _____

6 visual _____

(F) Replace the underlined words in the sentences with antonyms from the list below. [5]

> An **antonym** is a word opposite in meaning to another.
>
> **Example:** 'big' is an antonym for 'small'

| huge | warm | wet | quiet | narrow |

1 I have a double bed, wardrobe and dressing table in my <u>tiny</u>

bedroom. _____

2 Usually you need to be really <u>loud</u> in the library. _____

3 I was feeling really <u>cold</u>, so I made myself a nice drink. _____

4 The audience were <u>dry</u> after standing right next to the swimming pool. _____

5 We had to walk single-file down the <u>wide</u> corridor. _____

(G) Place a different time adverbial from the list at the beginning of each sentence to show the sequence of events. One has been done as an example. [4]

| After that | Finally | ~~First~~ | Meanwhile | Second |

First, take the printer and its documentation out of the box and attach the plug to the back of the printer.

1 _____, insert the coloured and black toners into the front of the printer.

2 _____, attach the USB from the printer to the computer.

3 _____, place the CD into the CD drive to allow the drivers to upload.

4 _____, follow the instructions on the CD to print out your test sheet.

💡 **Helpful Hint**

Remember that **time adverbials** help to show the order in which something happens. When you use **time adverbials**, always read through the sequence to make sure that you have put them in the correct order and the text makes sense.

9

Quick quiz

1–3 Place the time adverbials in the correct order to show the sequence of events.

Finally   Next   Second

First, read the information. _____, make sure that you understand it.

_____, answer each question. _____, mark your work.

4–6 Turn these words into verbs by adding a suffix: '-ate', '-en', '-ify' or '-ise'.

false _____   real _____   identity _____

7–10 Underline the formal phrases to make this text impersonal.
(I can't/It is not possible to) avoid the (road congestion/traffic jam) but (hopefully/it is hoped that)

(we'll be back by/the estimated time of arrival will be) midday.

11–13 Join the informal phrases with their formal phrases.

I wash my hands of you.   Remain quiet.

It's nice and toasty.   I want nothing more to do with you.

Shut up!   It is lovely and warm.

14–20 Underline the seven spelling or grammar mistakes in the following text. Then write the original word and the correct word below. [7]
North Sentinel Island lies in the Bay of Bengal. It is only around 72 square kilometres in area and

consists of deep forests surounded by thin beaches. The Sentinelese people that inhabat the

island has no contact at all with anyone else so nobody know anything about them. How many

people their are, what language they speak, what culture they have and what they eat is totally

unknown. Because of the dense forestation they can't even be observe from the air. An amazing

feet in a world of so many technological advances.

_____   _____

_____   _____

_____   _____

_____   _____

_____   _____

_____   _____

_____   _____

30

20

Ⓐ Underline the most appropriate modal verb each time so that the sentences make sense. [5]

Example: *I (couldn't/won't/can't) go to the tournament because I was ill.*

1 I (may not/will/wouldn't) pay even half the price for that!

2 (Might not/Won't/May) you come and sit down?

3 I (won't/will/can't) believe it – I haven't seen him since nursery!

4 I (can't/might/don't) mind coming to the park if I can sit down somewhere.

5 When I am in a silly mood, you (mustn't/wouldn't/couldn't) take any notice of me.

💡 **Helpful Hint**

Remember that **modal verbs** are 'helper' **verbs** that work with other **verbs**.
Modal verbs can include the negative: can't, couldn't, may not, might not,
mustn't, shan't, shouldn't, won't, wouldn't.

Ⓑ Write out these sentences, adding a bracket before and after the parenthesis in each sentence. [5]

Example: *Male bees called drones do not gather nectar and pollen.*

Male bees (called drones) do not gather nectar and pollen.

1 The baby who gurgled happily cuddled a teddy bear.

_____

2 The Nile in North-East Africa is the longest river in the world.

_____

3 King John who signed the Magna Carta was the son of Henry II.

_____

4 A volcano usually a mountain is where magma erupts so that lava and gas escapes.

_____

5 The Yorkshire Blue and White a breed of British pig is now extinct.

_____

10

(c) Underline the preposition phrases. There are two in each sentence. [5]

Example: *We crossed <u>over the bridge</u> and walked <u>along the footpath</u>.*

1   The robin sat outside the window, his feathers fluffed up against his body.

2   The rat scampered across the grass and back to its nest.

3   Max weaved fairy lights around the Christmas tree, then he placed a star on the top.

4   The pen from Dad's desk was placed beside the notepad.

5   Mr Legge, from the bakery, completed a charity climb up Ben Nevis.

 Helpful Hint

Remember that **prepositions** describe where the **noun** is.

(d) Add a pronoun in each space so that these sentences make sense. [4]

Example: *My holiday was great, but yours sounds fantastic!*

1   When Michael won the maths certificate, he was very proud of _____.

2   _____ both enjoyed our fish and chips.

3   Although the sofa was huge, _____ looked lost in the enormous room.

4   Iryna, _____ has moved into a new flat, is now much happier.

(e) Underline the adverb and circle the adjective in these sentences. [4]

Example: *The (spacious) apartment stood <u>proudly</u> on Baker Street.*

1   The invasive ivy crept steadily over the garden fence.

2   The prehistoric dinosaur hunted stealthily for food.

3   I vividly dreamed of paradise – what a beautiful dream it was.

4   Those hurtful words were said spitefully.

 Helpful Hint

Remember that an **adverb** can describe the **verb** and often ends in 'ly'.
An **adjective** describes the **noun**.

Ⓕ Write whether these sentences are simple, compound or complex. [6]

Example: *The water boiled rapidly.* *simple*

1 Rita placed her teabags in a tin, which sat on the dresser.

_____

2 Shakira galloped across the open fields. _____

3 Walid knelt on the ground but he did not make a sound.

_____

4 We cut the paper, we chose pink, into a semi-circle.

_____

5 Our skin is amazing as it is waterproof, tough yet sensitive.

_____

6 The new bed, with matching bedding, stood proudly in the

bedroom. _____

> A **simple sentence** has one **subject** and one **verb** and does not contain a **conjunction** (joining word).
>
> A **compound sentence** has two **main clauses** linked with a joining word. **Example:** The bird's nest was in the tree and the cat watched it intently.
>
> A **complex sentence** has a **main clause** with a **subordinate clause** that gives additional information. **Example:** The cat that I loved dearly was a menace!

Helpful Hint

If the **main clause** is the whole sentence, it is a **simple sentence**. If there is more than one **main clause** joined together, it is a **compound sentence**. If there is only one **main clause** and some additional information, it is a **complex sentence**.

Ⓖ Underline the conditional phrases in this paragraph. One has been done as an example. [4]

<u>If you could imagine what it is like to spend half of the year in almost total darkness</u> and the rest of the year in almost continuous daylight, the north of Norway is the place to be. The winter is dark with just a few hours of daylight when the land lies under thick snow. Although the winter is long and hard, the summer months have very little darkness. When the seasons change, the sun melts the snow leaving a lush, sunny landscape. The waters provide dramatic waterfalls and fjords, once the ice melts. Even so, the tops of the mountains always remain snowy.

10

(H) Underline the seven spelling or grammar mistakes in the following text. Then write the original word and the correct word below. One has been done as an example. [7]

The winter was setting in as the bitter wind howled down the <u>desserted</u> street. Litter from the overflowing bin moved in an eratic manner, wipped cruelly by the wind. As he walking unhurriedly up the road, he became aware of someone following him. He chanced his pace, moving just a little faster. He could now here the footsteps increasing their speed. He breaked into a jog. The footsteps behind him persisting and now they were getting closer and closer and closer ...

Example: *desserted*   *deserted*

1 _____   _____

2 _____   _____

3 _____   _____

4 _____   _____

5 _____   _____

6 _____   _____

7 _____   _____

(I) Choose one prefix, one root word and one suffix to make a new word. The spelling will sometimes need to change when the suffix is added. One has been done as an example. [4]

> A **prefix** can be added to the beginning of a **root word** and a **suffix** can be added to the end of a **root word**. A **root word** can have both a **prefix** and a **suffix**.

Example: *(pre, mis, dis) + (take, bring, caught) + (ing, ment, fully) =*
         mistaking

1   (inter, pre, il) + (ant, act, art) + (ious, tion, sion) =

_____

2   (ir, in, im) + (real, read, response) + (ible, able, uble) =

_____

3   (co, en, un) + (test, sent, race) + (ed, al, ive) =

_____

4   (en, inter, ir) + (side, chant, form) + (ation, fully, ment) =

_____

(A) Turn these present progressive sentences into the past tense. [5]

Example: *They are cooking pasta for their tea.*   *They cooked pasta for their tea.*

1   Pip is buying the ingredients for a fish pie.

_____

2   Jon is teaching Michael how to play the piano.

_____

3   The ice cream is melting in the sunshine.

_____

4   Ishmael is thinking about his friend who is on holiday in Australia.

_____

5   Abdullah and Talal are visiting their brother in hospital.

_____

(B) Add the correct pronoun in each space so that the paragraphs make sense. One has been done as an example. [11]

1–2 "I wonder where *that* book has got to?" Dad said. _____ was wandering around

the room looking everywhere for _____.

3–4 Mrs Hoskins made sandwiches for _____ son, Tom, who always ate

_____ in the school canteen.

5–9 Alfie was running late. _____ had accidentally cut _____ while

doing some gardening. _____ finger had stopped bleeding and _____

had cleaned the wound and put a plaster on _____ to stop any infection.

10–11 "_____ path should I take to get to the playing fields?

Is _____ very far?"

16

(c) Add a semi-colon in the correct places so that these sentences make sense. [7]

A **semi-colon** (;) can link related clauses together and can separate a list when **commas** are already being used.

Example: *The desk was covered in papers she really needed to have a sort through everything.*

> *The desk was covered in papers; she really needed to have a sort through everything.*

1   The suitcase, its lid open, was full of clothes the chest of drawers, by the bed, was almost empty her shoes were carefully packed in boxes.

2   The garden was beautiful the flower beds were in full bloom.

3   Lily was a talented dancer she appeared in many productions.

4   We read Michael Morpurgo, *War Horse* and *Private Peaceful* David Walliams, *Gangsta Granny* and *The Demon Dentist* Anthony Horowitz, *Granny* and *Stormbreaker* Michelle Magorian, *Goodnight Mister Tom* and *Just Henry*.

5   The town hall was packed the audience were eagerly waiting for the comedian to begin.

6   With their glorious feathers on show, the peacocks wandered proudly through the park they had escaped from their enclosure.

7   We visited several historic houses: Croft Castle in Herefordshire Attingtham Park in Shropshire Kenilworth Castle in Warwickshire.

(d) Underline the conditional word or words and circle the modal verbs, in these sentences. [8]

Example: *Should you accept the offer, we will send the money immediately.*

1   As long as I close the window, I can stop the birds flying in!

2   Unless you hear otherwise, the disco will be in the school hall next Friday.

3   If you help me sort out this mess I would be most grateful.

4   We might arrive at the party late if the train is delayed much longer.

5   I ought to resist another biscuit if I want to eat healthily.

6   Providing I set the alarm, I should be able to set off early to meet my friend.

7   I may be able to finish the puzzle as long as everyone leaves me alone!

8   If she wants to successfully complete the triathlon, she must train more regularly.

15

E Put a hyphen in the correct place so that each sentence makes sense. [6]

> **Hyphens** have many uses, including linking a **prefix** to a **proper noun**.
>
> **Example**: pro-European, un-American.

Example: *The company had to readvertise the job.* *re-advertise*

1 The area has some semiindustrial centres. _____

2 Mrs Preston, an exteacher, won the Artist of the Year award.

   _____

3 Fortunately the copilot took control of the plane.

   _____

4 The antipoverty protest was a success. _____

5 Although the car was preowned, it was in very good condition.

   _____

6 PreRoman Britain had a thriving culture. _____

💡 **Helpful Hint**

Remember that **hyphens** can join a **prefix** to a **root word** (such as, 'pre-cook') and they can help to make the meaning clear.

F Underline the informal phrases so that this email is written in a personal style. One has been done as an example. [7]

Hi Dad

Thanks for the email. (Yes I got the photos/I can confirm that the photographs were received) – aren't they great? It looks as though that course has (provided inspiration/done you the world of good). You've really (got the hang of landscape pictures!/succeeded in landscape photography). I am (tickled pink/so pleased to hear) that the art gallery wants to sell your work. (Your ability is unquestionable./What d'you mean, are you good enough?) Are you joking? The picture of the ice cave is fantastic. I (bet that's popular/feel sure that it will be desirable) and will make great postcards.

(In conclusion/Anyhow, must dash) – we're taking the rabbit to have his claws clipped at the vet's.

(See you Sunday!/I look forward to our meeting on Sunday.)

Lots of love

Sanjit

13

(G) Underline the main clauses in this paragraph. One has been done as an example. [6]

It was so hot in the mine, but it was too dangerous not to wear a hard hat and protective gear. Although it was hot, safety had to come first. The lift raised the men back to ground level and the smell of fresh air was truly wonderful. The man wiped the thick film of black dust from his face as he set off towards home.

(H) Use words from the following text to complete the table. [9]

The Faroe Islands consist of eighteen islands yet they are home to fewer than 50,000 people. Their name means "Sheep Islands" and this should give the visitor a clue. There must be at least twice the number of sheep than people! The islands are a dependency of Denmark, but the inhabitants govern themselves. The capital city, Torshavn, might be the smallest capital in the world.

Conjunction	Pronoun	Modal verb

(I) Write the following sentences formally, in the subjunctive form. [4]

Example: *If I was President, I would visit lots of different countries.*

If I were President, I would visit lots of different countries.

1 If I was tired enough, I might be able to fall asleep.

_____

2 If ballet was easier everyone could do it.

_____

3 I would find out interesting things if I was someone's pen pal.

_____

4 I wish I was playing football this weekend, if only I didn't have a broken leg.

_____

19

(A) Replace the underlined words in the sentences with synonyms from the list below. [4]

> difficult   sad   scared   fantastic

1 I love books and think reading is <u>brilliant</u>. _____

2 Tess went sailing at the weekend and said it was <u>hard</u>. _____

3 Jamie was <u>upset</u> that he didn't get a puppy for his birthday. _____

4 I'm <u>terrified</u> of the dark! _____

(B) Write whether the use of ellipsis in these sentences shows suspense, omission or stopping. [3]

Example: *Well, um … I just don't know.* *stopping*

1 Trying to keep his fears under control, he knelt down on the bedroom floor and slowly peered

under the bed … _____

2 I need make a start on the washing up but will put on rubber gloves before I do.

_____

3 Ali took four books out of the library at her school but must remember to return them.

_____

(C) Underline the preposition phrases. There are two in each sentence. [8]

Example: *I brushed my teeth <u>after supper</u> and <u>before bed</u>.*

1 That dog growls at the postman every time he walks up the path.

2 Mrs Hudson works at the information centre next to the church.

3 My cousin lives just outside Dudley in the West Midlands.

4 We stood beneath the big top as jugglers paraded through the crowds.

5 We swam around the pool then dived off the diving board.

6 The Mad Hatter's guests sat around the table as they ate from huge plates.

7 After music practice, I waited for Mum outside the hall.

8 The plane flew over the ocean and through the clouds.

15

(D) Place a different time adverbial from the list at the beginning of each sentence to show the sequence of events. One has been done as an example. [5]

Finally   ~~Firstly~~   Meanwhile   Secondly   Then   Thirdly

Firstly, Dad and I collected some decorations: glitter, fluff, paint, threads, and so on.

1 _____, I put the bubble wrap in front of me, bubbles facing up.

2 _____, I put the decorations onto the bubble wrap and carefully folded the bubble wrap in half to sandwich the decorations.

3 _____, Dad turned on the iron and let it reach a hot temperature.

4 _____, he put the bubble wrap on some cardboard, put an old tea towel on top of the bubble wrap and then applied the hot iron.

5 _____, when it had cooled, we took off the tea towel to reveal a piece of decorative, flat plastic I could make into cards.

(E) Underline the subordinate clause in these sentences. [8]

Example: *She loved the movies, <u>and the games</u>, of her favourite books.*

1 Seeing the ice cream van, the girls ran across the road.

2 I cut myself another piece of chocolate cake because I was still hungry.

3 We arranged to meet at the cinema in town, where I work on Saturdays.

4 After the play, we went out for dinner at an Italian restaurant.

5 The football match was cancelled because of the rain.

6 The parcel, ordered the day before, arrived at the time she had requested.

7 Before she could save her work, her computer crashed.

8 The garden, at its best in the spring, looks bare in the winter.

> A **subordinate clause** gives us additional information about the **main clause**. It cannot stand alone as a sentence and needs to go with a **main clause** to make sense.

13

F Choose one prefix, one root word and one suffix to make a new word. The spelling will sometimes need to change when the suffix is added. One has been done as an example. [7]

Example: (<u>in</u>, im, dis) + (<u>decide</u>, think, be) + (<u>sion</u>, tion, ful) = *indecision*

1   (mono, re, anti) + (form, spend, sad) + (ed, ful, sion) =   _____

2   (en, mis, un) + (sun, fun, joy) + (sion, ious, ment) =   _____

3   (per, ir, im) + (pose, present, set) + (ing, ful, tion) =   _____

4   (in, il, anti) + (art, act, and) + (ious, fully, ive) =   _____

5   (re, mis, dis) + (sing, agree, sign) + (ful, able, sion) =   _____

6   (in, un, pre) + (avoid, ease, life) + (ing, ful, able) =   _____

7   (im, re, pre) + (side, precise, perfect) + (tion, ful, sion) =   _____

G Write whether these sentences are simple, compound or complex. [7]

Example: *Dad did the dusting and Mum did the vacuuming.* *compound*

1   We tiptoed quietly down the carpeted stairs.   _____

2   Jayden was angry because he couldn't go outside to play.   _____

3   Floating like feathers, the snowflakes silently fell.   _____

4   The wind whipped the back of his legs.   _____

5   Lady Melchid always took tea on a Sunday, even
    when travelling.   _____

6   The lights went out because there was a power cut.   _____

7   The cat, slinking down the path like a hunter, prepared
    to pounce after the bird.   _____

💡 **Helpful Hint**

Remember that a **simple sentence** has a **subject**, a **verb** and no **conjunction**. A **compound sentence** has a **conjunction** that joins two or more **main clauses**. A **complex sentence** has one or more **main clauses** with **subordinate clauses** that give extra information.

14

(H) Turn these present tense sentences into the past progressive form using 'was' or 'were' and the 'ing' ending of the verb. [5]

Example: *Philip checks the map.*   *Philip was checking the map.*

1   Dr Delaney sees her patients at the surgery.

_____

2   The chef prepares the food in the kitchen.

_____

3   Our friend completes the crossword during his morning break.

_____

4   The elephants walk around the enclosure.

_____

5   The receptionist prints out the information for the customer.

_____

(I) Underline the six spelling or grammar mistakes in the following text. Then write the original word and the correct word below. One has been done as an example. [6]

On <u>friday</u> 4th July my family joined the cue for the Tropical Parrot Water Park. As there were five cashiers available, the procedure was very quick and easily. We'all enjoyed the 'Parrot Splash' pool with it's dives and tubes, but there are so many activitiies for the hole family to join in that you could spend all weekend here and still not see everything!

Example: *friday*   *Friday*

1   _____   _____

2   _____   _____

3   _____   _____

4   _____   _____

5   _____   _____

6   _____   _____

11

Test your skills

1–2 Underline the most appropriate modal verb each time so that the sentences make sense.

I (can/mustn't/wouldn't) mind having my hair cut like that.

We (will/won't/should) stay long as Samuel needs an early night.

Write out these sentences, adding a comma before and after the parenthesis in each sentence.

3   It was now July and coming from the west the storm looked foreboding.

_____

4   I looked up shielding my eyes against the sun and saw the aeroplane.

_____

5   The summer fete has with regret been postponed until further notice.

_____

Underline the preposition phrases. There are two in each sentence.

6   From base camp came the explorers, their belongings pulled by huskies.

7   The documents at the archives were stored with local history records.

Underline the informal phrases so that this text is written in a personal style.

8–11

(Happy Birthday!/Best wishes on your special day.) I hope that whatever you do, you (enjoy the occasion/have a super fun day.)

(Yours sincerely/ Hugs and kisses)

(Aunty Mimi/ Mrs M Houghton)

11

Write whether these sentences are simple, compound or complex.

12 We made our own kulfi, pistachio flavoured, for pudding. _____

13 She looked at the mess with absolute horror. _____

14 There was a gentle breeze but the dog still felt too hot. _____

Choose one prefix, one root word and one suffix to make a new word. The spelling will sometimes need to change when the suffix is added.

15 (mis, pre, im) + (specify, happy, sent) + (ing, ful, sion) = _____

16 (anti, il, un) + (help, joy, friend) + (ly, able, sion) = _____

17 (ir, in, re) + (cover, possible, know) + (ful, ing, cian) = _____

Underline the adverb and circle the adjective in these sentences.

18 The boy foolishly climbed over the broken fence.

19 I stuck with my initial plan after I had carefully considered the alternatives.

20 We successfully found lots of beautiful shells on the beach.

21 She threw the slender dart skilfully and it hit the target.

Turn these past tense sentences into the present progressive form.

22 Joan joked with her old friend Derek.

_____

23 Anders carried the boxes from the car.

_____

Add the correct pronoun in each space so that the sentences make sense.

24 The bears roamed around _____ enclosure.

25 She could see _____ reflected in the mirror.

26 Orin, _____ first day at the school was finally over, arrived home with relief.

27 "Everyone, remember to leave_____ plenty of time to clear up when you've finished."

28 Gareth forgot to lock the door. _____ was going to be in such trouble when he got home.

29 "I can't find my pencil sharpener," exclaimed Jo. "Can I borrow _____?"

18

Underline the conditional word or words and circle the modal verbs in these sentences.

30 When we get to the zoo, you can buy some food for the animals.

31 If the wind blows enough, we could put up the sail.

32 Providing there is a parking space, we will call in at the library.

33 Children may not leave the premises unless they have permission.

34 I ought to tidy up this morning but I may leave it until later.

Put a hyphen in the correct place so that each sentence makes sense.

35 Kelly has an autoimmune condition so she needs some treatment.

36 There were twenty odd members of staff at the party.

_____

37 I had to ask Mum to resign the form for school.

_____

38 After she dropped the children's books, Miss Lewis had to resort them in alphabetical order.

_____

39 Simon was a hard working member of the customer services team.

_____

Underline the main clauses in this paragraph.

40–45 As it was already quite late, the horses were in their stables. Although we were tired, we tramped along the road, more an unmade track, to check the other animals. The ducks and geese were all settled down and the chickens just needed rounding up and securing in their hen house. The final stage of the nightly ritual was to feed the cat and then we went to bed.

Write whether the use of ellipsis in these sentences shows suspense, omission or stopping.

46 He breathed with relief, until he felt a hand upon his shoulder … _____

47 "Well, I … um," hesitated Georgia. _____

48 "We need half a dozen eggs. Will you go and get some?" _____

19

Underline the subordinate clause in these sentences.

49 Watching the mouse, the cat crept silently across the road.

50 She loves to ride her bike when the sun is shining.

Underline the five spelling, grammar or punctuation mistakes in the following text. Then write the original word and the correct word below.

Mary Anning contributed hugely to our know of prehistoric life. She was a British collector and dealer of fossils that she found around the cost of Lyme Regis in dorset. She put her life in jeopardy many times as she often collected her fossils during landslides. As a woman, she was shunning by the scientists of the day. She lived in poverty until the British Association for the Advancement of Science was persuaded to award her a small annual pension. Mary died when she was only 47. At St Michael's Church, in Lyme, theres a stained-glass window in her memory.

51 _____   _____

52 _____   _____

53 _____   _____

54 _____   _____

55 _____   _____

Key words

abstract noun abstract nouns are ideas or feelings and cannot be touched, seen or heard, for example *anger, beauty*

active a sentence in which the subject is who or what does something

adjective a word that describes a noun

adverb a word that describes a verb

antonym a word that is opposite in meaning to another word

bullet point (•) a punctuation mark used to draw attention to key information

collective noun collective nouns refer to groups of people or things

colon (:) two dots used to introduce lists, examples or explanations

comma (,) a punctuation mark used to separate items in a list

common noun the name of an object, for example *book, apple*

complex sentence a sentence with a main clause and a subordinate clause

compound sentence a sentence with two main clauses linked by a joining word

conditional sentence a sentence with two clauses, the main clause is dependent on the other clause

conjunction a word that joins two clauses together

ellipsis (pl. ellipses) (...) a set of three dots to show omission, stopping or suspense in a sentence

formal (impersonal) writing using a formal tone and language

hyphen (-) a punctuation mark used to join words or join prefixes to words

informal (personal) writing using an informal tone and language

main clause a clause that makes sense on its own

modal verbs words that help to change the meaning of other verbs, for example *might, could*

non-restrictive clause part of a sentence that adds non-essential information

noun words that identify or name things, for example *girl, peony*

noun phrase a group of words that has a noun as its key word

object a noun, noun phrase or pronoun which comes just after the verb in a sentence

parenthesis (pl. parentheses) ( ) – , brackets, dashes or commas used to separate a word or phrase that has been added to a sentence as an explanation or afterthought

passive a sentence in which the focus is on what happens rather than who or what does it

past progressive describing something that was not finished when something else happened or something that continued for some time

personal pronoun words that replace names of people, places or objects, for example *her, it*

possessive pronoun words that show ownership, for example *hers, mine*

prefix a group of letters added before a root word to make a new word

preposition a word that describes the location of the noun

preposition phrase part of a sentence that begins with a preposition, followed by a noun, pronoun or noun phrase

present perfect describing something that happened and is still relevant now or is still happening now

present progressive describing something happening now and continuing over a longer period

pronoun a word that can replace a noun, for example *she, it*

proper noun names of people and places, days of the week, months of the year, titles and organisations

reflexive pronoun words that are used when the object of the verb is the same as the subject of the verb

relative clause a subordinate clause that is introduced using a relative pronoun

relative pronoun words that introduce a clause that gives more information about a noun, for example *that, which*

restrictive clause part of a sentence that adds essential information

root word a word that can have a prefix or suffix added to it

semi-colon (;) a punctuation mark used to separate two sentences or main clauses of equal importance

simple sentence a sentence with a verb, noun and sometimes adverbs and adjectives but no conjunctions

subject a noun, noun phrase or pronoun that comes before the verb in a sentence

subjunctive mood formal language used to express a wish or suggestion, for example *If I were a queen, I'd wear a crown every day*

subordinate clause part of a sentence that adds meaning to the main clause but cannot be used as a sentence on its own

suffix a group of letters added to the end of a root word to make a new word

synonym a word that is similar in meaning to another word

time adverbial words that help link ideas together and show the order in which things happen, for example *next, finally*

verb a word that identifies an action

Progress chart

How did you do? Fill in your score below and shade in the corresponding boxes to compare your progress across the different tests and units.

50% 100%   50% 100%

Unit 1, p3 Score __ / 11

Unit 1, p4 Score __ / 10

Unit 1, p5 Score __ / 11

Unit 1, p6 Score __ / 13

Unit 2, p7 Score __ / 20

Unit 2, p8 Score __ / 9

Unit 2, p9 Score __ / 13

Unit 2, p10 Score __ / 5

Unit 3, p11 Score __ / 9

Unit 3, p12 Score __ / 16

Unit 3, p13 Score __ / 15

Quick quiz, p14 Score __ / 17

Unit 4, p15 Score __ / 10

Unit 4, p16 Score __ / 16

Unit 4, p17 Score __ / 14

Unit 4, p18 Score __ / 11

Unit 5, p19 Score __ / 10

Unit 5, p20 Score __ / 13

Unit 5, p21 Score __ / 17

Unit 5, p22 Score __ / 12

Unit 6, p27 Score __ / 14

Unit 6, p28 Score __ / 14

Unit 6, p29 Score __ / 9

Quick quiz, p30 Score __ / 20

Unit 7, p31 Score __ / 10

Unit 7, p32 Score __ / 13

Unit 7, p33 Score __ / 10

Unit 7, p34 Score __ / 11

Unit 8, p35 Score __ / 16

Unit 8, p36 Score __ / 15

Unit 8, p37 Score __ / 13

Unit 8, p38 Score __ / 19

Unit 9, p39 Score __ / 15

Unit 9, p40 Score __ / 13

Unit 9, p41 Score __ / 14

Unit 9, p42 Score __ / 11

Unit 10, p43 Score __ / 11

Unit 10, p44 Score __ / 18

Unit 10, p45 Score __ / 19

Unit 10, p46 Score __ / 7

Slow Living

Slow Living

The Secrets to Slowing Down and
Noticing the Simple Joys Anywhere

Helena Woods

CORAL GABLES

Cover Design: Elina Diaz
Cover Photo/illustration: Helena Woods
Layout & Design: Elina Diaz

For permission requests, please contact the publisher at:
Mango Publishing Group
2850 S Douglas Road, 4th Floor
Coral Gables, FL 33134 USA
info@mango.bz

For special orders, quantity sales, course adoptions and corporate sales, please email the publisher at sales@mango.bz. For trade and wholesale sales, please contact Ingram Publisher Services at customer.service@ingramcontent.com or +1.800.509.4887.

Slow Living: The Secrets to Slowing Down and Noticing the Simple Joys Anywhere

Library of Congress Cataloging-in-Publication number: 2022948785
ISBN: (print) 978-1-68481-164-9, (ebook) 978-1-68481-165-6
BISAC category code CRA005000, CRAFTS & HOBBIES / Decorating

Printed in China

Dedicated to my husband and the love of my life, Alex. And to all the gentle and passionate kindred spirits who yearn to live slowly and feel connected with life. Shine bright, shine true.

"I believe the nicest and sweetest days are not those on which anything very splendid or wonderful or exciting happens, but just those that bring simple little pleasures, following one another softly like pearls slipping off a string."

—Anne of Avonlea

Table of Contents

Introduction

The years of the pandemic taught us how imperative it is to slow down and enjoy the small, simple things in life—not the things in the distant future, but those that are right in front of us. We've learned more doesn't mean better, and that striving is, quite frankly, overruled and depleting us of our natural energies. We've learned that sometimes the best thing to do in times of crisis is rest—guilt-free.

All things in life are in a constant state of flux. If there's one thing that's certain, it's that all of this is impermanent. Waves come and go, joy rises and falls, events and situations are often outside of our control. Some things we can control, however, like our speed, our intentions, and our awareness. We can choose to see the light in the ordinary, the magic in the mundane. When we appreciate what we have within, and in our own homes, we appreciate the process of life more.

Over the past several years of creating videos on YouTube around slow living and presence, I've observed how many people yearn to live slowly. It seems that, now more than ever, people are awakening to the idea that there is another way to live—one that is more peaceful, present, and light. Living slowly is quite simple to do once you form that mind-body-heart connection. When you listen to your intuition first, life's decisions become easier. There's less overwhelm, less overthinking.

But if slowing down and enjoying life fully is so simple, why is it so hard for many of us to do?

I wanted to share with you some simple and easy ways I have learned to slow my life down, and how I've come to feel lighter in my daily life since simplifying the excess.

So many of us are burning the candle at both ends, afraid of the unknown. We've forgotten what freedom feels like because we feel stuck in situations we don't want to be in. We've lost that sense of childlike curiosity because of life's inevitable challenges. The truth is that we don't ever walk out of this life without any scars. Life will always present obstacles and transformative experiences to grow from. And as the years go by, our shells begin to harden, the softness melts away. Our minds are no longer open, our hearts no longer tender.

But there is a way to soften the gentle spirit of our natural-born hearts, and it's through slow, intuitive living.

This book is an exploration of the ways I have enhanced my life by slowing it down and designing it around my own inner voice so I can live fully in the present, each and every day. In this book, I share all the ways you can live slowly, compassionately, and authentically with your inner voice. We will cover everything from crafting daily slow living routines and creating space in order to lighten your spark to navigating boundaries and seeing the big picture of this magnificent universe with which you're co-creating. In these pages are words of both simplicity and depth.

It is my hope that this book gives you the inspiration and motivation to question the lifestyles flooding your newsfeed, to inquire within your own intuition first, and to explore a new approach, if the way of life you're currently living doesn't serve you. If your current situation isn't bringing you the life experience you want to have, I hope you harness the courage to quit buying into it, simplify the excess, and question everything you've been taught to believe about success, happiness, and fulfillment. You have the power to decide how the rest of your life goes, and living slowly is one way to get there with a peaceful heart.

I'm so excited to share it all with you. Let's begin.

"The miracle is not to walk on water. The miracle is to walk on the green earth, dwelling deeply in the present moment and feeling truly alive."

—Thich Nhat Hanh

1
—

The Art of Slow Living

Mmmmm, *slow living*.

Doesn't it feel so cozy and wholesome just reading those words?

Living slowly has taught me a lot about patience and enjoying where I'm at now in my life. I'm no longer chasing, but rather delighting in the process, in the unfolding of life. At the end of the day, the results of the journey don't matter. What matters is that we're excited and innately fulfilled in the process of doing it all. Living slowly is disciplining our minds to not be so easily distracted by constant stimulation, but instead to find enjoyment in silent moments and simple joys.

Slow living is a lifestyle that appears to be the opposite of mainstream society. Instead of needing to be seen as productive or successful, you simply enjoy your life, without regard to what other people think of your lifestyle, how you look, or what you have. Slow living is about pacing yourself, going at your own natural rhythm. It's living in your own harmony, allowing yourself to fully be the main character of your own life story, and not deviating from the wisdom of your heart. As a collective, many of us are walking around this life half-asleep. Even if you're busy, if you're doing or producing things that seem important, it's very easy to start chasing the wrong things. But living slowly helps us live our lives more fully, because there is intentionality, a clear focus and purpose behind each decision. In a way, slow living resembles intuitive living, in that, when you know yourself and what you inherently value in life, everything around you becomes clear. In that stillness lies clarity.

Living slowly is a gentler path, one in which you regularly check in and ask yourself, "Does this feel *good* to do? Does this work *for me*?" The result might not be quick. The success might not be instant. But the more you prioritize your higher self and the callings of your heart, you'll find yourself starting to tune out the noise of the world telling you to go faster, to push harder. The traditional "girlboss" narrative says, "Fake it till you make it." It says that if you're feeling the dreaded imposter syndrome, just barrel on through and push that fear aside! If your desired outcome doesn't pan out the way you'd like, it's on *you*; you just need to keep pushing, keep doing, and make it happen!

But slow living is a more peaceful and present way to live, one in which we honor our energy as it is, without needing to guilt or shame it into doing or feeling something different. We accept our emotions, our fears, and our intuitive nudges as they are. There's no barreling on through. There's no hustle and grind. And there's a whole lot less burnout as a result. Instead, we embody a slow and steadfast movement, one in which we prioritize endurance over speed. We rest when needed. We pivot and change direction when it feels aligning to do so. We prioritize strategy and reflection over churning out action and output. Living slowly is about becoming aware, asking yourself *why* you do the things you do. It's getting curious, getting comfortable with not knowing the future, and it's about peeling away the layers to discover the masterpiece within.

Slow living is about becoming conscious. It's waking up from the programs we've been fed. It's embodying a steady awareness. Awareness is simply the quality we perceive as the present reality. Awareness is you noticing yourself reading this book right now, pausing often to observe the space between the words, between the lines, between the soft rolling of your thoughts, and placing it back gently into the stillness of the moment. The only moment that exists: *the now*.

I love this Helen Keller quote. She said, "I long to accomplish a great and noble task, but it is my chief duty to accomplish small tasks as if they were great and noble." There's immense joy gained from enjoying the experience of taking small action steps each day, while also being fully connected to our five senses. I feel more joy daily when I take delight in small tasks—whether it's washing the dishes with a foamy sponge and my favorite lemon-scented soap, turning the crisp pages of a library book, or listening to a cat purr. Placing our focus and awareness on those small acts dials us into the present moment.

When living slowly, know that you don't need to have your whole life figured out. You don't even need to have a plan. You *do* need to know what you value in life and what matters most to you though. Clarity is essential here. But it's quite easily found, I've noticed, when you slow down and connect with your senses.

Misconceptions about Slow Living

First, we must get an important key point out of the way: living slowly is a mindset. It doesn't have to *look* any certain way. There are a lot of misconceptions about what it means to live a slow, simple lifestyle. Know that slow living isn't a style or an aesthetic. You don't need to buy a linen apron and a beautiful wicker basket and frolic through fields, picking berries like a Disney princess, to live slowly. While I think that aesthetic is certainly beautiful to look at—romanticizing our everyday makes the small moments much more joyful, don't you think?—this book outlines a much more relatable and accessible approach to slow living, one that anyone and everyone can incorporate into their life, no matter their financial means or surrounding environment.

Slow living has become very popular online in recent years, particularly due to the pandemic. Like all things in life, when a certain lifestyle begins to trend, we start to see it through the filter of a certain aesthetic. Just look at minimalism! Originally based on embracing certain values and living a simplified life, it soon spiraled into a lifestyle that looks like a life with bare white walls, a capsule wardrobe, and wearing neutrals. When you first hear the word "minimalism," does a similar image pop into your head? The internet has made a caricature of a valuable and constructive lifestyle movement, so that it now resembles an aesthetic with very little personality or individuality. *Quel dommage!*

I challenge the notion that slow living must look the same for all who choose it. Know this: You can live slowly without living the off-grid, farming lifestyle. You don't need to cook or bake from scratch or frolic in fine linen dresses with flowers in your hair. You don't need to be a mother, be a traditional homemaker, or have a minimalist wardrobe in a minimalist home. You can if it feels genuine and joyful! If it's an expression of your authentic self, go all out! But you don't *have* to. There's no prerequisite. Many who discover and fall in love with living a slower life think they need to look a certain way or engage in particular hobbies in order to feel like they belong. Slow living has become a community, but I encourage you to express *your* version of living slowly that caters to your individuality and uniqueness of spirit.

There's also no need to move to the countryside; you can live in a busy city and *love it!* You can be a big dreamer with mighty ambitions and live a productive life *while also* living slowly. This lifestyle isn't reserved for certain personalities or energy types. One doesn't need to be quiet, calm, or an introverted hermit to live slowly and simply; vivacious, bubbly extroverts can live slow too. You can be child-free by choice, an adrenaline junkie, a frequent concertgoer, or a heavy metal lover! Slow living is a lifestyle anyone can access and practice.

See where I'm going with this?

Slow living is often misidentified with minimalism, cottage core, and other old-fashioned-style aesthetics sweeping the internet trends. While you can surely enjoy wearing thrifted finds, Scandinavian-inspired *hygge* decor, and tending to your balcony garden, that is entirely missing the deeper meaning of what it is to live a slow life. *There is so much more to it.*

Slow living is about living in tune with your intuition, going about your life at a pace that works for you, and not getting distracted by the speed at which our world is moving. It's making time to sit in silence, be in nature, and go inward to receive the answers that are meant for you. It's questioning whether things are true for you and honoring that—*full stop*. Slow living is intuitive living, intentional living, and simple living all in one. It's about connecting with yourself and honoring your needs while resisting the pressure to speed up and do what everyone else is doing.

By sharing these misconceptions, I hope to encourage you too to live in a slow, peaceful, and present way, while still embodying your most authentic, joyful self in whatever way looks and feels honest to you!

For the last five years, I have been learning what it means to live slowly. And in the past several years, as I've noticed the term "slow living" becoming more mainstream, I can't help but wonder if slow living is yet another trendy self-improvement train to hop onto. While I'm overjoyed by the excitement and enthusiasm over living a slower-paced life, I also feel it's pertinent to recognize that slow living isn't a trend. It's a philosophy and an enduring way of approaching life that extends beyond aesthetics. It's a way of being that brings immense peace and inner fulfillment. Because at the root of slow living is *presence*.

Slow Living Is a Present Life

A slow life is a present life. An intuitive life. It's focused on presence, not perfection. It's a mindset that values moving in harmony with one's natural rhythms. It's living simply with what is essential and what is important to *you*. In essence, slow living is like intentional living, but it differs in that it's living a life that matches your own speed and personal values, and not chasing after what everyone else and society values. It's no surprise that the world currently moves fast. People are moving faster every day and we're consuming at mind-numbing speeds.

When we choose to live slower, we prioritize our own intuition and our own internal guidance system first, before looking at and gaining inspiration from the external world. It's an internal-first way of viewing the world. From that inner peace, we can then expand our energy outward to live fully vibrant and inspiring lives.

Slow living is also not an alternative lifestyle, but it can seem curious and odd to many people who are living the fast life. A fast life of achievement and expensive travels may look identical to what Instagram and Hollywood shows as "living your best life." It can look a myriad of different ways, but it's often seen as accumulating fancy cars and up-to-date gadgets, constantly booking dream vacations, never feeling fully satisfied with one's dreams and accomplishments. A life that consists of racking up countless productive achievements, while never taking proper restful breaks. We're told to build our confidence, to pretend we know what we're doing to combat our imposter syndrome, to "fake it till we make it!" But the key we're missing in all of this is a lack of acknowledgment and appreciation for where we are now.

We aren't enjoying our *becoming*. We're restlessly pursuing our "peak."

In today's modern go-go-go world, choosing to live at a speed that best matches your unique personality, temperament, and natural rhythm feels odd. It may seem like we're the outsider, old-fashioned, or behind the times. Choosing to live slowly might seem old-school. But now, more than ever, we need healing. We need to find stillness, to get quiet and listen to the inner whispers within our own bodies. We need to commune once again with that childlike part of us, the joyful, silly essence that wishes to laugh, to wonder, to play. By choosing a slow and intentional life, we begin to live in accordance with our internal compass, our intuition that is always showing us the way home.

But somewhere along this windy road, we lost this connection.

How We've Been Taught to Be Happy

"I was part of that strange race of people aptly described as spending their lives doing things they detest, to make money they don't want, to buy things they don't need, to impress people they don't like."

—Emile Gauvreau

We're living in a time of extreme self-improvement. Everywhere we look, people are trying to find quick solutions to ameliorate their lives. It's natural, even normal, to feel like we should always be doing more. We *should* be improving ourselves. We *should* be making more money. We *should* be actively doing more in our days. "*Should.*" It truly is one of the most harmful words in the English language. By saying—even thinking—this word often in our everyday language, we are placing pressure on ourselves and guilting and shaming ourselves into doing things that don't actually lift our energies up. When we use the word "should," it implies punishment—that if an action isn't completed, we're not doing our absolute best. But there's no need to punish ourselves. What if, instead of pressuring ourselves to do more, we express compassion to ourselves? What if we *held* our tender selves, *allowed* ourselves to feel whatever it is we need to feel? And what if we made space for ourselves to heal?

We don't do enough of this in our fast-paced, hustle-obsessed culture. We don't allow ourselves to sit still, to daydream, to watch the wind in the leaves, to just stare up at the ceiling while lost in thought. Instead, there's always an unnecessary errand to run. There's always a phone screen glaring back at us. *There's always more to be done.*

The result is often full days, yet a persistent feeling of always being unsatisfied. *It's never enough.* So we continue to do more tasks and buy more things to satisfy the endless lack of personal contentment.

But perhaps, being present in our lives is enough.

We've been told that if we *have* everything we want and *do* everything we want, then we'll be happy in life. Take a look at our society, for instance. Society values and relies on how well we accomplish certain tasks. Are we efficient? Can we do things quickly? Are those actions leading to results? The problem with this is that, once we accomplish one thing, another thing always replaces it. It's a hamster wheel we can't ever get off. The cycle is never-ending and it's a dangerous trap many of us fall into. So we force ourselves to keep going. We tell ourselves, "Once I get through this busy season and achieve this, then I can take an actual break." We need to stop telling ourselves the lie that we can only rest when we've *done* enough.

Go soft, go gentle on yourself.

Our Worth Is Not in Our Work

The current trends reflect our values as a collective. In our digital age, it seems everyone online is screaming at us to start a side hustle, monetize our hobbies, earn multiple streams of passive income to pay off our student debt, take that promotion, and be constantly "upleveling." Today, aspiring to a "glow up" in life is expected. Even young teenagers, many of whom aren't yet aware of their values, are growing up watching productivity YouTubers and "girlboss" content creators, believing their paths are the expected way to live—perhaps the only way to live. When we're younger, we don't often question what we see as truth. When someone we admire lives a certain lifestyle, we presume we need to as well. But every person is different in their energy. Everyone has different values and personal dreams for themselves.

I remember reading an interaction in an online thread where someone mentioned they wanted to take up knitting, to which another person responded, "Oh, for like Etsy?" The simple and seemingly harmless romanticization of productivity in our current society shows us that, internally, we believe our inherent value is tied to what we *produce*, not *who we are*. We start to believe we aren't enough, aren't meaningful enough, if we don't produce good work. We believe our worth and purpose are tied to our productivity. Because then—at least, in our work—we can show how valuable our existence is. At last, we have purpose.

So what do we do? We fall into typical people-pleasing habits. We aim to please, to prove we are valuable workers and employees. It's why far too many Americans in the United States work long after hours, respond to emails on the weekends, and don't take their full vacation time. It's why so many people feel this subtle background noise of guilt when they aren't being productive. *Because nothing is worth doing if it doesn't make you money or help you be seen, right?*

More and more people are monetizing their hobbies for financial gain these days. But hobbies can very quickly, yet ever so subtly, transition into a pressurized career to sustain one's livelihood. Even I, as a YouTuber, earn an income making videos on slow living and have found myself at times feeling like my work as a creative isn't valued enough when my views drop. When the views drop, the money diminishes. The simple act of checking my analytics to see how my videos are performing that week to determine my income for the month can diminish my entire mood and make me feel like I'm not living to my fullest potential, that I'm *good* enough or *doing* enough. It's exhausting.

There is a certain pressure that happens when we over-identify with our careers, equating them with our self-worth. We lose perspective, lose touch with the big picture of our life's time on earth.

We can *all* fall into this trap, if we aren't careful. In these instances, I look back to the values of my core self as a reminder. I place my focus on my daily habits of taking care of myself, journaling, meditating, walking in nature. In moments when I start to believe my worth is in my output, I call upon my inner voice. I ask her to shed some light and give me guidance. I allow my intuition the space to drop in and provide the answers.

Redefining "What Do You Do?"

It takes courage to speak up and redefine societal norms, especially in a time when money and status seem to be prized above all else. The question "What do you do?" is so culturally ingrained in our social habits, it's become automatic. When we're meeting people for the first time, it feels like an innocent question to ask. It feels *safe*. It wasn't until I moved to France a few years ago that I realized how this simple question can spur different reactions among different cultures. In France, as well as many other countries in Europe, it's considered impolite to ask such a question at parties or social gatherings. When asked, I notice a silence fall over conversations. In my first year living abroad, I had to slowly start reprogramming my ideas of casual conversation starters. In Europe, there is this unspoken agreement that one doesn't need to understand or even know what someone else does for a living.

It's taken me several years to remove my belief that my worth and value as a person is tied to my work. And one of the ways I've adjusted my language to align with my new beliefs is to avoid the question altogether, or to answer it differently when people do ask.

Instead of identifying yourself by what you do, you can say, "Right now, I'm passionate about _____," or "I enjoy _____." You can also say, "I help people by _____," or "Currently, I'm offering services in _____." Simply asking people what they enjoy and are passionate about is a great way to learn more about a person, without automatically tying their value as a person to what they do for work.

The truth is, people don't remember what you do, they remember how you made them feel. And what one person finds valuable and fulfilling may look completely different to someone else. That's what makes people so interesting and multifaceted.

I believe the drive to accomplish and achieve things—not aligned with our core truth and values—actually stems from a fear of not being significant in life. Many of us fear death and living a life of little to no value. Morrie once said, in the book *Tuesdays with Morrie*, "If you accept you are going to die at any time, then you might not be as ambitious." This is a hard pill to swallow. While I believe many achievers find joy in the process of striving (which I share more on later in this book), I also know many people are constantly in a state of *doing* because of the fear of time's ticking hands. We find our worth in our work because it's something we can control. In those moments, we feel a sense of purpose. But if more of us were fully aware of death, I believe most of us would be doing this life a little differently—a bit more slowly and present-focused.

The simple act of awareness, of *observing* the fears that trickle through our minds, is a way to alleviate this fear. If death were never a factor, if we never feared being insignificant or unimportant, if we just lived our truth and followed our inner compass one single minute at a time, would we even chase achievement? Would we measure our worth with our work? Would we truly even *care* whether or not we were seen or recognized?

Here's a simple thought: *What if we were just here to have fun?* What if we were here to explore life's complexities and just learn and evolve *with* life? Living slowly helps us do that: to enjoy each precious moment and have fun while we can.

There is this idea spreading on social media that we need to chase something. That we need to strive and hustle and do something *big* with our lives. That we need to dream bigger, aim higher and never settle for anything less than mediocre. That we need to have an impact. There are so many songs that glorify this sentiment: Beyoncé's "I Was Here" or The Script's "Hall of Fame." Everything from social media to songs, Hollywood biopics, viral TikTok fame, reality TV shows—heck, even the *traditional education system* glamorizes and encourages us to strive to be achievers. But the problem with that is that most of us grow up to become burnt out adults who have no idea what they want to do with their lives. *Intuition? What's that?*

Here's a li'l refresher: If all you want is peace, if all you value and dream of is a simple life of presence and joy, that is okay too. If your inner being seeks simplicity, seek simplicity. That is a value worth celebrating. You, living, showing up, being present, are worthy. *Enjoy this life.* Have fun and throw all the paint on your life's canvas.

A few words that have colored my adult life, reminding me to loosen up and delight in this worldly experiment, are Danny Kaye's: "Life is a great big canvas, and you should throw all the paint on it you can." *Color your life!* Live it as you choose to live.

Why Do You Live Fast?

Here's a question to get you pondering: What is the intent behind your desire to live fast? What is the core desire to live a life constantly on the go *stemming from*? And why do you feel the need to always be doing?

It's hard for many people to slow down because we feel a lack of self-acceptance, of approving and loving ourselves for exactly who we are and where we are in our life's story. Perhaps we feel a desire for perfection—that nagging perfectionist within telling us we can't slow down or opportunities will pass us by, leaving us in the dust. That life will move on if we take a pause. Many of us don't slow down because we are afraid of falling behind, the fear of failure trailing our every move.

But what if we gave ourselves some compassion? What if we loved, approved, and accepted ourselves for exactly who we are, for exactly where we are in this present moment in time? Would we continue chasing? Would we keep hustling, rushing, craving? Would we keep feeling this internal pressure to *go*? To speed up? To do more? Or would we just stop? Would we just look around and take it all in? Would we just take a moment to look and revel at it all—the marvelous existence that swirls around us?

When we slow down, we enjoy the unfolding of our lives more. When we take mindful pauses, we enjoy the process of life's delicate and divine timing. When we accept ourselves for where we are in our life's trajectory, we appreciate it more. There is no longer a need to move quickly. The desire for perfection fades, because we are already whole and complete.

Our Dual Natures

We have two energies residing within us: feminine and masculine. When I say masculinity and femininity, I'm not talking about gender or social constructs. I mean *energy*. Energy is nonphysical, and we have both energies within us at all times. We can use these dual energies at any given moment. One is fast, and one is slow. One is yin, and one is yang. One is initiative, and one is intuitive. One is lunar and connected to the moon—our more nurturing energy, that which is more inward and internal. The other is solar and connected to the sun—our more energizing self, that which is initiative- and action-oriented. We have both energies residing within us, and one is not better or worse than the other. But for too long, solar, masculine energy has predominated in our societal narrative. We've been glorifying and praising those who are more energetic, initiating, and driven. But anything taken to an extreme is something to be wary of. Balance is necessary in our lives. We thrive when we have a balance between masculine energy and feminine energy.

Fast Life: The Masculine Mode

The fast life, or masculine mode, is *mind-led.* This is how we've been taught to live over the last hundred years or so. Pick up any self-help book, or watch any Hollywood movie or Netflix show, and you'll see what I mean. You'll see these cartoon-like, overly dramatic versions of characters, such as Cameron Diaz's charming portrayal of Amanda in *The Holiday*, or the likable mania of Sarah Jessica Parker's character in *I Don't Know How She Does It*. These characters are ultimately engaging, appealing, and relatable to the times. But these times are on their way out the door, as more and more people tap into their intuitive energies. What's needed most in our present day is a gentler, softer, more intuitive approach, one in which we feel more peace in our undertakings.

Our masculine mode is focused on initiative, rather than intuition. It has its benefits, and when we tap into it, we can really get a lot accomplished! We can act from a place of service. It's in our masculine energy that we create, and much can be contributed to our world and others when we tap into our masculine nature. But it can very easily take a dark turn when left unchecked. When we constantly live in our masculine mode, we can become detrimental to ourselves and those around us.

Living in a constant state of masculine energy looks like measuring our worth by our productivity, living in a constant state of hustle and to-do lists that need to be checked off as we wonder, "What next?" There's never a feeling of satisfaction and pride in our past achievements because there's always something *new* to do. The horizon is our only focus.

Living in a constant state of initiating feels draining, and we often feel tired, dehydrated, and overly serious because of it. We're glued to our phones, always feeling the temptation to be "on" and connected to the world, because if we aren't tuned in, we'll miss out—on an opportunity, an offer, or a chance to network.

We might possibly overthink things, resulting in chronic pain and trouble turning off at night. In fact, our phone feels like our sleeping buddy: It feels *awkward* going to bed without checking the latest updates. We even check our emails and social media first thing when we wake up and scour the news before drifting off. We feel a need to be constantly responding to emails, texts, and DMs, and we're stressed as a result.

When it comes to love, we're skeptical of it. Sex and pleasure? Who has time for that?! We can't even relax. Libido? *What's that?* We might not believe long-lasting marriages or true love exist, so we feel bitter about dating and opening up to others, and consequently pour our hearts into our careers. Perhaps we feel that people can always leave us, but our treasured belongings are here to stay, so we shop and surround ourselves in shiny new trinkets, feeling safe and secure in the ownership of what we gave to ourselves. We feel the need to protect and shield our vulnerable hearts from the heartbreakers of the world, always looking out for secret motives and reasons one can't be trusted. The assertive, take-life-by-the-reins, trust-nobody, masculine energy we've been taught to strengthen floats around in our subconscious. We were taught as kids to defend, protect, and work hard, but we lose our authenticity that way—the part of us that makes us so very *human*.

When we live in our masculine mode, we feel we can't trust others or trust that life will support us. We don't believe in miracles nor in the idea that life can shower us with blessings. We don't feel comfortable delegating tasks, so we tell ourselves, "If I want it done properly, I'll just do this myself!" We don't feel safe and secure in the present moment, and we don't feel safe in life. In fact, those living in their masculine energy see the gentle, feminine, go-with-the-flow-types as naïve, innocent, and weak. Their thinking is, "They *clearly* haven't had any real-world experiences to knock some cold, hard sense into them. They obviously haven't experienced any trauma. They're just romanticizing life and seeing the world with rose-colored glasses."

Can you *feel* that heaviness? The extremes we go to when we live this way cause us to have no enriching female friendships, no inspiring female expanders, and a lack of love, pleasure, and an enjoyable sex life. In an endless state of masculine energy, we constantly feel like we're on high alert, living in a state of fight-or-flight and seeing what we can *get* from other people instead of what we can *give*. Those who often live exclusively in masculine mode are so deeply enriched in this societally programmed way of living, they don't believe having "balance" in life is a thing.

But there *is* balance, and there's a way to tap into it.

Slow Life: The Feminine Mode

The slow life, or feminine mode, is *heart-led*. The feminine nature is playful, curious, and open with oneself and others. It is asking for what we want with clarity and confidence, without demanding it. This confidence is *quiet*. It's simplifying our life by doing what feels good and exciting! Instead of being hustling entrepreneurs, we're calm and efficient chill-preneurs. We set aside time to relax, unwind, feel pleasure, and do all the things that bring us joy. Instead of constantly feeling like we never have to time for sex, we actively engage in pursuing pleasure, sexual intimacy, and the sensual experience, alone and/or with a partner.

Make no mistake: The feminine mode gets stuff done! We can be productive, efficient, *and* aligned with our feminine energy, but the key difference is that we have lighthearted fun while doing it. We're ambitious, but there's an air of leisure when we go about our goals. We think, "Everything meant to get done will get done. All things have their divine time." We accomplish much, but we go about tackling our goals in a slow, peaceful manner, one that is trusting, calm, and self-assured. There's no need to rush, no need to compete. We don't feel the need to control every microscopic aspect of our work. Instead, we delegate easily and with joy! We hire out help if we need it, and we trust that others can support us in our growth.

Our playful, lighthearted nature allows creativity to *flow* through with ease. It's not effortful because creative ideas are always flowing in, and we've cultivated spaciousness in our minds to recognize them when they drop in. We feel excitement to pursue new creative interests and hobbies, even if they are unpaid and aren't part of our long-term goals.

When we tap into our feminine, receptive mode, we are gentle with our hearts and develop a strong relationship with our inner child, setting aside time to heal, journal, meditate, and be patient with ourselves. We put our health first, and we make sure we're feeling good before we take on the energies of others. Alignment before action is the name of the game!

In our feminine mode, we don't eat, breathe, and sleep with our phone. We may delete social media on the weekends (seriously, one of the best things ever—go try it) or take periodic breaks from Instagram so we can cater to our quiet, inner world. We check our email only at designated times every day, and we don't feel the need to always respond right away. We know that in patience and thoughtfulness, our best responses flow through.

When we've slowed down and connected with our gentle nature, we feel deeply worthy, and we allow ourselves to rest when we want. We say no to other people's demands because we understand our physical, mental, and emotional health is our priority. Without our energy and vitality, we know we have nothing to offer others, so we cater to our own needs first. Our feminine nature is also service-led, giving, and helping others when our cup is full.

When we connect with this more feminine aspect within us, we feel intrinsically *proud* of our growth and *satisfied* with our past accomplishments, without feeling that we could or should be doing more. We no longer experience the nagging feeling of, "I *could* be doing this right now...." When we rest, we rest. We don't question our motives, or wonder if we're fulfilling our future potential. Instead, we relish the moment, feeling grateful for what we've done. We know our worth isn't in what we produce, but in *who we are*.

Rather than being competitive, aggressive, and controlling, we trust ourselves and others. We live and let others live as they see fit. We view the world as a fun playground to explore, and we're open to new people and new experiences that feel foreign and different. When we feel competitive or triggered by others, we implore deep within ourselves and ask *why* we feel the way we do. We act patiently and kindly with ourselves, expressing compassion toward ourselves in moments of healing. We recognize that comparison and jealousy yield no benefit to anyone and are a complete waste of our precious life force. Instead of seeing how we are different, we see how we are similar. We recognize that celebrating other people's success doesn't hurt our own. Instead of comparing, we notice the good we have in our own lives (we are the main characters of our own stories, after all). Instead of feeling bitter, we see opportunities for expansion. Instead of charging ahead out of desperation, we slow down and look within.

When it comes to relationships, we allow ourselves to be vulnerable with others. We wear our hearts on our sleeves because our power is unwavering in its strength. We know being honest and authentic with others attracts like-minded kindred spirits. We know love flourishes in vulnerability, in honesty. We don't feel fear, we only feel trust—in ourselves, in others, in life. We date and befriend people who are uplifting and inspiring, and we cultivate quality female friendships that help nurture our minds, hearts, and spirits.

Our feminine nature is trusting. It's intuitive, sensitive, and so very *connected*. We listen more and talk less. These energies are softer, more harmonious, and ultimately more supportive in our quest to live slow.

The Beauty in Our Duality

As mentioned previously, masculine energy is more initiative, while feminine energy is more intuitive. Both energies are helpful in different ways, but collectively our society tends to applaud "girlboss"

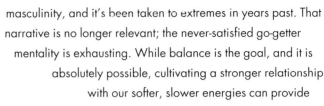

masculinity, and it's been taken to extremes in years past. That narrative is no longer relevant; the never-satisfied go-getter mentality is exhausting. While balance is the goal, and it is absolutely possible, cultivating a stronger relationship with our softer, slower energies can provide maximum benefits as we go through life. There is an ease, an openness, a childlike innocence with which we view life. It's the clearest path to experiencing joy every day.

We often think that, by doing and taking on more, we will accomplish and achieve more. However, when we slow down, we are infinitely more magnetic in attracting our desires. Honoring our sacred rhythms is how we magnetize. When we listen to our inner voice and lead with a pure, open heart, life is exceedingly more abundant.

Burnout: My Journey to Living Slow

If you're reading this book, like me, you may have a gentle heart or an intuitive spirit. In a sense, living slowly is living opposite to the way our world is currently progressing. Life is speeding up, and many of us yearn to slow it down. Technology is moving at a faster rate than ever before, and even the ways we purchase, communicate with one another, and

consume information seem to be moving at warp speed. For a soft and gentle soul, this fast-paced life is overwhelming. Do we need to keep up? How can we press pause? How do we carve out the time to relax and unwind the way we did before? How can we forge deeper relationships and better relate to others in such fast times?

We desire to relish simple moments, and many of us begin to appreciate slow living when we've reached a period of overwhelm in our lives. This is also known as burnout.

Many of us notice our growing interest in slow living in one of two ways:

1. We've lived a long and full life chasing money, achievements, relationships, awards, success, vacations, applause, and/or new shiny objects. We've experienced it all, yet we're still not happy.

2. We sense life doesn't *have* to be so effortful and hard. On a gut level, we just sense there's another way to go about this thing we call "life"—and that it can be simpler!

Or perhaps, like me, you've become aware of these two at the same time. My own life looked like a mix of each. After living a fast and hustle-focused life in New York City in attempts to be a successful performer and actress-turned-entrepreneur, I reached a point of burnout that I needed to address. Having always been a deeply intuitive person, I knew life didn't have to feel so hard. I knew life could be simpler and more free-flowing. I knew life wasn't meant to revolve around the constant striving that the cultural narrative glamorized. When I was twenty-three, the romanticization of productivity, entrepreneurship, and Instagram influencers was all the rage. It was the "four-hour workweek" and "girlboss" era. The lifestyle catered to the #GottaGrind storyline to fully align with my value of living a life of "freedom," and I felt I had to join the crowd.

After hustling it out, spending fifteen-hour days running around the city, it was rather suddenly that I thought, "Enough is enough!" The moment was clear. Watching throngs of people spill across the crosswalks, I sat on the crosstown M50 bus and experienced a serene moment of crystal clarity, one that would change my life and get me off the hamster wheel. In that moment, I wasn't thinking about the future, and I wasn't reminiscing about the past. I was fully in the present moment. Clarity, I later discovered, only comes in moments of total presence. This is how our intuition communicates with us. In that moment of presence, a peacefulness spread across my entire body. The sudden thought—that *knowingness,* gentle and soothing in nature, almost like a tiny water droplet spilling from the crown of my head—lasted no more than a second. But in that moment, I knew I had to slow my life down and leave New York.

The action was quick and effortless. I immediately jumped ship, used my extra babysitting money to buy a ticket to Bali, and began dedicating my free time to learning about meditation, healing modalities, and the slow-living lifestyle. After traveling and living slowly and frugally in Bali, I moved with my boyfriend to a charming, sleepy town in Virginia to start my life over after an ambitious and aggressively paced five years in New York. I was ready to live a creative life doing what I loved as a blogger and photographer, but I didn't want to live so fast-and-hustle and grind-it-out as all the influencers and business coaches on social media were touting. They kept telling us—their followers—that we had *big* things to do with our lives! That we shouldn't waste our potential. But I just felt overwhelmed by all the messaging. I just wanted to enjoy my life in all its simplicity.

Some serious unlearning must take place, I thought. If I read one more caption that read "Rise and grind!" or "If your dreams don't scare you, they aren't *big* enough!" my head was going to explode. Couldn't I do both? Couldn't I live comfortably working for myself as a creative storyteller and *also* live a slower-paced life in alignment with my intuition? It was at this time, while soaking in a steaming bubble bath after a long day of biking and juggling four part-time jobs (at minimum wage), that I picked up Erin Lochenor's *Chasing Slow*, a memoir detailing her journey learning to slow down and simplify her life. Erin's heart and spirit resonated with me on a deep level. Suddenly I felt *seen*. Finally there was someone out there like me who was *doing it,* living that gentler, more peaceful life while also writing and creating online. I knew I didn't need to aim higher, work harder, or strive for bigger. I could *chase slower.*

This, I later learned, was my expander. I knew if someone else was able to see through the murky fog and live life at a slower pace, I could find a way to live it as well. What I didn't know was that my life was about to change forever.

Moving Abroad

A year later, my boyfriend got a job teaching English in France. Within a matter of months, we got married in his parents' tiny backyard, sold all our furniture and belongings, and made the move to France. In a country where the culture and lifestyle were so different in speed, I was forced to adapt and put into practice everything I had been learning about slow, intentional living.

Living in France that first year was a challenge. I had to adjust my pace, inquire about my sense of immediacy, and seriously question the roots of my ambition for the first time. I spent afternoons wandering around Strasbourg, with a notebook tucked under my arm and a camera strapped over my shoulder. I observed and studied the people around me, intrigued by the difference in pace and energy from what I was used to.

While one can certainly live slowly anywhere in the world, not just in France, there is less of an obsession with money, goals, and "leveling up" in Europe than I observed in the United States—so much so, it's noticeably apparent.

The French don't live to work; rather, *they work to live*. Of course, they work hard in their occupations, but the insatiable desire for fame, accumulation, and excess abundance isn't as prevalent. There isn't an obsession with such things. (With the exception of Paris—Parisians have their own unique culture with its own lifestyle. I don't include Paris when I speak of the entirety of France.) Entrepreneurship and social media fame are also not hugely desired in France as they are in the United States. The French live for three things: family, long holidays every August, and interesting conversational debate over good food and wine. Many of the French people I've befriended over the years also happen to be very creative in their occupations, but not for the purpose of being seen or acquiring fame. Paying bills and living a comfortable life are all that's of interest.

It goes without saying that a lot of my passion for sharing about slow living is rooted and inspired by the French way of life. Living in France long-term has certainly shaped my own ideas and way of viewing the world, but so have my travels to the rolling hills and quiet villages of Tuscany or Puglia in Italy, the seaside villages along the Red Sea in Egypt, my aunt and uncle's farm in West Virginia, the quiet isolation in Iceland. It is our environment and cultural experience that shape who we are. And we can decide where we call home in this great big world.

What I'm *Doing* in France

"So what's your plan? What are you doing in France?" I get asked these questions often.

I'm venturing away from what I know, what I was taught. I'm learning to be quiet and observant, curious and patient. Trusting and content with the unknown future. I'm getting accustomed to small-town living, where shops and boulangeries close for two to three hours every afternoon and everything is closed on Sundays. I'm realizing, as I've lived here, how much I used to distract myself, how often I sought motion and movement just to feel settled. I realize how sensitive I have become to noise and content, and how much I *thrive* in silence. And I realize how deeply I crave it, how much I need it to feel connected to life.

In France, I'm learning to slow down, intentionally and mindfully.

My journey living slowly isn't perfect. It isn't aesthetically beautiful. I talk a mile a minute, am naturally very hummingbird-like in energy, and I often get completely and passionately carried away with my work, unaware of the day's passing when I'm in a creative flow state. But all in all, I'm living and unlearning the ideals my home culture has instilled in me. I needed to experience something different to see what I missed. Living in the US, I've been raised with the American belief that any dream is possible, that you must work hard and put in effort to achieve your goals in life, and that a certain measure of success is having enough money to cover all your expenses and then some. I grew up believing ownership of things (a house, car, pension) and titles (CEO, PhD, graduate) were the measure of success. I was programmed to believe that having a full schedule, being involved in plans, and being "busy" meant you were doing well in life. The biggest difference between my life in the US and my life in France is I no longer have a jam-packed calendar of social events and a list of friends to see. And yet, somehow I'm happier here.

What I've learned while living in France is that having less and quietly appreciating the little you do have is the actual secret. Relishing the small things, humming a song, allowing yourself to laugh loudly and openly, to dance when you feel joyous, to overhear yourself mutter words of awe as you notice the natural beauty around you.

France has taught me to let go of the attachments I used to hold so near and dear to my heart—to cultivate a healthy relationship with impermanence and to let go of anything that doesn't bring me inner peace. To embrace the new—new environments, new people, new languages, new cultures, new customs, new belief systems.

France has taught me to live well. While living here, I taught myself how to enjoy the feeling of progress, slow momentum, and joy in moving at the pace that feels right for *me*. I now bask in that delight of *not knowing* and then being surprised by what life has in store for me! I do this by honoring the messages that are coming through for me, from within me. Not questioning myself or doubting what I receive, but listening and honoring my inner voice first. Not every day is perfect. I have my hard seasons, I experience frustration like everyone does, and I'm no enlightened being. But I acquired a morsel of wisdom living abroad that can be learned and experienced anywhere in the world. And it's all rather simple: it's all rooted in listening to the quiet whispers within you, trusting in your unique path and then relaxing into a state of surrender and ease.

Yes, it is easier to live slowly in France. I would be dishonest in saying that location doesn't at all help, even if just a tiny bit. There are systems in place in France that make it easier to live slowly and simply. For example, the salaries are significantly lower in France than in the US for high-paying jobs. No matter the increase in job title or education level, the income ceiling is significantly lower than in the US. There isn't an extreme gap in pay between a teacher and a scientist, or a doctor and an administrator. The gap between the rich and the poor is smaller. As a result, everyone can meet their basic needs. Stress, overall, is lower, and worries associated with living expenses, education, and medical care costs are fewer. Healthcare costs are significantly less in France (for example, twenty euros will cover the cost of a cavity filling). The cost of housing is proportionate to salaries, and education costs are also lower. Crippling student debt isn't a thing in France. Students can get their university degree very cheaply (or for free) so more people have an opportunity to be successful later in life and to have stability in their careers and finances.

Now, it would be naïve for me to say finances don't contribute to living a slower pace of life, because they do. Without having our basic needs met, we would always be hustling to survive. Without structural support, we would fear the unknown, fear the future, and fear slowing down. Fear is what leads us to live the fast life. Fear of death, fear of illness, fear of poverty, fear of missing out, fear of being left behind.

Fear is why most people are afraid to slow down and move at an intuitive pace.

When healthy food options, safe and affordable housing, and universal healthcare are accessible for everyone, it is easier to slow down and desire less. You don't need to go faster, hustle harder, or achieve more to move up the ladder, because the rewards are fewer. Unlike in the US, where higher education is equated with a higher-status job title and higher salary, living in France offers far less lofty, shiny opportunities for growth, but it does provide a sense of comfort and, most importantly, peace of mind.

While you can live slowly and simply anywhere in the world, it *is* easier to adjust to a slower pace in France, because the systems and structures in place there support it. Access to a slower pace of living doesn't make France perfect, as there are also a lot of things about life here that are not ideal, but the structural support does help.

While there is much to be said about what I've learned in France, perhaps the single most important thing I've embraced is the slow-living lifestyle.

Life moves fast, and slowing it down allows you to fully appreciate the small wonders around you and to remember what joy, fun, and presence feel like. Living slowly has changed my life in more ways than one, and you too can live slowly *anywhere* in the world.

Here's how.

"Peace of mind comes when your life is in harmony with true principles and values."

–Stephen R. Covey

2
—

Your Core Essence

If you had one day, what would you do?

We often think of all the big things we want to do and have in our lives: see the pyramids, travel the world, own a house, write a book. We create these bucket lists and vision boards and, dreaming bigger than our parents, we chase *progress*. But our truest, most authentic selves come forward when we ask ourselves this one question: If I had one day, how would I *choose* to spend it? What would I do with my time? Would I spend it with other people, or would I spend it by myself? Would chasing that one goal really matter to me in the grand scheme of my life, or am I doing it for someone else?

So often we carry values and dreams from our childhood into our present without realizing those dreams were developed out of fear or a need to prove something.

I left home at eighteen to pursue a career in New York City that would most satisfy the hopes my teachers, parents, peers, and mentors had for me. Over the years, the dream fell away from me, but I kept holding on. I soon realized I wasn't "chasing the dream" to make myself happy. I was doing it to fulfill an identity I created. A lot of us stick with things for years because we feel guilty about quitting. I rationalized that I was making so many people proud, so I couldn't quit. I had to prove my value to others and show them I could see the dream through to the very end. A few years later, when I finally mustered up the courage to leave that childhood dream behind, I was surprised to hear how many people back home told my mom that it was such a shame I had left that pursuit, such wasted talent. "A waste of potential," they said.

But I was rejuvenated. I was filled with a new vigor for life, a sense of aliveness I hadn't felt in *years*. This experience made me realize how personal and subjective values are. The values of one person might not be the same as those of another. While some may value talent and accomplishment, others may value simplicity and personal joy. Perhaps some value health and wellness, a deeply fulfilling marriage, or a circle of friends. One might honor spiritual growth over physical health. What do you value most? What in your life do you naturally find yourself prioritizing over other things? And what would you drop everything for in a moment—your friends, your sibling, your mother, your partner, your audience?

Knowing what is most important to you gives you clarity, so you can prioritize the essential. Everything in our lives blooms when we have clarity.

As I grew into my twenties, I realized I had placed a deep value on my career and public reputation because those were the values my peers celebrated and encouraged in me. It's what I was shown and taught. When you're routinely told where your talents lie and how you should spend your time to maximize your "potential," you start to go along with it blindly, ignoring the light pings in your heart asking you to reconsider. You nod your head, telling yourself how you *should* be spending your time, what you *should* prioritize. The programming we receive in childhood can last a lifetime, unless we have the courage to examine and question its source.

Anytime we do this sort of inner work, there needs to be a momentary pause. Reflection is paramount. Your route must be reevaluated: *Is this the direction I want to go? Does this feel right?*

Your days matter. Life's joys are *in* the day-to-day. If there's no enjoying the process and the daily happenings of life, what's the point of it all?

The Success Myth: How We've Been Taught to Be Happy

Everyone views success differently. Success is not defined by a particular award, a high number of social media followers, or even if one is married. It doesn't equate to a certain amount of money earned or countries visited. Success can be a rather simple, ordinary life, one filled with small joys and ample leisure time to enjoy your hobbies. For some, having the freedom to dedicate more time to their hobbies, health, and wellness is valued more highly than earning a six-figure salary. For others, earning a $40,000 salary is perfect. Some consider success to be earning enough money to own a few houses in different parts of the world. To others, success is having enough money to afford a trip to Disneyland once a year! To some, success is in *being rooted*, and for others, it's in *being rootless*. We each have a personal definition of what equates to happiness and fulfillment, and it's largely based on our values.

Perhaps you value contribution in life. Contribution can look like being an active member of your neighborhood or community. It can look like living a life that feels fun and authentic to the dreams of your inner world. It can be as simple as sleeping in every morning, or waking up every day to purring cats kneading at your feet and enjoying time spent curling up with a book in bed. Success can be as simple as waking up healthy, alive, and grateful that the sun has risen another day and it is warm enough to enjoy it. Success can be having the freedom in your morning to start your workday slowly, with a cup of hot chocolate, a journal jot, a tarot-card pull, a stretch on your yoga mat, or a favorite library book.

It's important that we each define success for ourselves. We must question everything society, our teachers, and even our favorite self-help authors have taught us over the years.

Let's slow down for a second, take a breather, and inquire deeper:

- Were the dreams expressed to you ever *your* dreams?
- *Where* did you get your identification of success?
- What did your first glimpse of success look like? Where was it? How did it make you feel? Who showed it to you?

Think back to the person who influenced your definition of success. Now, where did *they* get their vision of success? Did they appear happy while chasing that version of success? Perhaps the *chasing* of a goal is their alignment. There are a lot of achievers out there (hello, enneagram type 3!), and achievers love a good goal to pursue. They genuinely relish the process of racing after something not yet acquired.

But that doesn't mean *you* have to chase.

Ask yourself: Is it possible *their* measure of success is someone else's, and they, too, are regurgitating values, dreams, and information that aren't even their own heart's desires? Knowing our values and remaining *still* enough to listen to our heart's wishes is so important. We waste more time being active and busy, accomplishing a list of checked-off to-do items, than when we are still, silent, and present in thought.

Many of us believe success means achieving desired outcomes. We feel we'll be happy when we *have* and *do* all the things that beckon us. We tell ourselves, "If only I had *this*, then I would be happy."

But what if, instead of focusing solely on having things and doing things, we focused on *being*?

Forget what the media presents, what influencers show you, what your peers dream of, what your parents taught you to believe. Success is not measurable, and it cannot be quantified. Slow living asks us to inquire more. No matter what your dream is, you'll only be satisfied with your success if you know what you *value*.

An Easier Way to Dance with Life

Instead of grasping for specific outcomes to be happy, our priorities must embody our values—*the feelings we most desire*. So much in life is outside of our control. There are principles at play, planets in orbit, puzzle pieces hidden. To pretend we are in total control of all the principles at play is a waste of our precious life energy. There is a certain beauty in humility—humility in the wonders of life and that there is so much we don't yet know.

Amor Fati. Love Your Fate.

It's silly to hold ourselves personally accountable for every single result or outcome. Outcomes are completely out of our hands, but what we *can* control is our actions. Showing up is enough.

Instead of measuring results, we can measure how aligned our values are with our daily choices. To live in alignment with your values is to flow with the natural current downstream. There's no effort, no resentment, no frustration, no bitterness, because you're dancing *with* life.

Instead of focusing strictly on achieving goals or judging our progress based on what we have, focus on *being*. "Being" is a state of presence. A feeling. It's being *fully present* in every moment, given the current circumstances of your life. Feelings of joy, fulfillment, and peace don't rely on having attained a specific outcome or result, but rather on fully expressing and living out your values every moment of your life. Expressing our values anywhere we live, in any situation, with any resource at our current disposal, is real freedom, real empowerment.

Values: Your Core Essence

Your values are the foundational aspects of *you*. They are the *feelings* you resonate with most and wish to embody. Let's call them your *core essence*. When you live true to your core essence, you feel connected to yourself and to life on a deep, *energetic* level. When you live in harmony with your essence, you start dancing with life. And it's just all around *way more fun!*

But how does one find their core values? Here are some questions to get you pondering…

- What do you spend a lot of your time thinking about, planning for?
- What are you often budgeting and saving your money for?
- If no one was watching you in your day-to-day life, what would you spend the most time doing? How do you spend your energy, and what fills your cup?
- When you're socializing with friends, what topics excite you? Light up your eyes? What do you find yourself talking about the most, or *wishing* you could say? What could you talk about for hours on end?
- What do you spend the most time researching, Googling, learning about? What books and classes catch your eye?
- What inspires you when you're browsing Pinterest, scrolling through Instagram, flipping through magazines? What pictures hold your attention? And what do those pictures have in common? What is the core energetic root of that visual, that color—what word comes to mind?
- What do you most dream about? While daydreaming, what is your future self doing? Where are they? How do they appear to be feeling?

These are all signs, hints leading you to the essence of who you are. All it takes is some pondering, light reflection, and journaling.

Your values are your foundational blocks—the core makeup of who you are and what you desire most in life. These qualities are most private and personal to you. No one needs to know what they are, or even recognize these aspects in you. All that matters is that your values reflect who you are deep down and not what you aspire to be. Values are always present-moment-focused; they live in the *here and now*.

Our core values should be innately fulfilling and an expression of our truest self. This requires you to be honest with yourself. Integrity is needed when digging! Clear out any expectations you may have for your future—any goals or measurable achievements you hope to get out of doing this inner work. Living slowly is not about living a life that looks good to others; it's about living a life of authentic truth, however that looks and feels to *you*. Your core values should feel ease-filled, a *natural* extension of your soul's essence and innermost expression. They should feel like home—a sigh of relief, a breath of fresh air. They should feel as snug as a cozy sweater, the perfect fit.

Your core values can also change with time and should remain flexible, focused on the present moment and where you are currently in this chapter of your life. Our values are like *feelings*—they cannot be crossed off a list and they aren't goals, because they can't be measured.

It's also important to note that there will be times when attaining certain outcomes does feel internally joyful and fulfilling to your core essence. But that's because there is a *deeper* value behind the action or outcome. For example, if you desire to have a large following on social media, the deeper value behind that outcome might be "being seen" or "recognition."

Goals are great to have, as long as they connect back to your values. But "success" should be based on the action taken, not on the result. What matters most is your own internal alignment and follow-through. Life becomes stressful when we focus on grasping for specific outcomes instead of enjoying the ride. Don't allow your imagination to get the best of you. *What is present now?* What action can you take now in your current reality? What is the path that feels most *ease*-filled, most aligning…most *fun?* And remember, values do not follow the traditional narrative we've been taught of, "When I get this, then I'll be content and satisfied with my life," because we can only live true to them today, *right now,* in this very moment. They're not focused on a target far off in the future. You can embody your core essence anywhere.

A Note on Desire

We don't chase after *things*; we chase after *feelings*. Feelings are our most powerful compass. Our emotions dictate how we think, feel, and believe. When we get to the root of *why* we crave something in life, it's always connected to a feeling we wish to have. It's never the *car* we want. It's not the *award* we deeply desire. It's not the beautiful house we want. Rather, it's the *feeling* of security, safety, and rootedness we crave. It's not the expensive *wardrobe* we wish to be able to afford; it's the style, comfort, and authentic self-expression we wish to embody.

We must first recognize it's not ever the thing we want, but the *essence* of it. We want to feel and embody the feeling—the value—the thing gives us.

Knowing your values is extremely helpful in slowing down and centering yourself to ground your actions in the present. It's the simplest, most effective way to live a life of intention and integrity. Knowing your values helps you zoom out and think about the big picture of your life and the direction in which you're headed.

To illustrate an example, below are my four current values and how I prioritize and express them in my life.

Freedom

Freedom of place, movement, finances, time, creativity. Having ample spaciousness in all my attachments. This looks like investing, finding ways to earn money passively, saying no more often than yes. This feels like a life of quiet, with plenty of spare time and empty days on the calendar to focus on my various interests and passions.

Creativity

Self-expression, speaking, writing, creating something daily, filming, decorating, sketching, watercolor painting, working with pastels, organizing, decluttering, letter-writing, flower arranging, scrapbooking, sharing with others online and in my local community. I prioritize and shape my lifestyle around a feeling of total heart-based, creative self-expression.

Growth

Learning, debating, taking classes, reading, researching, challenging, and having conversations. I love to be challenged, and I seek new experiences, people, places, and lessons because I desire to feel a sense of growth, to feel stretched in all areas of my life. I seek to always be expanding.

Play

Leisure, games, outdoor activities, spontaneity, road trips, local adventures, belly laughs, lighthearted fun, fostering kittens, spending time with animals and children! I want to feel a sense of lightness, humor and playfulness as a reminder that life doesn't have to be so serious!

Discover Your Core

Here are some ways to discover, connect, and live out your core essence.

Quiet the Mind

Look inward before you start searching through lists and trying on words for size. I find this little exercise helpful: Close your eyes, take a few deep breaths, and ask yourself, "How do I want to feel in my life?" On the exhale, wait for the answer to bubble up to the surface. Sit patiently and ask again if necessary. Then, ask yourself, "How can I best embody my authentic self?" Listen to your intuition, and wait patiently for a word or feeling to come forward. Hash it out in your journal and keep a record of what came up for you.

Break Out a List

After you've meditated on it, it's time to pull out the list! If you need help discovering your values and don't know where to begin, peruse a list of values or feelings and circle all the words that resonate with you on a deep, heartfelt, *gut* level. Danielle Laporte has an incredible list of values, or "core desired feelings" as she calls them, in her book *The Desire Map*. You can also find extensive lists online via Google. Scan the words one by one and wait for a feeling of, "*Yes,* this is *so* me!" If you have a hard time picking a few from the list, narrow them down by crossing off those that don't speak to you. Repeat the process a few times and keep eliminating until only a handful remain.

Know What You *Don't* Desire

When discovering your core, it's helpful to know what you *don't* want to feel. What lifestyle or feelings make you want to turn around and walk—perhaps *run*—the other way? Do you want a feeling of spontaneity and adventure in your present life, or would you prefer a quiet, calm, and cozy lifestyle that's predictable, secure, and gives you a sense of routine and stability?

My husband and I, for example, want a life of stillness, peace and quiet, nonattachment and freedom—in essence, a life free from serious responsibilities—so we can prioritize our own personal interests, hobbies, and travels. We've always known that our mutual values and long-term vision meant choosing not to have children. Not because we don't love kids (I'm a total kid magnet and we both love spending time with children!), but because the *feeling* and lifestyle that having a family entails does not match the values we wish to feel in our life together. *Clarity is powerful.* This simple act of knowing very clearly what you don't want to have in your life helps you zero your focus in on what you *do* want, to narrow down your most treasured values. Knowing we don't want to have children points us toward our most cherished value: freedom.

Break It Down

It's easy to lose track of your values when you have more than five of them, so narrow them down to four or five and ask yourself what you'd like to do to express and embody those values within a specific timeframe. If one of your values is "minimal" or "spacious" and your goal is to feel less cluttered in your home, you might donate items you no longer love, paint your walls a lighter neutral tone, and get rid of excess pieces to budget for a single piece you really love instead. Some habits might include washing your dishes as soon as you eat, putting things away in their proper place immediately upon entering the home, or regularly clearing out high-traffic areas. Create some space and break your actions into small, manageable tasks to get you closer to embodying your core essence.

Baby Steps

If you don't know which action steps to take, start small. One small step at a time in the right direction is better than taking no steps at all. When you take steps that are aligned with your core, they should feel peaceful and natural, not forced or overwhelming. If it feels forced, or like you're swimming upstream against the current, revisit your approach and strategy. Don't try to force these values to work. If they don't fit you perfectly, try something new!

Memorize 'Em!

It's important to memorize your values—the words you identify with your core essence—because you'll need to remind yourself of them when making decisions. Every decision, commitment, and choice in life should reflect your core essence. When times are busy, having values in the back of your mind is an easy way to recenter and ground. Write your values in your journal or on a Post-it note and place it somewhere you'll catch a glimpse of it often.

Stack Habits On

Next are habits! *My favorite part.* Start to ponder what habits you can implement to express your core essence. Habits are different from actions: actions may occur once, but habits are recurring actions or routines we do regularly. Habits are much more important than actions. Instead of creating multiple habits at once, stick with one new habit that is aligning until you start to do it without thinking. I find habit tracking incredibly helpful in getting started with new routines and habits that feel foreign. If you find yourself getting off track with your new habits, don't feel guilty! Be easy on yourself, take it slow, and start again the next day. Habits take time to build. Our motivation will wane and wander, but returning to it, and to our values, is most important.

Once the habit becomes second nature, you can stack on more habits. For example, if your value is to feel "energized," you can take your vitamins or B12 supplement immediately upon walking in the door after your run outside! A *triple-stacked* habit might look like putting on uplifting music, dancing in your living room, and drinking a tall glass of water—these three habits will simultaneously help you embody a feeling of energy. Whatever habits help you *feel* your chosen value, stacking them onto each other at the same time and in the same place every day helps you ingrain those new patterns. Make habits easy and fun!

A Note on Habits

Make Habits Obvious

Set your daily intentions for your value-based habits at certain times of the day.
Example: I will do ___ habit at ___ time in ___ location.

Make Habits Easy

The easier and more obvious you make a habit, the more likely you are to do it. Making habits convenient will keep resistance at bay.

- Example: Set your cute workout clothes by the door the night before, place your meditation pillow and favorite journal on your bedside table, schedule time for nature walks in your daily planner, or fill your water bottle the night before and place it in the fridge for easy access in the morning.

Make Habits Attractive

Create ease-filled *transitions* to move you into each habit. Pair an action you *want* to do (example: listen to music/podcast) with an action you *must* do (example: drive to work). On those extra-hard days when you feel additional resistance to following through on your value-based habits, simply listening to feel-good music or a podcast works wonders in lifting your mood or mindset.

Review and Reflect

Our values change with time, so it's important to periodically check back in with yourself. If you currently desire a life filled with adventure, but you once valued a lifestyle rooted in rest and relaxation, you need to swap out the old values that no longer align with the *current* you. We are growth-seeking beings, forever morphing into new versions of ourselves. As we grow older, our circumstances change. Be open and flexible to this change in your values, and the process will feel much easier! If we don't periodically reflect and review, we'll never be able to expand. If we don't adapt, we risk becoming stagnant. As growth-seeking beings, nothing is more painful than stagnation.

Resistance & Finding Our Way Home

Just because we are consciously aware of our values and know the actions we need to take to embody those values, it doesn't mean we *do* them consistently. We feel resistance when our fears, doubts, and worries start to float to the surface. Resistance may feel like you're stuck, pinned down, or held back from any forward movement. It's a feeling of stagnation or delay, because while we *know* what we need to do, we feel the pangs of doubt holding us back and keeping us small. Then, we stop ourselves from fully expressing our values. We dim our lights from shining bright. We tone ourselves down, hiding our core essence as a result. It'll cause us to overthink, question ourselves, and justify or rationalize the things we really want. We'll fall into a pit of deep despair: the holy grail of scarcity-thinking. *There isn't enough time. I don't have the right tools, the right equipment, or the resources to follow through on any of this. What's the point?*

This is the ego talking, not the core essence or the radiant spirit and soul that is *you*! Resistance is rooted in fear. It looks like limiting beliefs, negative self-talk, imposter syndrome, and endless procrastination, and it fears disapproval and rejection. We overthink when we live in fear of what other people think. When resistance flares up, which is inevitable, we revert back to our old habits—habits that are easy and comforting and bring us temporary relief, such as procrastination, binge-watching television or media, scrolling on our phones, shopping, drinking, avoiding, etc. Basically, we'll do *anything but* the thing we really want and need to do. Short-term, it feels great! Momentarily, we feel a sweet sigh of escape. Long-term, we miss out on living in harmony with our highest self—the version that deeply desires to live in tandem with its innermost truth. This is the meaning of living a slow, intentional, and deliberate life—one in which we prioritize the person we want to become, the soul essence we know and *feel* deep down is within us, but are too afraid to see flourish. To live slowly and intentionally implies living a values-led life, frequently referring to them to remind us of the long-term big picture of our lives and, ultimately, to what really matters to our highest self.

When You Feel Stuck

When you find resistance flaring up, try some of these little actions to realign with your core essence.

- Physicalize it! Get your body movin' and groovin'!
- Make a playlist with songs that embody your core essence, soul, and feelings. Play it whenever you want to activate your highest self.
- Channel your core essence in the present moment, no matter your current circumstances. Ask yourself, "What can I do *now*?"
- Notice the feeling. Observe it, label it, and say it aloud.
- Become aware of your habitual thoughts, specifically the negative ones that play on a loop. Write them down and reflect.
- Question negative thoughts. Ask yourself: "Is this true? Do I have evidence of this?"
- Catch the negative thought and immediately replace it.
- Pick up "morning pages" and get in the habit of doing three pages of rampant journaling first thing in the morning.
- Get an accountability partner; send voice memos to one another.
- Take consistent baby steps. Instead of blaming yourself for failing, redirect yourself to the present moment and take the next baby step in alignment with your core essence.
- Learn new skills and continue to expand your knowledge.
- Join a community.
- Create joyful morning habits.
- Delegate tasks or ask for help.
- Get still and write to your inner voice.
- Data-collect: Experiment with new habits, hobbies, and interests, and keep an open mind.
- Accept and celebrate your desire to pivot. Change up your habits, actions, and routines if they no longer feel aligned. Switch up your values if they no longer resonate.

Truthfully, we all have times when we fall, fail, and need to start over, times when we need to ask for help or support. When we are fully aware of our core essence and what's most important, and take tangible actions that are value-driven, we are always exactly where we are meant to be.

Let go of the reins of life and trust that you'll be okay, even if your mind initially encounters resistance. You can always take a pause. You can always pivot and make a detour. Slow down, look around, and refigure your next steps. Adjustment is a possibility at any given time. Opportunity renews daily.

A Note on Purpose

Our purpose is not always in the *thing* we do. Some of us aren't here on earth to make or invent a specific thing. Some of us aren't here to perform or spread a certain message or to be remembered for our role as parent, spouse, caregiver, or teacher. Our purpose is never attached to earning a certain amount of money or owning an amount of land, buildings, capital, you name it. Our purpose goes deeper than that.

In my own life, I've realized my purpose is not in the actions I take; my purpose is *my energy.* My energy, when rested, nourished, and replenished, is joyful and easily contagious to those around me. I can light up a room immediately upon walking into it. I can turn a stranger's day around after a few minutes of conversation. From teachers and baristas to strangers in the park and people I've served at restaurants, I've been told, "Your joy is infectious!" and "Your energy is contagious!" This is not something I ever think about or a quality I ever need to work on. It is my natural essence, my purpose, and my soul's gift. It's something that comes naturally and easily to me, and when harnessed in a positive way, it uplifts other people's energy when I am around them. This is my purpose, and there's never a need to attach it to my self-worth or income. I don't need to win awards for it, or even be recognized for it. I don't need to *do* or *earn* anything. I must simply be myself and remove the fears and blocks that get in the way of it shining. This is just one example of how a purpose doesn't have to be something we do, earn money from, or tied to a family role. *Our purpose can be in our energy alone.* Perhaps, like me, your purpose is also to uplift people by simply being yourself. Or maybe your gift is your humor, your quick-wittedness, your intensity, your stoic nature, or your depth of feeling. Some of us, like my husband, are here to be grounding forces, to help root and connect others with their calming nature. We all are unique and have individual gifts we came to earth with. What's yours?

Often what we see and like in other people serves as a mirror, reflecting that which we have in ourselves. Look around at the personalities that attract you. What is it about their energy that connects you with them? Do you notice a trend? If we think about people we admire and those who inspire us, we'll find distinct correlations between them all. You'll find a similar theme at their core. It reflects what you have within yourself—perhaps that which needs more nurturing, honoring, and sharing. Caring for yourself, upholding your boundaries, and understanding what *you need* most to embody your highest self is your ultimate form of healing and nourishment.

Lastly, you fulfill your soul's mission and your purpose in small, incremental ways. It's not in the big action steps or the grand achievements that you accomplish your purpose, but rather in little everyday things. You can live out your purpose *now.* You don't need the fanciest resources or environment to live it. Our purpose is to show up consistently with integrity, and we do this by living our truth fully and unabashedly, with our values acting as the compass pointing us to our true north.

☼

Regardless of our environment, circumstances, and daily happenings, what matters most is living true to our core essence. You successfully operate as your highest self when your life is aligned with your values. A feeling of accomplishment and possession can be felt long before we receive anything. We can feel joy while we're in the process of it. The joy must be in the *work*, not the result of it.

Living a slow, value-driven life requires patience. Instead of living fast, walk steadily and water your garden. With each new day, a new brick is being laid. What you plant each day will bloom.

It Starts Here-It Starts Within

"There are two ways to get enough: one is to continue to accumulate more and more. The other is to desire less."

—G. K. Chesterton

3
—

Simplicity

Michelangelo once said that, before he started work on his *David*, the sculpture was already complete within the marble block. It was already there, and he just had to chisel away the excess material. He said, "I saw the angel in the marble and carved until I set him free."

Our lives show astounding parallels. Instead of always adding more to our lives, what if the simplest way to free ourselves from overwhelm is to *subtract*? To remove that which is clouding up our focus, to rid ourselves of that which is hiding our gifts? What we need is to clear the decks, scrub the floorboards, sweep out the cobwebs of fear, and clear out the unhealthy habits we routinely fall back on when life presents obstacles.

The ego, the manic chatterbox that is the mind, always wants to add more to our lives. So we pile more things on—food, shopping, social events, obligations, responsibilities, television—to escape that which we don't want to see. Excess is how we cover fear. Fear lives in a state of insatiable *desire*; it will always want more and will never be happy with less. But what if we flipped it? What if we chose to uncover the *root* of our lives, to take away that which is blinding us to our truth?

The answer lies in simplicity.

Everything you need to know, you already have. What you seek, you already know. All you need to do is remove what covers it. Remove the excess and discover the core—the radiance within you.

Notice where your time goes. Where do you place most of your focus in your day? Be gently aware of *what* you give your attention to repeatedly, and *how* you replenish that energy. Time is not a renewable resource. It is your most valuable currency. Your energetic life force, and the time you get to utilize that force, is immensely valuable. *How* you choose to spend your time dictates how you spend your life. Having too many faucets running will deplete your energy, whether it's the attention you're giving to someone in person, online, or in your thoughts. What you *think* about is where you deposit your energy, and we have a limited amount of energy. The key to living a simple life is to mindfully manage your energy, know your values and non-negotiables, and stop giving your excess energy, time, and attention to things that aren't beneficial.

While I certainly love the idea of always having an infinite amount of time and resources (and in essence, this is true—we *do* live in an abundant universe), we must also realistically look at what we have in the present moment: twenty-four hours in each day. Everyone, excluding time travelers, has a certain amount of time allotted to them daily. There are only so many places we can be at a given time, and there are only so many resources we can use in a single given moment. We can't give our attention to everything and everyone all the time.

It goes without saying that we must eliminate certain things to create space for the things we want to prioritize. The aim is to remove things in our lives that are not personally important or *life-giving* to us and replace them with value-led actions. For example, if "creativity" is an important value to you and you sign up for a painting class on Thursday nights from six to eight o'clock in the evening, you'll need to *remove* the items on your current schedule at that time during the week. If you want to dedicate more time to your children, you'll need to cut back on after-hours drinks with your colleagues. If freedom is an important aspect of your core essence and you wish to travel more or live abroad and own less possessions, buying property in the United States might cause additional resistance and block you from living your core essence.

We want to keep things as simple as possible.

Understanding your core values is the first step. Upon discovery, you must remove what hinders you or holds you back from taking *ease-filled* action. Resistance will always find a way to creep in, but with our values set firmly in our mind's eye, we can remind ourselves of our priorities and simplify the important and mundane decisions in our everyday lives.

Now, if you're saying, "Yeah, sure, but I don't have *time* to live slowly and embody my values right now, Helena!" I hear you. But I also find there are always *pockets* of time we can use to our advantage. It can be one hour in the early morning before the kids wake up, or late at night when the dishes are cleaned and the kitchen put to rest, when a clear moment of time presents itself to you.

Depending on your situation, however, there may be things in your life right now that you can't say no to— things that aren't aligning but that you can't actively change in your life in the present. This is okay. Baby steps are great for this! Instead of taking drastic measures and changing your life by leaps and bounds, commit to taking small daily actions with what you *can*. Habit tracking works wonders.

Taking fifteen minutes to engage in an activity that helps you embody your values is better than no time spent at all. Give yourself grace, be gentle on yourself, and do what you can with what you're given.

Chances are, most of us spend time doing things that are not value-driven or personally important to us. We overcommit ourselves to things that are not important, thus overcomplicating our lives and overwhelming in the process. Many of us fill every inch of our schedule, taking on more responsibilities than are physically and mentally feasible. We're afraid of confrontation, of saying no and putting ourselves first. Then, there's also the fear of missing out—a strong one, indeed. This is why embracing simplicity is important.

Embrace Simplicity

When we embrace simplicity in our lives, we realize less is more. The more we have, the higher the possibility that confusion and overwhelm can occur. The more options we have while shopping, the higher the chance we'll have a bout of buyer's remorse afterwards. The more options we have in our lives, the less fulfilling the outcome will be, because we'll always have something to compare it to. Comparison is the *ultimate* taker of gratitude. We can't appreciate what we have in our lives if we are always looking outside of us. By appreciating what we have and *tempering* the desire to have more in our lives, we learn to be grateful for the things we have in the present. With fewer options, we have fewer comparisons.

Doing less is not lazy; it's intentional and wise. Don't allow society's constant striving to distract you from the pangs of your heart, the callings deep within you to eliminate and simplify. Honor yourself, because honoring your desire to do less actually gifts you with the discernment and openness to soar through life with ease, to live in total alignment with your unique truth, to be the main character of *your* story! When we apply discernment to our time, energy, and resources, we step fully into our power. Living intentionally is empowering. Saying no to excess is rooted in a place of power. When we say no and honor our time and boundaries, we are living in our self-worth. That empowerment is contagious! It inspires others to live their truth as well. Our aim should no longer be to please people or take on *more* than we have space for. Our goal is to live in total harmony with what we need and what brings us joy, because that joy boosts our own life force and sends a ripple effect to everyone watching our lives, empowering others to honor and respect themselves and live their truths.

When we simplify our lives, we open doorways for things that aren't intrinsically joyful to flow out with ease. When we know our worth and live with simplicity, we open new windows for the light to get in, for new opportunities and positive experiences that are perfectly, divinely meant for us. Simplifying creates that space. Beautiful gifts can't fall into our orbit when our lives are crowded with excess. Without awareness, we automatically block the good from coming to us. We turn ourselves off, blocking out the good, the magic we can't see yet, because we're so busy looking at the clutter.

You can't be fully present in your life if your mind is somewhere else, constantly seeking approval from others. You can't live a life of integrity and truth if you are distracted by the unnecessary excess that continues to tempt you. Allow the universe to shower you with blessings by getting rid of mental clutter and simplifying.

Slow It Down

Slowing down doesn't mean accomplishing less. Simplifying is discerning the essential from the unnecessary. It's cutting out the distractions and unhelpful options that are inimical to enjoying the process. It's about eliminating the need to rush, whether that be literal or the mere perception of it, and choosing to see the beauty in the simplicity of the moment. *Slow it down.* Instead of being stressed or annoyed by a train delay, rebrand it as a gift, a chance to enjoy some restful moments. While waiting in line, instead of immediately scrolling on your phone, allow your mind to wander. Go for a short walk without your phone. Daydream. Lie down on your living room floor and gaze up at the ceiling for a few moments. Close your eyes and feel the sun on your face. Consider attending a meditation retreat, or listening to silence for the entire afternoon. Cut out media on Sundays. Create space in your day to *appreciate* more before piling on more things to *do*. Slow it down by finding pockets of empty space.

Write It Out

For some of us, our brains go into hyperdrive at night. A simple way to ameliorate and simplify this mental chatter is to keep a notebook and pen near your bedside. Get in the habit of writing out the emotions and thoughts bottled up within you when you find yourself overthinking. Pour out the excess onto the page: the worries, the doubts, the dreams, the hopes, the fears, the to-do lists, the pro/con lists, the grocery lists, the shopping lists. Just get it out of your body and put it somewhere else. Make space in your mind by moving these thoughts elsewhere. Aside from simplifying our thoughts, writing has also been shown to reprogram fears and limiting beliefs. Our hands and fingertips form a connection to our hearts when we write. We move the excess energy from our minds and into the body. After writing in a stream of consciousness style for a few minutes, it's quite easy to enter a state of hypnosis, an alpha brain-state associated with deep physical and mental relaxation, like when we daydream or engage in light meditation. It is through the act of handwriting that we access the gateway to our subconscious mind and strengthen our relationship to our inner voice. When we write on paper and access this peaceful hypnotic state, studies have shown it's the optimal time to reprogram the mind with new beliefs and improve learning and focus.

So pour your thoughts and emotions onto the page, first thing in the morning and right before falling asleep. When you're worried or stressed, I encourage you to write until there are no words left. Get in the habit of simplifying your life by taking your thoughts out of your mind and putting it all onto the page. Physicalize it. Journaling is my life's greatest joy, and as an active diarist of over twenty years, I can say it is the best way to remove the heaviness of thought, simplify excess worries, and ultimately feel lighter.

Be Okay with Good Enough

Perfection is nonexistent. We'll never reach a state of perfection, no matter how hard we try or how thorough our observations. Instead of focusing on being the absolute *best*, pick a few things you can be great at and leave the rest to being good enough. Learn to be content with doing *good*. In some ways, striving for perfection is a nice direction to aim for. Noble even. Wanting achievement isn't a bad thing, and one we shouldn't feel guilt for. But perfection is an impossible reach—one we seek but will never attain. At the end of the day, we won't remember how perfect, polished, or pulled-together someone is—we remember how people make us *feel*, not their superiority. Eliminate the unnecessary perfection that plagues your consciousness and aim for *good*.

Simplify Your Desires

Try this little experiment: Spend a full forty-eight hours consciously noting all the little hopes, dreams, wants, and desires that float across your mind. Write them down if you want. Then roll a bracelet onto your wrist and turn it every time you find yourself desiring something new in your day. Notice how many times you want something new. Chances are, it's probably often. The mind is constantly in want of more. Now, try noticing the things you have already, the small things you appreciate now. What things in your life already give you a warmth in your heart or a pep in your step? Quit focusing on the problems. Quit paying attention to what's going wrong or what you don't have. At the end of the day, what we all really want is to deeply feel the beauty in our lives. But that can only happen when we pause and observe. When we simplify our desires, we also simplify our need to compare ourselves to others in the process. Here's the thing about comparison: We will always be aware of people who have more than us. There will always be people we're jealous of, because *no one* has it all. There will always be someone who has more or does more than you. You can unfollow them and block them out of your life, pretending they don't exist, but there will *always* be someone else to take their place. Instead of ignoring, unfollowing, and averting your attention, focus on what you already have. Celebrate the small things in your *own* life. This is the best way to cure comparison and to simplify an emotional state of desire. Train your mind to notice the abundance you have now, and your thoughts of comparison and scarcity will shrink. The sooner you realize how valuable your life is, how much you already have presently, the less thirsty you'll feel, the less you'll desire, the more you'll dance with life.

Simplify the Need to Possess

Do you ever wonder why we find it socially acceptable to have huge piles of stuff in our homes that never get used? Why do we continue to clutter our sanctuary with things that don't add any benefit to our lives? It's because we live in a speed- and size-obsessed culture, where bigger and more is better. We fear scarcity, so we bury it in excess. But we'll never liberate ourselves from the feelings of overwhelm if we continue to be addicted to material things. If we continue to accumulate things we don't need, we will be forever confined to this hamster wheel—like mice in a maze, constantly seeking the next cheese cube or the next shiny object to quench our desire. It's a cycle only *we* can stop. It's time to simplify our need to possess. If you find yourself holding onto physical items that create clutter and don't give you a rush of joy in your heart when you look at them, it's time to clear them out.

Living Simply vs. Minimally

There's a difference between living simply and living minimally. Minimalism is centered around the idea of only having what you need. The bare minimum. It's living with the minimal essentials so you can remain free from the constraints of materialism. I'm not a minimalist, but rather, I live simply. Living simply is living within your means, appreciating what you have, and not restricting yourself from buying things that bring you simple pleasures. It's actively enjoying your present possessions.

I don't resonate with the limitations minimalism can bring because I enjoy having a variety of options to choose from in my own life. One or two choices per item just doesn't cut it for me. Give me all the colorful highlighters, spring dresses, and dish sponges, please! I also love bold colors, busy patterns, and eclectic, funky finds that can't be found anywhere else! I collect stamps and Polaroid pictures, and I have way more jewelry than I probably need. But while I love and appreciate the bountiful material beauties this earth has to offer, I find living simply and appreciating the things we already own is essential to a slow lifestyle. If you don't have room to appreciate it, you probably don't have room to keep it.

We live in a time when fashion and product hauls are common, even glorified. We live in a time when you can buy whatever you want at the click of a button (literally, one-click purchases on Amazon!). *The real self-mastery is knowing you don't need to own everything you want.* You don't have to own something to appreciate it. You don't have to buy things to feel good about yourself. Our consumerist world has affected our ability to feel grateful, whether we own something or not. Just because we like the cute Anthropology Christmas salt and pepper shakers doesn't mean we need to own them. Buying them may just be an impulse purchase. I find it's helpful to wait forty-eight hours before making a purchase on an impulse find. So often we see something we love and we feel we've just *gotta* have it! What if we first took a moment to pause? Let's choose discernment. If something brings us joy and it's still on our minds after forty-eight hours, by all means, let's go for it!

Appreciation Doesn't Imply Ownership

We don't ever need to own something in order to admire it. We always have the ability to use our imaginations, to *imagine* having wonderful things, to *imagine* what joyful experiences must feel like. In life, we are not victims of our circumstances. We can train ourselves to see the beautiful, to find magic in the mundane. *Even in a jail cell, you can still use your imagination.* You can choose to free your mind from worry.

The same is true with possessions and people online. We can imagine having something, but it doesn't mean we need to take it home with us. We can follow people's lives online and feel happy for them without feeling envious. There are so many people having deliciously rich experiences. What if we could join in, cheer them on, and fully experience the magic and mystery of our own lives — without comparison?

Can you appreciate and have gratitude for things that are *not* in your life?

Right now, a lot of my friends are starting to have children. It doesn't sway my own choice of living a child-free lifestyle, despite *adoring* kids. My friends can have children and love being parents, but it doesn't mean I want the same. We can be happy for others without wanting the same things for ourselves. This is true for everything in life: possessions, income, attained dreams, relationships, circumstances. We don't need to possess these things ourselves to appreciate them. We don't need to get triggered by others who have what we don't. In moments of comparison, I find it helpful to remember that everyone's path in life is divinely chosen and meant for them. That is their own unique life journey. What's meant to be will be — for them and for you. Their path cannot be replicated, because your path cannot be replicated. Knowing that takes all the frustration out it. And it's also quite a magical thought to ponder!

Essentialism

"Learning to ignore things is one of the great paths to inner peace."

—Robert J. Sawyer

We're all on a quest to feel inner peace, but peace is only fully experienced when we feel present in our lives. And that presence is found in *simplicity*.

One of the reasons we seek simplicity in our lives is because we're overwhelmed. In these fast times, there's a plethora of things to do, places to travel to, people to see, and books to read, so it feels as if there's never enough time to do it all—but that's the key: There *isn't* enough time to do all of it. Realistically, there are not enough hours, days, or years to see and do everything this magical earth has to offer.

The more stressed you are, the less you need to do. When our hearts are working overtime or our minds are operating in fight-or-flight mode, there's a lack of clarity and focus. In these states, we rush, making more errors and mistakes and not doing our health and physical bodies any favors! Stress is life's clear signal to slow down and simplify.

The only way to limit overwhelm is to limit your options—don't do more, add more to your plate, or juggle the myriad of tasks, but do find more efficient ways to be productive with your time. Stress melts away when we have a very clear *focus*. When we define the few things that are most important, the unnecessary drops away. This is how empty space is created.

Few people are liberated from the noise of this world, the hum of its static. But you can turn off the sound at any time. You can dim it down and simplify your environment. If you're someone with a lot of family responsibilities or work obligations and still don't think you have time, I hear you and I urge you to look out for those quiet moments in your busy day, because *they are there*. If you want to live intentionally, you will make time.

Tim Ferriss once wrote, "A lack of time is a lack of priorities." Many of us overestimate the time we work each day and the time it takes to get things accomplished. Many of us aren't using our spare moments effectively. Instead, we're distracting ourselves with our phones, and when we aren't watching, scrolling, or consuming, we're thinking of things on our to-do list that need to get done. We're contemplating next steps and writing lists, instead of taking a moment to *breathe.* Stillness breeds breakthroughs. To make clear and intentional choices, we must recenter. We need to simplify and remind ourselves of what's essential and take a step toward it.

Miners, for example, don't fill their backpacks to the brim with every single stone or rock that catches their eye. There's not enough space for that. It would completely detract from the job at hand. Instead, they distinguish between the rocks and the valuable stones. Always keep your eyes wide open. Always keep a look out for the red herrings. To live in full alignment with your truth, you must distinguish between the helpful and the unnecessary, the gold and the rocks, the valuable and the distractions.

The Truth About Time

You have enough time to do the things that are *important* to you.

It's safe for you to slow down.

Slow doesn't mean unproductive.

You're productive when you're intentional with your energy and time.

You don't need to work quickly.

You don't have to get everything done today.

Eliminate the Unnecessary

What tasks in your life can you eliminate, automate, or delegate to someone else? Physicalize this next step and write it down on a piece of paper. Within three columns, designate one column for each, and stay objective. It's only when we remain objective, with a clear level-headedness, that we can calmly recognize what is unnecessary and nonessential.

Look at your values and the activities, tasks, and obligations filling up your day. Do they align? Are they working in tandem? Are those tasks and activities an honest expression of your core essence? If anything is taking valuable time away from that which is vital and important, scratch it off. Eliminate it and let it go completely. After you eliminate, automate the necessary things that need to get done but don't need to be done *by you.* You can automate things with an app, or even set automatic monthly financial investments. You can have your ink cartridges automatically ordered and delivered, pet supplies delivered, even groceries and cooked meals sent to your doorstep.

Lastly, delegate by asking for help from a friend, partner, colleague, or neighbor. You can hire out help, trade tasks with friends, or even get your mom friends together and have everyone chip in for a babysitter! What's important is simplifying your must-dos, those things which are intrinsically joyful and energizing and actually move the needle. Eliminate the rest.

Get It Over With

This one is an absolute game-changer. It is the equivalent to ripping the Band-Aid off. Don't postpone decisions or uncomfortable conversations. Deliberation silently complicates our lives, when often the answer is quite straightforward. Listen to your intuition. Note your first gut response. If your first instinct— your first bodily reaction—clearly communicates with you, do not complicate things by taking more time to think about it. Don't deliberate on something for longer than necessary, just get it over with. Less overthinking, more action.

One of the easiest ways to complicate your life and live out of alignment with your inner voice is to wonder what everyone else wants. Follow your first instinct. Have the hard, important conversations right away. Exhale deeply and send the text. Strike a power pose and make the phone call. When we deepen our relationship with our intuition, the need to spend a lot of time deliberating and thinking about what to say or which actions to take falls away. *Life becomes simple.* We stop overthinking and avoid unnecessary complications. Simplify your days by being honest with those around you. You can start the more difficult conversations with a simple, "I'm going to be honest with you." A simple and nice way to say no to someone's request is, "I honor your (project) so much. However, I don't have the capacity to give it the full attention it deserves." When we are honest with those around us, we are honest with ourselves. The more we honor our inner voice, the more we strengthen that connection and integrity.

Set Limits

Have full awareness of your goals and values and set strict limits on your non-negotiables. To create an abundance of time and enjoyment in our lives, we must cut out the pesky distractions that take our attention away from enjoying the present. One of the best ways to eliminate the unnecessary is to set strict limits. These could be financial limits ("I will not spend more than x on this item"), relational limits ("I will not tolerate this *specific* behavior or action from others in my relationships"), option limits ("I'm only going to try on and decide between this many outfits") and time limits ("This project will not take more than x hours of dedicated, focused, and uninterrupted attention"). I love using timers when doing small tasks I need to get done. Not only does it give me a burst of motivation, but I always find the task itself takes way less time than I expect it to. When we set and adhere to these limits with ourselves and others, we stay in full alignment with our self-worth, and we create ample space for other wonderful things in our lives to flow in. Simplifying our lives requires us to know our worth and what we want, and to adhere to the limits that cost us more time and attention than we'd like when ignored.

Quit Multitasking

It's a tip we all know brings us greater focus and productivity, but it's one I will continue to reiterate in this book because it's so important. Do not multi-task. Embrace single-tasking. Go all in and commit yourself fully. Be so fully committed to whatever single task you're doing, so fully immersed in that *one* experience, that the world around you starts to blur. *Glide* into that flow state. It's one of the most deliciously wonderful and addictive feelings to experience. Once you enter that flow state, the distractions, sounds, and things vying for your attention will dim, and present-moment awareness will settle in. We find appreciation in these moments of presence and full mind-body-heart awareness. That feeling of total presence deepens with focus and concentration, so quit racing between tasks and forget trying to switch between those ten tabs on your computer. Be fully committed to *one*.

Know Priority Number One

Living simplified lives requires us to know our priorities. We must have a full awareness of the essential components that bring value and joy to our daily lives. Self-awareness is imperative. No sweeping things under the rug or spiritual bypassing here! When it comes to your daily tasks, it's very important to keep your list small, realistic, and with a clear and actionable strategy. There's no need to have a laundry list of to-do items. It'll only overwhelm you!

One of the best ways to narrow down your choices and prioritize your day is to ask yourself, "If this is the only thing I accomplish today, will I be satisfied with my day?" In this moment, forget the long list of to-do items and the healthy habit trackers. Pare it down. What is essential *today*? The best antidote to a life of overwhelm is simplifying. What is the one and only thing that needs to happen each day, both for your enjoyment and for your forward momentum?

Remember the Big Picture

Forward momentum is imperative for a life of growth. As growth-seeking beings, we will always feel joy and contentment in our lives when 1) we are continually growing, evolving, and learning, and 2) we contribute and serve others.

Evolution is part of life and it's what we're here to do. Evolution is the opposite of stagnation. To grow, we must stay mindful of the big picture and what's most important in our lives. Ask yourself, "What if, in putting this off and waiting until I'm older, I don't make it to that age?" It likely won't be done. Are you content knowing you may never do it? If you are, continue as you are, but if that one thing is important to you in the grand scheme of your life, start moving forward, one baby step each day. Gather momentum and enjoy the process as it unfolds. Thinking of the big picture of your life is the best way to reduce it to the basics: *what matters to you most?*

Create a Habit of Frequent Elimination

Clear the clutter on your computer. Move photos into folders and close out all the unnecessary tabs, windows, and programs on your desktop. Trash the nonessential. Go through your phone every Sunday and delete all the old photos and screenshots taking up space! Choose to live in the present and move on from the past. Do the same with email, YouTube, and people you follow and are subscribed to online. If someone doesn't resonate with you anymore, unfollow them and don't give it a second thought. If a newsletter is no longer helpful on your journey, unsubscribe and don't look back. *Move forward.* Aim for a new horizon! You do not need to read every email that makes its way into your inbox. You do not need to stay in the know about every person you admire online. Set the notifications on your phone so only phone calls and text messages can come through. Eliminate the distractions by eliminating those *dings!* Set those boundaries and clear that clutter! Get in the habit of doing this ruthlessly (and weekly).

There's No Need to Do It All

We often put immense pressure on ourselves to do things in the present that we said we'd do in the past, but do those things match what is important to us *now?* We're constantly changing and evolving. Give yourself permission to shift your priorities, and don't turn your "want to do" tasks into "have to do" tasks. Write a list of all the things you do in a week, then ask yourself if you're doing something because you want to do it or because you have to do it. Make a list of all things you "have" to do, check in with your heart (chest) or gut (stomach), and cross 'em out one by one. Slow living leads with intentionality. What can you delegate? Where can you simplify?

Wanting something doesn't imply it *must* be done. While checking off that one thing on your to-do list might be nice, if it's causing you stress, simplify your schedule and don't turn your want-to-do items into have-to-do items. Wanting to cook a nice meal for your partner after work is not worth the extra stress on your tender heart if it's been a long day and you have the option to order in. Hosting your friends for the weekend doesn't imply you need to get some fresh flowers for their guest room or redecorate the house to spruce it up. Just because something seems fun and like a nice thing to do in the moment doesn't make it a requirement. Simplify your must-do tasks. Release that pressure on yourself, sweet soul. There's no obligation to *have* to do something. On the days you feel overwhelmed or pressed for time, instead of cooking an elaborate meal, opt to order in. Pick up the already-made baked goods at the grocery store instead of baking your kid's muffins for the bake sale. Release the pressure. There's no need to be perfect. Choose simplicity over obligation.

The honest truth is that we may not be able to do *all* the things we want to do in one lifetime. And that's okay! Make peace with the idea that some things are meant to be created and done by you, and others may need to take a back seat. Learn to be okay with the fact that not every idea of yours is meant to be carried out to completion. Not every travel destination is meant to be seen by you. Not every dream is a *have-to*. What's meant for you will not miss you. If it's meant to be, it will be. For those of you who often feel scattered and overwhelmed by options, finding acceptance *for what is* really helps.

There are so many careers I would like to dabble in during my lifetime: librarian, scuba-diving instructor, skydiving photographer, bookshop owner, papermaker, filmmaker, author, teacher, magician, journalist, detective—the list goes on! There are so many classes I want to take, and there never seems to be enough time for all the books I want to absorb. Living a slow life requires focus. It's living one step at a time and accepting that we might not get to everything. Make peace with what you have and prioritize what gives you the *most* joy and fulfillment.

A Note on Perfectionism

As perfectionists, we berate ourselves when things aren't going well. But know that perfectionism occurs on behalf of the ego. Our *mind* causes the problem, not our heart. To gain a bit of control of this, first breathe. Breathing is such an integral part of remaining peaceful during stressful moments. Second, don't try to label it. And quit viewing perfectionism as a bad thing. The mind tries to create an identity around perfectionism, labeling it as a negative. What if you tried honoring it? Instead of trying to eliminate your perfectionistic tendencies, learn to manage them. Recognize that when we overthink things or worry about what other people will think of us, know that it's just perfectionism rearing its ugly head. Perfectionism is really just plain ol' insecurity at the end of the day. It's a fear of not being seen as pulled-together, accomplished, or "right" by society's standards. Wanting to be perfect can be as simple as wanting to always dress in a way that is polished and impressive, or wanting everything to go exactly according to plan.

Imposter syndrome is another way perfectionism manifests itself in our conscious minds. We fear we aren't good enough, that we aren't knowledgeable, skilled or talented enough. And then our insecurities lead us to never wanting to be found out. Take three deep breaths and ask yourself if worrying about this thing will matter a week or month from now. Recognize that done is better than perfect, and *let go*.

Power Down to Live a Brighter Life

We are possessed by our thoughts. And many of us don't intentionally pick our thoughts, but rather, it often seems as if the thoughts pick us. One of the ways this plays out in our lives is in our screen time. Automatically we pick up our phones, veg out on the couch, or binge a show after a long day of work. So many of us spend our entire workday staring at a computer screen, whether in a Zoom meeting, creating a project, or answering emails. We spend an inordinate amount of time with our eyes glued to the glow of our laptops. But what if we filled our remaining hours with more tactile endeavors and projects—ones that connect us with our surroundings, local community, and physical senses?

I began to incorporate more of this way of living into my life when I moved to the countryside. As I write this, I live on a quiet island in the Mediterranean called Corsica. During my time here, I've befriended myriad characters, all of whom inspire me to spend my free moments away from the internet. There's the jewelry-maker, who hand-bends brass wires to form delicate bracelets and necklaces for the locals in town; a painter who swirls colors with his brush when he's inspired by the surrounding sea and cliffs; a tanner who crafts leather belts in her small mountain cottage surrounded by towering trees; and a friend who designs and decorates elaborate cheese boards with wildflowers picked from her sunrise hikes. These are just a few of the people I've met in my area who spend their spare time making things with their hands.

There is a whole *world* outside of the news. We flick on our phones or glance at Twitter, and the world looks like a scary place. And everyone seems to be doing the same things: posting about the same products, following the same social media trends, advertising the same sponsor, traveling to the same places, holding the same opinions. Social media reflects the bubble in which we live. Staying plugged into this "matrix" only reinforces what *we* think, what *we* believe, and what *we* feel and know to be true. But when we drop our phones and scan the headlines less, we awaken to the fact that there are millions of people living their lives differently and who, ultimately, *see the world differently*.

You can choose to simplify and cut things down to the essential and joyful. This doesn't imply that we necessarily need to live on a low-information diet. On the contrary, information can be a great inspiration, a powerful motivator to try new things and expand our horizons! But change up your sources often. Frequently clear out the people and content you follow and actively look for new perspectives, new lifestyles, and new approaches to topics. Frequently reflect and question what you take in. This is ultimately how you grow.

How to Simplify Screen Time

Here are some practical ways to simplify your screen time and live a brighter life by powering down.

Get to the Root

Inquire within frequently, and be conscious of your motivations. We must get to the root of our problems in order to understand them. Ask yourself what triggers you to stay on the couch a little longer than needed. As you sit there, gently move your focus from the program to your thoughts and ask yourself what you are avoiding, trying to escape, or numb out from when you're consuming media. Distractions occur on the surface, and they grow to epic proportions when we don't take the time to examine what is growing underneath. Every distraction is rooted in something. Often, these distractions, when boiled down to their core essence, are rooted in fear, and they express themselves in myriad ways, like online shopping, excess TV and media consumption, cycling through negative thought patterns, sugar and alcohol addictions, needless comparisons, and worrying over things outside of our control. It can manifest in an obsessive need to be perfect, to always appear unbothered. When we harness the courage to sit with our fears and acknowledge them, the less we fear, and we ultimately become less dependent on distractions to keep us feeling safe and secure.

Remove and Include

Grab your journal or a piece of paper and review your daily habits. Which habits do you constantly fall into when you want to escape or numb yourself? Write 'em down! Consuming similar stories and opinions from other sources that are not our own, even conversations we repeatedly have with people in our lives, keep us further from attaining our own wisdom. Some stories make you feel good, as escapism is wonderful to a degree. It is through storytelling, escapism, and comedy that we can feel a sense of lightness in the darkest times. I believe storytellers and comedians are the true healers of our world, because they're able to make us laugh and feel *joy* through their various artforms. Films can help us empathize, relate, and see the beauty in life. Comedians help us lighten up, laugh, and relax. There's truly nothing more joyful than curling up on the couch at the end of the day with a new novel to escape into. *But to what extent?* The key takeaway here is not to overdo it. You'll know when your escapist habits turn unhealthy because you'll *feel* it. Intuitively, you'll sense that getting up to do something else feels more energizing. Your mind will start to wander over to other things you could do, activities that feel more rejuvenating, more restful.

After Consumption, Ask Yourself

How do I feel after consuming this?

Is this the energy I want to take into my life?

What would my life feel like one month, one year, ten years from now, if I *continued* with this?

Ease Off Slowly

Sometimes eliminating screen time completely is difficult, and you may need to slowly ease off it. Use a daily habit tracker to help you track the days you've gone without resorting to old habits and patterns. Preferably, handwrite it in a bullet journal, notebook, or tracking sheet to avoid utilizing a screen to manage tracking.

Then, write down a list of the new habits or activities you could engage in to replace your distracting habits. What if, instead of watching another episode, you replaced it with a book, a puzzle, or a gentle stretch? Leave your yoga mat unrolled on the floor as a reminder to venture toward it. Place your favorite books, watercolors, paint brushes, oracle cards, and/or candles around it. Keep it easy and in sight. Replace Pinterest scrolling with a ten-minute journal jot. What's important to remember is that there is *always* something else, something more supportive and life-giving, that we could be doing.

Simply writing other habits down and keeping them in sight is an easy way to remind yourself of the alternatives. Buy yourself a beautiful pen or notepad. Get yourself a fun notebook or sticky notes that are lovely to glance at! Tape it to your bulletin board so you can be reminded of it daily. Stick a pretty Post-it note on your desk, your bathroom mirror, or on your laptop. Keep it in sight, and you'll always be reminded of all the magical ways you could be spending your time. Take small, consistent baby steps. Replace an old activity with a new, aligning one. Sign up for a class, try a new hobby, pick up a new skill, connect with friends or loved ones, read books, practice self-care, and do the necessary healing work.

Ruthlessly Unfollow

Decide to clear out your social media. Go through the accounts you follow and unfollow anyone who doesn't bring something positive or educational to your life. Unfollow anyone who disconnects you from your brightest self. Tune out the drama. Lay off the chaos! Then find three to five new accounts, shows, movies, podcasts, or YouTube channels that are uplifting, inspiring, expansive, educational, or fun! During any given season, I follow three to five influencers and creators who are inspiring and help me grow at that particular time in life. Those creators are frequently let go and replaced by new creators for me to learn from. Just because you found yourself inspired and uplifted by a creator at one point doesn't mean you need to continue to follow them years later. *Allow yourself space to evolve.* Give yourself grace and move on to new expanders and *new* expansions. Find channels, movies, and podcasts that align with your current highest self or reflect who or what you desire to grow into down the road. Look to content that expands you and illustrates where you *aspire* to go. These are the stories, humans, and sources that will progress you forward to your highest evolvement. You have full permission to ruthlessly unfollow anyone or any source that doesn't gift you this expansion.

Out of Sight, Out of Mind

We have *more* than enough time to hold space for activities that bring us joy; it's simply a matter of looking at where we spend our remaining hours, minutes, and seconds and using that time intentionally. Forming a habit certainly takes time to hone, but more than that, it takes intention. If you removed social media, the news, Facebook, and/or your daily ritual of watching a show and replaced it with a non-screen-related activity, think of how much lighter you would feel. The less we consume, thus giving our eyes a break from screens, the more we commune with our inner voice, a knowingness that thrives in silence, stillness, and simplicity. Start by keeping the phone in the other room, both when working and when spending time with loved ones. If you need to, go so far as to leave it in the glove compartment of your car in the garage. Don't bring your phone with you on date night. If you're going out to a restaurant, challenge yourself to leave your phone at home. Overall, the goal is to keep your phone out of sight.

Habits become built-in when they are easy and accessible. The more we see something, the more likely we are to think about it and pick it up. If you don't see it, you won't think about it. For example, you could have a "bathroom book" where, instead of bringing your phone with you, you read the book you keep in the bathroom. This is such an easy way to read more and scroll less! The more you see your book lying about, the more likely you are to pick it up.

Set Personal Challenges

There is something undeniable about the intrinsic fulfillment that comes from setting personal challenges and overcoming them. How gratifying it is to solve problems that once felt like massive hurdles! One personal challenge that feels *deeply* gratifying is following through on a social media detox. It's a challenge that never gets stale! I set social media-free challenges for myself personally, and I always come out of them feeling refreshed and renewed.

Establish a goal of not going on social media one day a week. Then, take it one step further and have social media-free weekends! Now, if you're wincing at the sight of these words, be honest with yourself and examine your heart. Get to the root and inquire further. Why are you so attached to it? Why is social media essential to your happiness? There's no need to make a hard and fast rule out of this, but I can attest that taking periodic breaks from social media helps us deepen our mental and emotional clarity. It helps us understand our attachments and why they exist to begin with, which is invaluable.

Boundaries

Living slowly and simply requires us to have boundaries that align with our core values and are an expression of our highest, most authentic selves. The more boundaries you put up that align with your spirit, the easier it will be to remain rooted in your core essence. Part of living a peaceful life is saying no to all the things that are not life-giving to you. What you feed your mind is in your control—you have the choice to feed it nourishing ideas or detrimental ones. You have full ownership over what you take in. Know that everything that you watch, read, and consume in your life seeps into your subconscious, guiding and inspiring new actions to take and new beliefs to reiterate back to you. Being able to distinguish between the helpful and the distracting is imperative to living a life of peaceful simplicity.

When we hear the word "boundaries," a lot of us wince or worry we won't be living vibrant, full-out, *fun* lives if we're always saying no to things. We don't want to be Debbie Downers! As someone who is the life of the party, I can assure you, having boundaries doesn't mean you won't ever have fun again or that you'll become uptight, constantly negating what everyone asks of you. It means you honor your energy first. You look within yourself first for answers that are right for you. It's choosing to consume less external information for more internal space.

This could be as simple as putting a boundary on phone scrolling and instead using your morning train commute to look out the window and enjoy the scenery. This could look like taking ten extra minutes in the morning to enjoy your morning coffee without distractions. Saying no doesn't mean literally saying no to someone (although that can apply as well); it means simplifying your life to remove the things draining your energy and including only the things that bring you peace.

For my people-pleaser readers, this will be a hard pill to swallow. We want to be liked, and putting up boundaries will make people uncomfortable. But know this: Those who can't respect your boundaries are those that have benefited from you having none to begin with—and those aren't people who will support you anyway!

Essentialism and boundary-setting are critical aspects of living slowly, because life is not naturally slow anymore—life is fast. Look at the current media trends and notice how limited our attention spans are becoming, how bored we become a week or two after a show premieres or a person rises to fame. We move on quicker than ever; our attention is constantly scanning headlines in search of something or someone new.

To live a slower-paced life that's different from the mainstream, you must stop caring about what everyone else thinks of your lifestyle. Slow living is not about keeping up with the Joneses. It's just you, living your life and possibly saying no to unnecessary distractions that arise. Upholding your own boundaries allows you to create your own narrative, rather than blindly agreeing to everyone else's. It's saying no *joyfully*, because your peace comes first.

Some of my boundaries include giving up trips to IKEA. After realizing how walking around busy shopping centers and stores give me more stress than peace, I now forgo those invites. I'd rather say no to busy, hectic environments in favor of a trip to the local park, an empty museum, or a quiet bookshop. My boundaries look like only agreeing to social invitations that *give* me energy rather than those that deplete me. It looks like keeping more space on the calendar wide open, only having one to three goals per day, and having one full day per week without consuming any media.

In your day, reflect on all the things you do, all the things you say yes to. What can you cross out to stay focused on what really matters? Zoom out and remember the essentials.

Carefully Reserve Your "Yes"

Living a simplified life requires us to prioritize things that are energizing and limit those that are draining. *Slow down your need to say yes.* Carefully reserve your "yes" for things that are vital to your joy. Your energy is precious. It's a form of currency. What you exchange for a fraction of life energy needs to be worth it. Only pursue things you *know* will bring you massive excitement when doing them. It's easy to jump into things that sound good or seem simple enough, but be wary of where you place your commitments.

Go back to your values. Does this activity align with your chosen values? Does it help you *embody* the energy you wish to hold space for? Activities that don't light you up or lift your energy make you a drag to be around. We are all intuitive beings; if you feel bored, you can bet other people feel bored, too. When we engage with others, we want to enjoy ourselves, but we also want to uplift others in the process!

For my ladies out there, if you know you'll be at the peak of your menstrual cycle when committing to a business launch, an important meeting, or a coffee date with a friend, it may feel more tiring than energizing, so slow down your "yes." Take a moment to regroup and simplify. Take a pause and go within. There's no need to rush it.

Another helpful tip: Use the magical 80/20 rule and schedule 80 percent of your day, while always leaving 20 percent of it open for last-minute changes, spontaneity, and in-the-moment decisions. Make room for flow by scheduling less. Slow down your need to say yes, stop taking on more than you can realistically do, and quit filling your calendar to the brim. Allow space in your day to do nothing, to follow the whims and winds of your spirit.

Be Unreachable

Yikes. This might make you wince, but let me tell you: this is one of the best ways to simplify your life and maintain your inner peace. Think about how accessible we are in today's world. At any time of day, someone can find us. Whether it be via email, text message, Instagram, Facebook, or through a good old-fashioned phone call, we are easily accessible—now more than ever before! It's no surprise that increased accessibility has us more overwhelmed than ever.

With every erupting ding from our phones, we feel the need to respond right away. So many young people feel social anxiety and hide from their phones, living in fear of checking their inbox. *I can attest to this!* There are far too many people wanting your attention all at once in today's world. But humans are not energetically capable of holding that amount of space for people. That's why I propose a little experiment for you: *Be unreachable.* Get comfortable with being unavailable. Train your brain to be content in not responding to people right away. We've become so programmed over the years to always be reachable, and we've trained our minds to always be "on." *Turn it off, friend.* This will take some time, and may need to be implemented slowly, but try this and tell me your feelings of social anxiety don't soften. When going out to dinner with your partner or friends, leave your phone at home. Allow your text messages to go unanswered for a full twenty-four hours. Start to only check your email twice a day: once at the start of your day and once again at the end. If you're going on vacation, tell your colleagues you won't be available to communicate via email while on vacation, and stick to your guns! (Responding to work emails while on vacation is a common habit I've witnessed and experienced personally while working in the United States, but one that is practically *unheard of* in Europe; the French find responding to work emails during the entire month of August utterly laughable!) Simplify your life and uninstall apps that distract you from your enjoyment. Only respond to private messages on social media once or twice a week, and do it in one grand ol' swoop! Not only does batching save us time in our days by creating space for us to do other things that are more enjoyable, we're also less overwhelmed and rushed in the process. Win-win! Be less accessible and take your time in getting back to people. If people don't respect your boundaries, *too bad.* Your health and staying power are more important in the long run.

Go Against Groupthink

To feel inner peace, there are certain boundaries that need to be upheld within the group. Society loves to separate groups of people and divide them into *teams*. It's the classic "us versus them" mentality. We are social beings, so naturally we're hardwired to always be thinking about the group. The problem lies in our inability to question things for ourselves.

When we constantly agree with the group—whether it be our peers, our colleagues, our neighbors, our families, even our online community—and we don't pause to question things for ourselves, we can easily lose our inner truth. We lose integrity within ourselves, with what makes our opinions individual. It can be as simple as highlighting a sentence on your Kindle, not because the point is important for you to remember, but because Kindle shows you that 894 other people highlighted it. It can be as complex as joining a widespread cancel culture tour just to feel included as part of a group. *If someone did something wrong and everyone else is bringing them down, I should too, right?*

In moments such as these, you must implement boundaries. Question groupthink. When we don't think for ourselves, when we blindly agree with what everyone else is doing, we bring ourselves lower energetically. We forget to think for ourselves and have thoughts of our own. Jumping on bandwagons is neither original nor instrumental to your growth. It was Haruki Murakami who said, "If you only read the books that everyone else is reading, you can only think what everyone else is thinking." Simplify your life by maintaining boundaries with the groups around you.

Be Patient in the Process

When we force the process to be faster than it was intended to be, we end up rushing the unfolding. When we force an outcome before it's ready, we end up making the process more complicated than it needs to be. We must extend patience to the process, like the way we wait for green bananas to ripen before we eat them. Simplify your hobbies and ambitious endeavors, and don't overthink things. Be careful not to turn a passion into a revenue source *before* you're ready. Otherwise, you may end up resenting the passion. Some bold leaps don't simplify; they pressurize. Force is a silent killer of passion. Instead, follow your excitements in the moment and take baby steps, moving one slow step at a time. Consistency always beats speed.

Eliminate What's No Longer Working

To simplify necessities from complicated distractions, we must regularly check back in with ourselves and reexamine the best use of our time through audits. We can do this by performing an 80/20 analysis. The 80/20 rule, also known as the Pareto principle, basically states that 20 percent of our input, or what we give to something, should result in 80 percent output, or what is given back to us as a result. This helps us make the best use of our time, money, and energy so that we aren't spinning our wheels taking action on things that aren't sustaining us financially and energetically, thus creating more space to do other things that are slow, restful, and nourishing.

Take time each month to sit down and write a list of the main tasks and activities taking up most of the time in your day. Are those things helping you move forward? Are they intrinsically fulfilling? Are they expanding you or helping you grow? Whether for work or business, your dating life, your cleaning routine, or even investing in your financial portfolio, take time to do a thorough audit every month to reexamine what's working and what's not. This is a step *so* many people skip in their lives, but it's one that makes our day-to-day more complicated when we don't consciously know where those time drainages are. Eliminate tasks that aren't moving the needle. Put up a boundary on anything taking valuable time from your day that doesn't bring you joy in the process.

A Note on Productivity

We also must talk about work and getting stuff done. This is reality. Bills need to be paid. A lot of people associate slow living with laziness or remaining idle, but slow living and productivity can coexist.

I live slowly every day by approaching life as a balancing act. I make it an intention to never go to extremes in any area of my life. Society pressures us to be overly ambitious and to chase for more when we're already happy with what we have. Collectively, when ambition is left unchecked, this can lead to a world filled with anxiety, stress, burnout, and depression, a life where one is never fully satisfied and can never fully "make it." On the other hand, we have slow living: a more grounded lifestyle lived consciously and simply. It sounds lovely, but if left unchecked and taken to the extreme, we may turn lethargic, lazy, or perhaps feel no need or desire to improve our lives at all.

Productive does not equal being busy. We can be productive without the need to rush or get ahead. Living fast tricks us into believing we are in control of everything in our lives. Being busy makes us feel important, sought-after, and desired. When we're busy, we often equate it to having a lot of things to do, but if those things aren't intentional and purposeful, we fall away from our values. We lose presence. Our aim isn't to be busy for the sake of being busy; that's just glorifying it. Mindless doing and unconscious productivity stem from fear—fear of not being enough, fear of the unknown, perhaps even a fear of being forgotten. Busy is, in a sense, striving.

Just because life has slowed down doesn't mean you need to fill that time with new projects and work activities. An empty space on your calendar doesn't mean you must go searching for something to fill it. Productivity looks different for every person. (Remember that joy and fulfillment come from living from *your* values.) Reading is productive. Spending time with your loved ones is productive. Taking a walk in the fresh air is productive. You do not need to be working nine-hour days to be productive. You don't need to work to be *deserving* of rest. You can take small steps, move at a snail's pace, and enjoy the small, simple details of the journey We are here to have fun. Fill your time up with things that make you joyous and grateful. Rest is our soul's refuge. It is how we heal ourselves and find strength to continue. The easiest way to burn out is to continue on an upward trajectory, in a straight line, without taking frequent restful breaks. Never resting leaves us drained and depleted of energy. Saying no to one thing is saying yes to another.

I encourage you, sweet soul, to have productive days, not busy ones. To notice the beauty in simplicity, and to uphold the boundaries that reflect your core essence. When we simplify the essentials, only then can we really slow down.

4

Slow Living in Practice

"How we spend our days is of course how we spend our lives."

—Annie Dillard

We live in a society that has an intense sense of urgency. We want things done quickly and efficiently. We want fast food and fast cars. We don't always celebrate the quiet things that develop slowly or that require patience, like jewelry-making or painting a work of art that takes meticulous detail and brush strokes. Look at growing a baby or tending to a garden. *These things take time.*

If you're someone who tends to say, "Where did the beginning of the year go? It feels like it was just yesterday," that's a clear indicator to slow down. Time doesn't move quickly. We just think it does. It's only when we rush through life that it seems to be passing quickly. We jam-pack our schedules, filling them to the brim with work meetings, side hustles, and social events, so that it does, indeed, appear that life is moving fast. But that's because we've made it so.

Slow Down Your Routine

What we do with our days is how we spend our short but beautiful existence. How we *start* our day is a great indicator of how the rest of the day will unfold. When we start our day slowly, we're living life deliberately, rather than living life by default. When we begin our day from a centered place of peace, we'll remember that initial feeling throughout the rest of the day. We'll have a marker, a setpoint, to remind us of the energy and values we want to embody for the remaining hours. To put it simply, when we wake up, it's time to hop on the appreciation train.

There are two rules to starting your day mindfully:

1. You need to feel good doing it.
2. Your routine needs to be completely and *entirely* focused on *you*.

Your mindful morning practice is not for anyone else. It's not to be seen by your friends, your partner, or your followers on social media. This is *your* sacred time. How many hours in our days are spent focusing on *other* people—responding to *other* people's emails, working and chatting with *others,* sharing life with someone *else*? There is plenty of time in the rest of the day to share and give, to reciprocate and serve. But this is not the time for that. This is a time for *you.*

This time in the morning is meant to dazzle and delight you. It's meant to open you up to the magical mysteries of your inner world, to nourish and remind you that life is worth celebrating. Your mindful morning practice is not the time to scroll on social media or respond to emails. It's a time to get quiet and listen to the inner whispers of your heart, the whispers that can only be heard when you get still and silent.

Speed is not our friend; it just poses as one. When we live quickly, we miss the quiet pleasures of life. One of the easiest ways to slow down your routine is to place your full attention on your senses. Connect with the feeling of touch—the hot ceramic cup of coffee in your hands, your favorite silk or linen pajamas you fell asleep in the night before. Allow your fingertips to linger on your crisp linen drapes as you open them in the morning, take a deep breath and soak in the morning air. When you wash your hands or take a shower, use your favorite scented soap and bath sponge and fully take in the scent, the textures, the temperature. Delight in the magical feeling of soapy, hot water! When you cook breakfast or drink your tea, bask in its sweet aroma, listen to relaxing classical music, and get lost in the beauty of your simple morning ritual. Be so fully present with your drink as you feel the warm liquid glide down your throat. Take a moment to look up at the clouds outside your window and soak up the warmth of the sun hitting your face.

See what I'm getting at?

This is, hands down, the simplest way to slow yourself down when you feel the need to rush or go at a faster pace than necessary. If we don't slow down, we'll miss the small, simple joys that abundantly fill our mornings! I always ask my husband to leave the window to our bedroom balcony open when he wakes up in the morning, so I can hear the distant cowbells in the fields. It's a simple thing, but when I'm deeply asleep, floating upon the surface of waking, listening to the tinkling bells and a melodic *moo* coming from somewhere outside brings me a feeling of ease. It's a delightful way to start my mindful morning.

There are simple things you can do to remain present, like take pleasure in the details of your clothing and wear an outfit that makes you feel beautiful. Put on the essential oil diffuser and soak up its lavender sweetness! Smell the fresh tulips on your bedside table, or keep a poetry journal for your hazy dreams. Spritz on your favorite perfume in the morning, and sniff your wrist occasionally to smell the fragrance you applied earlier. Let your gaze linger on the sunbeams sprinkling across your porch. Take notice of the dust on your houseplants and dust them. Put on joyful music and open your hips, your heart. These are small acts that take less than a few minutes. But the small acts make the biggest difference in our day.

Slow Down Your Morning

Starting my morning nurturing my inner world without my phone nearby helps me sustain my peaceful state longer throughout the day. When I begin my morning without perusing social media and *The New York Times*, not only do I feel calmer and more in control of my mood, I am infinitely more productive for the rest of the day. With less consumption comes more creativity; less input results in more output. When we give more, to others and ourselves, it's easier to rest easy at the end of the day, knowing we gave the day our very best. We gave our fullest, brightest spirit for one precious day on earth. *A valuable exchange.*

Mornings are more peaceful when I turn off all notifications on my phone and switch it to airplane mode the night before. We all fall into our bad habits occasionally, so if you do end up falling back into the rabbit hole of grabbing your phone first thing in the morning, you won't see any notifications or missed text messages if it's on airplane mode. This is essential to starting your day off slowly. If you want to take it a step further, delete the email app on your phone and move all your apps to the second or third screen, so when you first click on your phone, the first screen or two are blank pictures. This is a simple trick I use that has stopped me in my tracks from opening my email and the news. We want to start our day in a place that *feels good*. One with no distractions, so we are better able to focus on the pleasures of this present-moment experience. Slap on a nature picture or a photo of a baby animal as your home screen and call it *delightful!*

If you are nocturnal, your slow living practice will begin in the afternoon. In this case, you might like to go outside and spend some ample time in the sun before sunset. For you early risers, the morning is your time. Connecting with the sun and getting vitamin D daily is so important for our overall health and mood. Being a night owl myself, I enjoy practicing yoga on my balcony and feeling the fresh air first thing in the morning, then going for an hour's walk or taking a swim in the sea before settling down for work in the evening.

No matter what time of day you rise to start your practice, it is imperative that you do what brings you joy. A lot of self-help gurus and spiritual influencers will tell you to meditate first thing in the morning, to work up a hard sweat, or to do a morning yoga flow with the rising sun. I'm not telling you to do that. In fact, intense workouts drain my energy more than peaceful, quiet strolls around the neighborhood. Instead, I suggest you do whatever is most aligning for *you*. If that looks like starting your day with a cup of hot cocoa and curling up in bed with your favorite book, then enjoy *that*! If it looks like watching an episode of *Gilmore Girls* or writing six pages in your journal, go for it! Whatever *you* do, make sure it satisfies two criteria: it feels good and it's centered around *you, lovely soul!*

While I love lighting a candle, doing five to ten minutes of meditation, and then dancing to uplifting music, I know that's not everyone's cup of cocoa! *Do you.* Get into alignment before acting. Before you can show up for others and be your most vibrant self, you must fill your cup first. This is where our mindful morning practice begins! For those with children, I highly recommend waking up one full hour before your kids wake up to center yourself and engage in the activities that bring you joy.

Here are just a few examples of some slow activities to get you into a feeling of peace, presence, and joy.

Rise

- Meditate or pray
- Light a candle
- Open the window and breathe
- Watch the colors bleed together in the sky at sunrise
- Sway to soft music
- Pull an oracle card and journal upon its meaning
- Stretch your muscles or practice yoga
- Take three deep breaths upon waking up
- Forage in the garden or local park
- Look outside and watch the rain
- Gaze up at the clouds passing by
- Hydrate and drink water, consciously connecting with its potency
- Write in appreciation or record a grateful voice memo

- Write to your intuition
- Write a letter to a pen pal
- Read a feel-good novel or spiritual book
- Watercolor paint, sketch, or work with pastels
- Sit with your coffee and observe your thoughts
- Take a candlelit bath
- Go for a walk to get some fresh air
- Dance to music
- Gather some fresh flowers, herbs, or veggies from your garden
- Water your plants
- Sit on your porch and listen to the morning songbirds

Slow Down Your Evening

Just as our morning has the potential to preface a deliberate day of delight, we must also wind down at the end of the day to reflect and put our witnessed experiences down to rest. Each day is a new beginning, a fresh way to step forward with your life. *A treasure!* And because of its sweet, delicious sacredness, we don't want to bring any of today's drama, fear, or stress into the following day. This is no *Groundhog Day*.

We need to put the day to bed. We need to close the chapter, so we can begin a new one. One of the best ways that I slow down at the end of a tiring and stressful day is to journal at length about it. Report on its comings and goings. Share your fleeting thoughts, your harbored emotions. If you've had a stressful day, it is even more important to vent it out on the page before slumber. Do a rampage of every little worry, every little stressor or negative thought that crept up on you from the day. Pour it *all* out on the page! Give yourself a good thirty minutes to release it all. The weight of the day will lighten, and you'll be better able to have a good night's rest before a new day in your life's story begins.

Light a candle on your bedside table and watch the flame before drifting off to sleep. Soften your gaze, observe the steady glow of the flame. Try this and *tell me* you don't notice your worries fading away. If a thought pops into your awareness, if a worry drip-drops to the surface, gently place your focus back on the flame. Watch the steady movements, the pivots, and the dazzling bluish mixture at the center. Keep your focus steady, soften your jaw, and notice as the present moment becomes crystal clear. You won't have to think about it; you'll just *feel* it.

We don't want to live life by default; rather, we want to live deliberately. The aim is to live with intention and present-moment awareness. Establishing an evening routine with rituals that put our mind at ease helps us develop that emotional and mental consistency. Habits are a powerful thing. Let's use them to our advantage, so we can fall back and lean on them when times get tough. Challenging moments will arise often, but having rituals and habits to support us during those times softens the blow.

There's no need to make your spiritual work a checklist of things to do. That zaps all the fun out of it! Have your rituals in place, but also be open to adapting to a new healthy habit if you desire a change.

Ask yourself, *What feels like the most fun thing I can do right now? What feels peaceful? What feels like a sigh of sweet relief?*

Here are a few examples of some of my favorite evening rituals.

Wind Down

- Put your phone on airplane mode
- Turn notifications off (minimum one hour before bedtime)
- Make yourself tea or hot cocoa
- Journal and reflect upon the day
- Soak your nails and give yourself a manicure
- Do a gentle facial massage
- Listen to classical music
- Write a letter to someone in your journal
- Watch a cozy film or wholesome TV show
- Listen to affirmations (Louise Hay is a gem!)
- Do a guided meditation
- Dance slowly and sway along to soft music
- Do a gentle yoga flow or evening vinyasa
- Practice breathwork
- Read a relaxing fiction or fantasy book
- Light a candle and watch the flame
- Observe the moment, your breath, your senses

Nature

Nature is one of our greatest teachers on our slow living journey. We can learn lessons from the flowers, the leaves, and the creatures that call the outdoors home. Nature is silent. It's slow, patient, and incredibly resilient. Even in the darkest times, nature finds it possible to rebuild after destruction and continue growing through the rubble of devastation. After horrific wildfires, the earth always starts growing again, the plant life flourishes abundant and lush, mere months after tragedy. It's enduring and steadfast. A gentle giant, the earth contains a quiet inner strength that is consistently a genuine marvel to behold.

Adopt the pace of nature, and you'll naturally feel a pull to slow down.

When we spend solitary time in nature, we receive nature's most abundant source of healing. Time spent alone with the earth is how we care for our souls. It's how we ground ourselves in life and the seasons. Give yourself every ounce of permission to be still and silent with the wind, trees, and sea. Stillness is what's required to come home to yourself, to your quiet strength and inner power.

We are just as resilient, just as resourceful as nature. While spending time meditating in nature, you may feel a sense of interconnectedness with all living things. The connection to all living creatures, insects, seasons, plant life, and weather intensifies when we commune with nature daily. An energy of love and unity grows when we spend time with the natural elements. Whether it's a fifteen-minute morning walk in your suburban neighborhood or a sunset stroll through your city's park, take time every day to listen to what lessons the earth must teach. Begin each day with the hopefulness that nature will bring you something: a blessing, an insight, an epiphany, a message that rings true to only you. Nature gifts us little clandestine messages every day, but so often we're too busy to commune with it, to be still within the silence nature offers.

Do you ever notice how nature whispers to us exactly what we need to know, right when we need to know it? The next time you go on a walk alone in nature, leave your headphones at home, leave the phone behind, and observe the teachings sent your way.

Nature signals to us that which floats in the background of our subconscious: the waves reflecting to us the need to adjust and flow with the tides of change; the ants working together to remind us that we aren't isolated islands and to partner up with others because we can't excel alone; the murmuration of birds gathering playfully in the fading vibrancy of the sun, signaling us to celebrate the end of another beautiful day. Nature teaches us the simplest but most profound things. When we spend time with nature, connecting with her, we tap into a greater awareness—our inner voice—and the part of us that is *pure connection*.

Being in nature can also frighten us. Oftentimes, I experience moments of loneliness in the first few days of camping outdoors because of the lack of the comforts I'm used to having available around me. With no internet connection, I must turn my gaze toward the silence and toward my thoughts, sometimes for longer periods than I would like. Silence can frighten us; the lack of options and hyper-connectivity can be bewildering and uncomfortable.

I find it curious how the lessons wild animals have for me meet me at the exact time I need to learn them. Whether it's a wild boar in the mountains of Corsica, an adorable hedgehog in the forest at night, or a fox in the city streets of London, I always find special messages and meanings that erupt from the deeper wells of my subconscious. When I encounter wild animals in my life, I find it helpful to study them, to observe them quietly and curiously, and to ponder the symbolism of what the animal represents. Note its speed, energy, and gifts. In the silence, what does our intuition sense? Where do our thoughts instinctually drift? What does this creature point to in our own lives? What message is this animal bringing? There is magic in every corner, symbolism behind every ordinary sighting.

One of my favorite creatures on earth is the common woodland snail. Every time I stumble upon one on my walks, I must slow down, stop, lie on the ground, and study its elegance and subtle sophistication. Snails exude quiet strength. With such tenacity and endurance, these underappreciated nocturnal creatures cover a lot of ground each evening. Every time I spot one, I am reminded to slow down and keep up a steady pace in my own life. Many times, my husband has had to remain patient with me, as I lug my camera out and film their slow movements, but it's a small, simple delight I've come to cherish dearly.

Ground Yourself in Nature

When you feel overwhelmed, go outside and place your palms on the soil and your back on a tree trunk. Drink in the earth's pulse through the soles of your bare feet. Allow the sand to bury itself comfortably beneath your fingernails. Wash your sorrows in the salty sea. Like a child, roll down the mossy hill, the sand dunes. Let the earth's pulse consume you. Feel the heartbeat of the soil, the life force buried deep within the snow. Nature replenishes and heals. It calms us when we're stressed, it soothes our broken hearts, it nourishes us when we need it most. The fresh air revitalizes our dreams, sparking inspiration as the stars remind us to gaze up, pause, and take in their splendor. Nature is the best medicine, our dearest friend in any hardship. Smile at it, weep on it, scream your anger into the dark abyss. Let the sky and soil cradle your broken heart, your deepest yearnings and frustrations. The earth is always here for you. It's here to soothe. Ground yourself with it, and you will never go hungry.

Listen to Nature's Music

Just as nature heals us, it also sings to us, scattering little whispers along our path. Leave the music and podcasts at home and just be *one* with nature. Listen to its sounds. Nature has the loveliest music, but in our hyper-connected world, where we often feel pressure to always be learning, improving, or entertained, we cover it up with earphones that *disconnect* us, tuning us out from the soothing lapping of the waves on the shore, the whisper of the winds, the sweet song of the birds. One of the easiest ways to slow down and ground with nature is to simply listen to it.

Allow the Light to Guide You

When you walk, allow the light to guide your steps along the way. Observe as the afternoon sun drenches the treetops in its rays, casting contrasting shadows on the footpath ahead. Take a city stroll at golden hour, when the dappled sunlight is soft and delicate. Let its misty haze beckon you to each new street, as you turn each new corner. Watch the reflection hit the glass skyscraper windows and cast its beauty, all the while informing you of a new direction to walk toward. We always have a direction in mind, a place to be and a time to be there. But what if we let nature guide the way? What if we allowed life, *the light*, to take us there instead?

Be Present with the Elements

When taking a nature walk, do you ever find yourself unable to *fully* bask in the beauty around you? Have you ever experienced the moment of divine presence while in nature, where you can feel yourself smiling—*actually smiling*—softly back at its wonder? These are some of my most precious moments, but so many don't get to experience nature. One can enjoy the sights, admire the beauty, but also not truly *feel* it. This happens because we are so trapped in the mind. Endless, repetitive thinking. We're obsessively thinking in circles, looking back to the past, imagining future scenarios, unwilling to surrender to the beauty that is right around us in the now. Our mind actively distances us from presence. It clings to what it knows and replays experiences that are no longer here, frozen in a time that no longer exists. This feeling isolates us, cutting us off from the present moment. So make it your aim to appreciate the fleetingness of this moment. Take special note of your surroundings, the environment, the sounds, the textures, and the feelings that arise. Make it a goal to be fully with nature when in nature. Connect with its divinity by being fully present with it.

Silence

"All profound things and emotions of things are preceded and attended by silence."

—Herman Melville

When was the last time you intentionally set aside time for silence? Silence is steadily disappearing from our lives. In today's modern age, we are inundated with information, content, and opinions. The amount of distractions available to us leads many of us to wonder what a life with silence even looks like. Whether it's a notification alerting you of a new text message, streaming services that provide myriad shows and movies to choose from (all while allowing you to skip straight to the next episode), or simply passing the time listening to a podcast while stuck in traffic, we are constantly listening to something or someone.

Where is the space in between all that noise? Have we forgotten about the lost but necessary art of listening to silence?

Silence scares people. It's an increasingly unknown phenomenon to many of us. We tend to fill any silent gap with entertainment or information. If a moment isn't used fully, we feel like we're not using it to its full potential. So we distract ourselves to the point that total silence is becoming a nonexistent part of everyday life. The word noise is literally actually derived from the Latin word *nausea* or seasickness. When our lives are filled with too much noise, it's easy to overstimulate ourselves to the point where we lose connection with ourself.

This is the information age. With the amount of music, podcasts, and other media available to us at any given moment, it takes *immense* courage and willpower to choose silence. And it feels uncomfortable. There is a literal tension that arises when we have total peace and quiet, especially if we're not used to it. It feels unsettling to have quiet introspection. But silence gives us a wonderful opportunity to deepen our relationship with ourselves and our inner voice. It gives us a chance to reflect honestly on our lives. Studies have shown that spending two minutes in silence is more relaxing than listening to relaxing music. While many of us are filling our minds with a steady stream of new information, our brains need times of idleness without having to react to anything external, to unwind in the absence of input. The internet is still very new in the grand scheme of life, and because it's so new, we aren't taught how to healthily consume it. But we do have the ability to cut down on the amount of sounds and stimulation we expose ourselves to and consume.

On especially busy days, when I find myself rushing from task to task, I often listen to podcasts. Putting on music in the morning gives me that jovial jolt to start the day, and podcasts keep me learning and entertained while I run errands. My work also entails a lot of listening and editing videos of people speaking, and then when my husband comes home from work, we like to talk and watch a show together. By the time I'm settling in for a night's slumber, that empty quiet reminds me: This is the first time, all day, that I'm listening to silence. And how soothing that quiet space feels. How much I've missed it!

Silence is becoming an increasingly uncommon and unknown phenomenon to us. Listening to total silence feels uncomfortable because, the more distractions we have available to us, the less we want to listen to silence. And the less we listen to it, the more we fear it. It goes without question that we are restless about rest and anxious about quiet. The things that leave us with nothing to do, even just for a few minutes, are viewed as wasted, dead time, and a frustrating delay. We associate silence with emptiness because we feel we aren't making the most of the spare time we have. But silence is necessary for our daily lives. It is when we ignore the silent moments that we miss out on this natural component of life: the contrast between doing and not doing. The lines become blurred—work and play, on and off. When we don't make time for silence, *that sweetness of hearing nothing*, we miss out on the in-betweens of life. And those in-betweens are the very best part.

Without silence, we forget to be present. It's always in that state of isolated presence that we feel deep gratitude for the simple joys in our lives. There are small, seemingly insignificant things vying for our attention, begging us to notice their beauty, but we're often too busy to stop and take notice.

It's also evident that inspiration and insight often strike when we are in total silence. It's when we allow our minds to wander, drift off into space, and daydream that fantastical ideas emerge. It's as if ideas just drop into our minds! Take author J. K. Rowling, for instance: The idea of Harry Potter emerged while she was sitting on an hours-long delayed train. This was in the '90s, when distractions weren't so readily available. She wasn't bingeing podcast episodes or distracting her mind by watching videos on her phone. *She was bored.* And that boredom was the gateway to a magical idea that contributed joy to millions of people's lives. That empty space was ample enough to drop in an idea, a story, that would change the world.

We don't have to be on a delayed train ride to carve out silence. Remember: spending just a *few* minutes of silence is more relaxing to our brains than listening to relaxing music.

Finding Silence in Our Busy Lives

Find Pockets of Quiet

One can live in the busiest and most bustling of cities and still find pockets of silence by simply being mindful of your surroundings—the hum of the air conditioning vent, the rise and fall of your breath, the flicker of the candle flame on your desk. Notice the sounds around you, for there is always empty space, momentary lapses of noise that create pockets of silence for us to find stillness.

Find Quiet Areas

If you live in the city, I highly encourage you to forgo eating lunch at your desk and instead, venture over to a local park on your lunch break. Don't take any calls. Instead, spend time alone in a quiet place where you can watch life go by. If you have a nearby church or cathedral, choose to spend some silent moments there. Find quiet streets in your city, cul-de-sacs or one-way streets, or visit public libraries, museums, and empty art galleries. Art galleries often don't play music and boy, do they feel like a sanctuary! You can also visit free botanical gardens, music-free cafes, or go along the waterfront for moments of quiet. When I travel, I often spend quite a bit of time in chapels, not because I'm religious, but because the silence and vast, empty space refill my energy cup. I always feel revitalized after taking some time in a silent gallery or chapel while visiting a busy city.

One such chapel I've visited was the Kamppi Chapel, or the Chapel of Silence, in the heart of Helsinki, Finland. Those wishing to meditate in the busy streets of the city are welcome there. As an introvert, I found myself bereft of energy in the crowds of people filling the streets. This was pre-pandemic and a popular time for tourists, as sightings of the Northern Lights were common around that time of year. The looming wooden structure stood before me, its simple, minimalist design a welcome sight after taking in the constant advertisements and corporate stores in the city. Out of curiosity, I ventured into the bare space. Immediately, I found the silence palpable. A wave of calm washed over me, and I was instantly enamored by this space, a chapel so "inactive" that only one scheduled devotion is held there every week. The soundproof room beckoned me, and I opened the heavy doors to find light flooding the white, barren room and meditation cushions scattered on the floor. Its immaculate silence, inviting presence (all faiths are welcome to practice there), and slightly eccentric minimalist design made it one of the most unique places I've meditated in in a large city. It's my favorite place to be when I visit Finland, and the first on my list to go back to someday. Silent places like this are common in even the unlikeliest of cities, but only if we have the courage to leave our comfort zones and the curiosity to explore them.

Noise-Canceling Headphones

Noise-canceling headphones will become your new best friend. They are truly a masterpiece of an invention. When I crave silence in loud areas, such as in airports, in cities, and on the train, these li'l darlings block out all the stimulation and help me find my breath, the steady beat of my heart. It's the easiest way to find total silence. If you have the funds, get yourself a pair of noise-canceling headphones. They are worth the investment.

Don't Fear Silence

There's something eerie about being alone in the silence of our thoughts, with no distractions, no noise, and nothing but our thoughts to pay attention to. When we spend time alone in silence, we are confronted with reality—and worst of all, our fears. We can't push aside our fears with the hum of a beat or the sound of someone else's voice. In the absence of noise, you're forced to listen to and address the life you've created, the thoughts that follow you, the past that haunts you. It takes courage to listen to silence. While it can be initially frightening, listening to the silence empowers us. Being alone with yourself in the quiet holds up a mirror to look at yourself and asks you to dig deeper, to ask the harder questions we often don't want to unravel. *In silence, we find ourselves.* This bare state is where our honest heart lies, where our truth is. And it's more human, more effervescent, and more *real* than anything we try to cover it up with. Don't fear the silence; it's asking you to go inward and be here, now. Silence asks us to slow down.

"Anything you want to ask a teacher, ask yourself, and wait for the answer in silence."

—Byron Katie

Slow Down Your Day

To appreciate the small wonders of your life, you must first notice them. Today, life feels like it's moving faster than ever. It's difficult to notice the beauty in the ordinary when you're rushed, stressed, or frustrated. I know what it's like to live fast. I lived the opposite of a slow life in New York City. Naturally, I am a future-oriented thinker. This has always been an aspect of my personality I've struggled with, because I'm always thinking ahead to the next thing. The past is long gone, but the future is being created now. Having that long-term vision, the endless potential on the horizon, can limit you in finding the beauty in the present. There is so much beauty, here, *now*, but looking to the horizon won't help you find it. In fact, it may even lead to anxiety, stress, or excess worrying over what you cannot control. This realization revealed what I was missing in my life. Through trial and error and a lot of experimenting, I discovered practical takeaways that helped me in my own journey of living slowly. If you're a creative, an artist, a visionary, a dreamer, or even just worried about the potential what-ifs of life, this is what's helped me in my five years of choosing to slow down and seek presence. Here are the ways I live slow every day.

Embrace Single-Tasking

Our powerful brains can handle a lot of external stimulation. As a result, we often feel the need to distract ourselves and do multiple things at once. Forcing ourselves to focus on one thing at a time can feel like we are underusing our mental capacity and not taking full advantage of our day. We often overcommit ourselves. We take on more than is desirable or necessary. Multitasking is not our friend. It might seem like we're saving time doing two things at once, but countless studies have shown that doing one thing at a time improves our focus, efficiency, and concentration. It brings us more peace in the present moment.

In addition to single-tasking, slow down your workload. Close all the nonessential tabs on your laptop and focus on switching between only two tabs. Three at the max! Reduce mental overwhelm by creating only two to three goals for the day, instead of a laundry list of to-do items. To slow down, I use the Pomodoro Technique, where I set a timer and work in twenty-five-minute increments, taking five-minute restful breaks in between. This method of working helps us dedicate attention to one task at a time and to access a flow state. Give the present moment your full attention by focusing entirely on one task until it's complete.

Go on a Slow-Living Date

What is a slow-living date, you may ask? It's, quite simply, *having nothing planned*. Just go where the wind takes you. This outing need not be fancy or complicated. Keep it simple and mindful. Go beachcombing along the sand, birdwatching at the nature reserve, or pack a picnic and a comforting novel. You may also feel called to have a dedicated "Slow-Living Sunday"—an entire day devoted to living simply, slowly, and mindfully. Whatever you do, take yourself on an intentional slow date one day a week, where you let life guide you along, with no distractions.

"It Is What It Is"

We've all said this before, right? It's one of the most soothing phrases we can say to ourselves when life isn't working out the way we'd like. Surrender to the unfolding of life and have patience and compassion for yourself. Keep the phrase "It is what it is" always ready at the back of your mind. When we accept life, we live peacefully within the present moment. We learn to love what is, instead of always seeking more. *It is what it is*. There's no need to fight life. If it were supposed to be different, it would be.

Read a Tangible Book

One of the most comforting simple joys is holding a book in your hand. An actual book that smells divine. Whether it smells like fresh ink or more like crisp paper, whether it smells like an old musty book that's been on the shelf at the library for years, or it smells like a new one with glossy, magazine-like pages and reminds you of a beloved textbook from your early school days, books are *everything*. Without our even realizing it, they help us slow down. They encourage us to sit in silence and gently focus on what is in front of us. Go to your local library and drag your finger across the spines, hold one in your hands, bend the spine, turn the crisp page. Check it out from the library and bring it home with you, curl up on the couch with it, and get lost in the beauty of losing track of time with a good story. Pick one you love, one that's inspiring, and one that speaks to you and everything you stand for. Read an actual book. You'll instantly feel a desire to check out of the fast-paced, bustlin' world we live in.

Move at a Snail's Pace

There's no need to go big or go home. There's no reason why you must accomplish everything all at once, or get your entire to-do list finished by the end of the day. Start small. Take single steps. Go at a pace that feels good to you. The road is long, and your only job is to take one single step every day. Consistency is more important than energy. Endurance is a better indicator of success than speed. Move at a snail's pace, and you'll always find yourself at the place you're meant to arrive.

Embrace Your Seasons of Waiting

We all go through different seasons of life—seasons of abundance and harvest, seasons of hardship and turmoil—and then we have the most ambiguous life season of all: a season of waiting. A season of waiting looks different to everyone. Perhaps it's as literal as waiting for the first day of university to begin, so you can get on with your studies, or waiting to have a healthy, strong, and growing baby. Perhaps it's a season of growing and maturing for you, spiritually, emotionally, or mentally. The one trend that characterizes a season of waiting is a feeling of being in the in-between: half-risen, half-falling. It's a feeling of emerging...but not quite being there yet.

A caterpillar, having just finished the arduous journey of crawling, eating, and spinning itself a silky cocoon, sits and waits to emerge, clear as day, as something more glorious than it was before. But will the transformation be certain? Naturally, we beings love progress. Desiring growth, expansion, and the *new, new, new* are key components of who we are as growth-seeking beings. As humans, that is what we are: seeking growth continuously. But some of the best things in life come from waiting patiently for a period of growth.

During these slower times, I enjoy seeking out ways to learn from this period of waiting—what can this teach? How can I grow from this? I always vow to leave this season better than the way I was before. A season of waiting is a beautiful time to practice being open to receiving lessons and teachings. I view this time of pause, of nonactivity, as a time to allow for more intentional rest. I use this time to connect with friends and loved ones, to make time for my passions, like letter-writing, and other neglected hobbies I've put on the back burner.

A season of waiting is also a time of ripening. If you are persistent, if you just wait it out, the reward feels far more delicious in the end because you've prepared and planned for it. When it does arrive, you'll be ready to take inspired action. You'll be ready to give generously. It's true that the greatest things in life are worth waiting for. This goes for the ideal partner, the dream job, and the perfect cup of cocoa. If you wait patiently, it will feel even more delightful when you receive it. Magically, when you finally receive it, it always feels exactly, perfectly, right on time. It comes when you are ready, when you will most delight and be at ease in having it. *I promise you.*

"Just Be" Time

I also make time to just live, to gaze out the window. I adore the moments in life when I sit on my bed, on the couch, on the shore, and I just *look up*. I study the ceiling, I feel the spaciousness in the air, my gaze softens, and I feel a steady peace. A quiet sinks in and, almost immediately, I feel grateful. I set aside time to simply breathe, feel the inhales in my chest. I dedicate time to watch the bees pollinate the flowers. I carve out minutes to watch the way the wind moves through the trees, the steady rhythm of the waves. To sit on a stoop and watch the people pass. There are small ways we can all do this. When you go to the beach, don't bring a book with you. Or, if you do, bring a cozy fiction novel, a story of make-believe, something that actively encourages your mind to imagine and create. *Think less self-help, more storytelling.* I challenge you to not look at your phone on your morning train, to listen to the silence for a few moments, instead of playing an information-packed podcast while driving to work. Sit and bask in the sunlight, observe the natural world around you—the bird on the branch, the clouds moving past. Just go and let the wind take you where you need to be. No plan, just the natural pace of your footsteps.

Get Physical

I live slowly every day by being fully in my body. Nothing snaps me back into the present like getting out of my head and physicalizing my energy through dancing, movement, dressing up, stretching, walking. The more we think and analyze everything going on in our lives, the more stuck we get in our minds, the more lost we become. Instead, let your heart lead the way. Try to let your gut make decisions. Life becomes easy when we lead with our heart and allow our body to tell us what to do, instead of rationalizing it all. Loosen up, dance it out, have pleasurable sex, do some jumping jacks, hop on your bike and venture to the library, put on some socks and slide across your living room floor! Whatever expression of movement is most *fun* to you, do this every day, and you'll feel lighter and more connected with your body *and* with life.

Relish the Process

Living slowly asks us to relish the process. If we don't enjoy the journey, we'll never enjoy being at the finish line. The energy we devote to something at the beginning and in the middle of the road is the same energy, or less, that we'll have at the end. This doesn't mean you don't have dreams; it's that you don't have an attachment to the outcome. The loss or lack of something doesn't affect your emotional well-being, because your well-being is already fully satiated. Getting a fun outcome is just *extra* joy on top of your already full heart. *Relish the process of your uniquely divine story.*

Stop and Smell the Roses

Literally, stop and smell the roses at the local bodega on your way to work. Pause to take in the scene around you. In other words, notice the simple joys.

Vitality

Be discerning and especially cautious about where you place your energy. It's so easy to get pulled out of a calm, peaceful state. Often, we meditate or do our self-care rituals in the morning and feel present and connected, only to carry on with our day getting out of that state. We start answering emails and running errands in a rushed manner, invariably losing touch with that peaceful, present part of ourselves. One of the ways we can bring on this feeling of peace, whether it's on our morning commute or scrolling on social media, is by taking deep breaths throughout our day, placing one hand on our heart and one on our stomach and asking ourselves questions like, "Why am I doing this right now? What is this giving me? Is this serving me? *Is this vital?*" Always ask yourself if the thing you're doing is *giving* you energy or taking it away. Be consistent with your questioning and ruthless with your eliminating.

Hydrate Often

This is a simple habit that's helped me have clarity, peace, and calm, and it's an important one. When we feel tired, bored, angry, or foggy, chances are we are dehydrated. Water is beauty juice. It cleanses our body and flushes out all the gunk that's causing us to feel unaligned. The next time you feel tired, stressed, or emotionally spent, load up on water. In fact, do me a favor right now, and *go drink a glass of water*. I'll be right here when you get back. Your hydration matters, and it sets you up with energy and vitality for the rest of the day. When you have clarity of focus, you're better able to make restful choices.

Electricity-Free Night

One of my favorites among the rituals I have with my husband is having a designated electricity-free night every other week. We turn off all the lights and screens in the house, light candles, and choose to either read aloud from a favorite book, play guitar, or talk. Replace your family movie night with a board game, Rummikub, or a card game. Interacting with one another is a better way of getting in that quality time than sitting down in front of a screen, and trust me, the silence and romance of not using electricity is so divine, soon you'll be looking forward to turning the screens and lights off!

Get a Hobby

And make it a physical one—one that's tangible and snaps you back to the present moment! *No media escapism here!* Opt for things you can do with your hands, like painting, creative writing, knitting, scrapbooking, jewelry-making, baking, yoga. Instead of watching Netflix, opt for a sudoku puzzle—and do it from an actual book, not an app! The point is, start incorporating a hobby into your everyday life that's tangible and connected to your five senses.

Some of the hobbies I've picked up over the years include flower arranging, jewelry-making, baking, flower-pressing, and taking physical Polaroids. Then there's the activity I cherish most: letter-writing. There's something delightfully heartwarming about pulling out a piece of crisp stationery and writing a long letter to a friend. It forges a deeper connection, and it requires us to be patient, slow, and deliberate with our words. Add the finishing touches of stickers, ribbon, and hot wax before stamping it with an artfully designed seal. This step, adding those final decorative touches, asks us to be present with each layer. It cements that bond—showing the other person you care enough about them to create it.

We write, jot in our journals, and type on our keyboards so quickly. What if, instead of snapping a quick photo for Instagram, we took the time to sketch it out? Taking a few minutes to be present and observe a scene before sketching it is a great way to slow down and pay closer attention to your surroundings.

Sketching, watercolor painting, and bullet journaling are some of my favorite tangible ways to slow down and be present. I also love to slow down by writing with a quill. Using a quill and a pot of ink to write my to-do list reminds me to slow my writing down. Plus, listening to the gentle scratches of the quill moving across the page is such a cozy, simple joy.

Sewing, knitting, and scrapbooking are favorites for many who connect with a slower, simpler life. Nature lovers may appreciate gardening, beachcombing, or simply going on an appreciation walk without a phone. Instead of taking pictures, connect with the earth, hold the trees, and feel the hum of the land.

These are intentional choices, ones that are thought out with deliberate intent. It's in the small daily choices: picking up a deck of cards instead of the remote control; going to the library and checking out some new books to read instead of perusing blog posts or Instagram captions; listening to a podcast or audiobook instead of watching a video to learn from while organizing and cleaning the house. Even something as simple as jotting down a list of things you're grateful for or what you're proud of yourself for throughout the day is a calming and appreciative way to end the night.

Carving out a little bit of time each week to engage in tangible hobbies that keep our eyes feeling light and bright, and our minds clear and open, is a great way to slow down. These are simple actions, backed by deliberate intent, which have a profound impact on the way we feel. When we spend time away from our screens, we feel healthier, lighter, and more energized. Our days are precious, our lives fragile. Let's celebrate this existence by honoring the time we have.

Slow Down Your Self-Care

While living in France, I've taken an interest in self-care practices. It's not that I didn't enjoy long baths before my move to France (a daily bath truly keeps stress at bay!), but I started paying more attention to my daily routines, noticing the little touches I'd once never paid attention to. I firmly believe our environment affects our mood and interests. We adapt to what is around us. I used to rush getting ready each morning. I'd quickly brush my hair, put on some clothes and bike to work: no makeup, no perfume, no peaceful routine to center me in preparation for the day. The French love to pamper themselves. Whether enjoying a deliciously languid breakfast at the dining room table with an assortment of croissants, *pain au chocolat,* and baguette with butter and jam, or spritzing on some Diptyque perfume before tying a floral scarf on their purse—the small details count. The French have taught me to take delight in my presentation, to not forgo beautiful lingerie, silk nightdresses, and other accoutrements that remind me to slow down and relish the simple pleasures of the physical experience. It is the little hints of bold color, scent, or red lipstick that set us up for the day with care.

Self-care may not be self-love, but we show up for our highest self in the daily ways we care for ourselves. French women don't wear a lot of makeup, but are rather natural in their presentation: natural nails, natural hair color, few to no lip injections. Rather, they add a few touches, like mascara, blush, and red lipstick, that highlight their natural features. We're living in a time when everyone is obsessed with staying young and looking like everyone else. But the French have inspired me to see things differently: Botox isn't highly valued here, and being 100 percent natural is preferred over trying to look younger. There is a certain elegance and sophistication in accepting and embracing the way your natural body looks. Wrinkles are a form of growth in our lives, a sign we've truly lived.

In French, the phrase *"se mettre en valeur"* means "to make the most of yourself," and it's a phrase that encapsulates the French approach to appearance and presentation. In France, being sloppy in your appearance is akin to letting yourself go. The daily act of taking ten extra minutes every morning to intentionally curate my outfit, add some lip color, add a colorful pin to my jacket, and style my hair has made each day a little bit more fun! I've learned to become more polished and pulled-together over the years, thanks to my time abroad.

Tasteful lingerie shops are plentiful on the French city streets, and owning beautiful pajama sets, like camisole nightdresses and silk robes, is common amongst the French women I've met. When I lived in the States, I slept in oversized T-shirts and shorts, never taking the time to pamper myself with beautiful and soft pieces that made me feel good in my body. While these details may seem superficial, they matter, because they remind us to pause and enjoy the beauty in the ordinary objects in our home.

When we wear nice things, we appreciate them more. We want to care for them. And the way we care for our objects reflects the way we care for ourselves.

One of the biggest things that has affected my overall feelings of joy and well-being is being mindful of what I consume, with both my physical body and my energetic body. This doesn't mean I don't have my vices (I love a good cup of hot cocoa, and I have my own guilty pleasures, ahem: Netflix's *Love is Blind* and tea-spillin' celebrity gossip), but I consciously think about what I'm giving to myself. When you love your vessel, you want to care for it. When you appreciate your heart, your mind, the sparkly essence that makes you *you*, you naturally want to give yourself love! Don't listen to negative media that makes you afraid of life. Quit listening to and absorbing content that leaves an icky taste in your mouth. Turn it off. Go back to your breath, look inward. Consume uplifting, inspiring content that makes you feel excited and eager for another day on this earth! Surround yourself with people who inspire you to love life and explore your world with new eyes!

What are you consuming? What foods and drinks and nutrients are you offering your physical containment, the soul that chose to be here at this moment in time? Are you blocking your connection, your level of present-moment awareness by bingeing a show or eating a meal that makes you feel tired and sluggish afterward? Take continuous note of what foods make you feel light and alive. Be aware of what foods zap your energy (hello white rice and buttered noodles) and what foods give you a boost of energy (mmmm chickpeas, quinoa, fresh greens, and hummus)!

In my past life of living fast, when it came to meals, I wouldn't think about what I consumed. As a child, I decided to become a vegetarian because of my love for animals, but aside from choosing not to eat meat, I ate fast. Fast food was standard for me growing up. As a young adult living on my own, I'd rely on frozen meals. For dinner, I'd throw a Trader Joe's frozen meal in the microwave. For lunch, I'd grab a quick slice of ninety-nine-cent pizza on my way to work. I'd shovel large quantities of food into my mouth, never slowing down to pause, ponder, be present with the flavors. At this period of my life, my checked-off to-do list was always more of a priority than sitting down to slowly enjoy a meal. I didn't savor it. Sometimes I'd eat a bagel or grab a donut from Dunkin' while walking to work and eat it in a handful of bites, with roaring heavy metal blaring through my headphones. I wasn't fully aware of what I was eating or even what it looked like. I didn't question what ingredients were put in it or express appreciation for the energetic fuel placed before me. Far from my experiences in France, where meals are treated as a delightful life affair, I consumed what was fast and good enough. *Good enough.* My most important priority was getting to work on time, not what I was putting into my body. Anything that barely passed the initial boundary threshold was allowed access into my life.

Looking back, I wonder: did I care about my life at all? Did I realize how precious my time was? Our energy is currency. Where we put our energy, focus, and attention is where the span of our lives goes. If we aren't selective, if we don't curate, our lives can easily be cluttered and overwhelmed with useless information that not only wastes our time, but slowly and surely takes our life away.

The more connected I am with my intuition, the more sensitive I am to food and media. When we deepen our relationship with our inner voice, it activates an awareness that wasn't there before. Certain ingredients make us feel wary, cause us to break out in hives or acne. Perhaps we notice that we feel more sluggish and tired after eating certain meals or consuming certain drinks. This is because we've deepened our awareness and established a closer connection with ourselves. When we live with intention, we become more aware.

If you want to live an energized life of deep presence and connection with yourself, you must engage in self-care and self-respect. Everything you desire in life must match the way you care about and tend to yourself, both mentally and physically—in the way you eat, in the way you nourish yourself, and in each small daily choice you're presented with.

Simple Ways to Add Self-Care to Your Day

- Drink a big glass of water
- Buy some flowers or plants for the house
- Light a candle and make a wish before falling asleep
- Read before bed
- Take a walk outside and breathe in the fresh air
- Stretch your body out or do some yoga
- Apply some lip color
- Take vitamins or supplements
- Wear an outfit that makes you feel dazzling
- Eat a big bowl of greens
- Allow yourself to cry; let it out as much as you need to
- Be honest with yourself and others
- Bake something sweet for yourself and your family
- Sit in the glorious sun
- Slather yourself with high-SPF sunscreen
- Look in the mirror and appreciate your beautiful body
- Say some positive affirmations aloud (that you truly believe!)
- Hold yourself, and tell yourself, "I love and approve of you"
- Take a nap in the middle of the afternoon
- Style your hair
- Sip some hot tea and watch the clouds pass by
- Rub your worn-out feet
- Write a letter to a friend or loved one
- Write a letter to your future self and attach it to your journal with a date to open it
- Play a musical instrument
- Run up a hill and sing, "The *hills* are alive!"
- Take your makeup off at the end of the day
- Watch funny videos of adorable cats
- Look at photographs of baby animals
- Write with colorful pens
- Listen to cozy ASMR on YouTube while studying or reading
- Dance and sway to the pleasure of your soul
- Kiss your skin, embrace and thank your beautiful body for hosting your spirit
- Refill your water bottle before bed and drink upon waking
- Invest in your IRA
- Express yourself creatively; share your voice
- Allow yourself to be seen
- Befriend people you want to be like (you are the five people you spend the most time with)
- Take small micro-actions every single day that reflect a sense of high self-worth
- Polish your shoes
- Write yourself loving words on Post-it notes and place them around your home
- Take note of your good qualities (literally write them down) and remind yourself of them often
- Talk to a friend
- Buy yourself some sparkly eyeshadow
- Cuddle under a warm blanket
- Crank up the music and boogie down!
- Invest in stocks and mutual funds for your future self
- Listen to relaxing music
- Buy yourself a new journal and devote some time to it
- Allow yourself to dream big
- Eat a piece of fruit
- Twirl in a dress
- Spritz some perfume in your house
- Sing your heart out!
- Do a facial massage
- Pull a tarot card and meditate on its meaning
- Write to your intuition
- Express your appreciation aloud; declare your joy!
- Make time to laugh, and laugh generously

Slow Down Your Consumption

Before I lived a slow, present-filled life, I consumed things quickly. An average day went like this: watch YouTube or Netflix in the morning before work, scroll through social media on my lunch break, play video games with Alex in the evening after dinner, scroll through Pinterest before bed. And repeat. I'd go online to write a blog post, only to get lost in the maze of opinions from strangers in Facebook groups. What did *I* think? What were *my* opinions? I didn't know. I was consuming at record speeds: I'd binge shows in a single sitting, churn through books one after the other, sometimes an entire book in a day.

I didn't pause to let ideas settle, never asked myself what I thought of the strings of words on the page before me. I didn't reflect upon the characters, their choices, their life paths. I would let Netflix carry me away to the next episode, one after the other.

Can you relate?

In our current times, this is the average life for many. We keep scrolling, we continue bingeing. We don't pause to ask ourselves whether this feels aligned enough for us to keep going. We consume fast, and we move on from it even faster. Trends no longer last seasons, they last *days*.

Growing up, I remember plopping down in front of the large box-like television set and watching the latest episode of *Lizzie McGuire*. Back in the early 2000s, we didn't binge, because new episodes came out weekly. Every Friday evening held a new storyline, a refreshing surprise. I remember excitedly arriving to school on Monday mornings, eager to see my friends so we could express our mutual joy over the latest episode. We had time to reflect, space to wonder what would happen next. Unanswered questions required our imaginations to sort through them. Life was slower then. Today, the media landscape has changed, and trends go in and out of style in less time than it takes to create the content itself. Our attention spans are growing shorter every day and many of my fellow millennials find it difficult to watch a full-length movie.

Daily intentional habits weigh ounces, but regret weighs tons. If we don't take an active role in carefully selecting what we give our time and attention to, the years will bleed together until we wake up one day and realize how much was spent consuming and not fully living.

Looking back at this chapter of my life, the fast days when I was more focused on climbing the ladder, being seen, being out and about at cool events with cool people, I see now what a complete 180 my life has taken. I don't care about consuming more; I care about consuming less. Less, but *better*. I have carefully curated my life to only include the best things for me. Instead of buying new outfits every week because they're on sale, cheaply made and easily accessible, I consume a handful of quality pieces once or twice a year that are harder to come by, more expensive, but will last me decades. Essentially, I consume intentionally. Instead of bingeing multiple shows on multiple media platforms, I only follow one to two shows I really love. I support and consume the content of three YouTubers. I follow about seventy people on Instagram, but I only consume the stories and photos of five. I'm discerning because my life and time are sacred.

Our most cherished friend is our inner voice. Our intuition, our wisest ally. So often, we forget to take the time to reflect on what we're consuming and ask ourselves first. Those reflective moments of respite are needed to commune with our intuition. We need to slow down our consumption to fully *live*.

Take Your Time

Honestly, *what's the rush?* Start asking yourself this regularly. When you zoom out and see the greater scope of your life, *how does rushing help you?* It only causes greater stress, it makes us more likely to fall or get into an accident, and our blood pressure is more likely to spike. When we rush, we operate in high-beta, the brain state that is hurried and manic. It's also *the* most unproductive, inefficient state to be in, causing unnecessary stress on the body. *Take your time.* Take your time walking your dog in the morning. (Let's be real: It's probably the highlight of your sweet pup's entire day!) Take your time having your glorious cup of coffee—cradle that delightful mug, and relish the freshly brewed aroma, *mmmm!* Take your time *drinking in* the colorful notes of your favorite song while stuck in traffic on the way to work. Take your time with everything. This is the life you came here to live: *enjoy it.*

The number of times I've caught myself rushing through my day in a fight-or-flight-esque mode has made me question a lot in my past. When we rush, we're running away from something deeper. At the root of hurry is a deep need to go faster to make up for something missing in our lives. Perhaps we're insecure or have low self-worth. Maybe we're perfectionists. Whatever it is, it stems from a place of fear. It doesn't feel good or peaceful. There is no need to rush through life. Start to ask yourself, and ask it often, "Is there a reason I need to be rushing here?"

Ask Questions After Consuming

Engage in conversation after consuming content. After finishing a movie or episode of your favorite show, turn to your roommate, partner, or family member and ask them what they thought of it. Text a friend and ask them who their favorite character was and why. Dig a little deeper: What was the general theme or message of the story? What can we take away from it? Is there a lesson to be learned from the characters and their experiences? If you're consuming content on YouTube, leave a thoughtful comment with your own questions and experiences, reflect on what the piece helped you with, express what exactly made you laugh or what you found insightful or entertaining. Make room for your own thoughts to express themselves.

Set Your Table

Prepare your meal, your place setting, with care. Pull out the fine china and use it weekly. Buy yourself a single teacup and saucer that makes you over-the-moon excited with glee when you sit down to have a cup of tea each morning. Sit down to eat and put media away. If you like to consume content while eating, opt for reading or listening to music. Put the screens away and read a book, or listen to classical music or peaceful movie soundtracks. Light a candle before eating, express appreciation for the nutrients and energy before you. There's nothing wrong with eating your meal while watching your favorite show, just don't do it every night. Make it a special occasion!

Don't Respond Right Away

Instead of responding to emails and text messages right away, step away and process. Allow yourself the time to reflect and think of a thoughtful response. Our society is obsessed with efficiency, but that doesn't mean you have to be efficient. Mention on your website or set up email automations to let senders know you will respond to business inquiries within seventy-two hours. If a friend starts getting antsy about you not texting back right away, tell them you're not active on your phone all the time and that you will get back to them soon. There's no need to explain yourself. Give yourself time to be where you are.

Zone Out with Intention

It's perfectly okay, healthy even, to zone out occasionally. If, at the end of the busy workday, nothing sounds more wonderful than plopping down on the couch and scrolling through Instagram or TikTok, then take that time to zone out and escape for a bit. The key takeaway is a *bit*. Zoning out is great, *if* we are intentional with that time and conscious about our choice to zone out. Instead of bingeing content, I encourage you to zone out with intention. To do this, simply go into consuming *knowing the intention is to zone out.* Carve out a designated amount of time to do so, set it in place either with an alarm or by asking your partner or roommate to remind you when that time is up. When the time is up, continue on with your day in presence.

Slow Down Your Social Media Consumption

When we watch television or scroll through social media, our minds enter a relaxed, hypnotic state. When we feel this relaxation, not only are we less intentional and conscious of our own thoughts when we consume the words and lives of others, but we are less present in our own lives as a result. If we're going to learn about slow living, we need to venture into social media territory.

In my own life, I've been on six-month social media detoxes and weekend detoxes (which I still practice quite regularly), and I've deleted personal accounts on Facebook and Twitter. I also don't consume content on TikTok, and while I can't compare what my life would be like if I did, I do believe with every fiber of my being that these intentional acts have given me an astronomical abundance of *time* in my life. Not being able to scroll, peer into the lives of others, or be inspired by other people's words and creations has opened immense space in my heart and mind. It's allowed me more time to be present and enjoy my real life and my relationships. It's given me the quiet gift of being bored. Without boredom, creativity has no space to drop in. When you're always looking outside of yourself, there's no room to be your original self. Unplugging keeps us from comparing ourselves to others, and we gain valuable time in our lives to do what brings us joy and fulfillment.

Here are some practical ways to begin living with social media intentionally.

Living *Intentionally* with Social Media

Start Small

Set up a new social media routine for yourself. This may appear challenging at first, but you can instate an easy rule, one that's manageable. This needs to be a routine you can realistically stick with. For example, your new rule might be, "No more Instagram after nine at night." Master this, then challenge yourself by knocking it down one more hour. Change nine to eight o'clock, and so on, until you've found the time that works best for you. Then, when you've found you're no longer attached to social media, challenge yourself to an entire day, then a weekend, then a week. Notice how you feel as you spend more and more time off your phone. Do you feel happier? Healthier? Do you have more time in your day to pursue your hobbies, interests, research projects? What does this time away from social media *add* to your life?

Take a Twenty-Four-Hour Digital Detox One Day Per Week

When you find it easier to lay off your social media accounts, I encourage you to take a twenty-four-hour digital detox from *all* media for one entire day per week. No phone, no streaming services, no YouTube, no media consumption. Instead, *make* something. Be creative. Spend time outdoors. Learn a new skill. Research. Delete all social media apps during this time, and immediately afterward, celebrate with a mini reward that will keep you interested and absorbed! Pick up a new book at the library, treat yourself to a magazine, pick up that hobby you've been wanting to experiment with. A full twenty-four hours away from your screens every week will give you the *glow* you've been looking for!

Check It Once

After your twenty-four-hour digital detox, when you log back into social media, make it a new habit to only check in once a day, preferably not in the morning or while at work. I've played and experimented with lots of different times, but I find it's easier to stick to this habit at the end of the day, once you've finished work and spent time with your family. Check in and post all in one time per day. You'll find you save more time in your life by doing it this way than logging back in multiple times throughout the day.

Set a Time Limit

Set a twenty-minute screen time limit in the app limits settings of your phone. When you get notified that your screen time is up, before automatically clicking to ignore the reminder, take three deep breaths. Just three breaths. Bring your attention inward for a moment. When we spend time on social media, we're putting our attention and energy on the lives of others through an app. We're consuming, instead of being mindful. And this can easily lead to mindless consumption that's largely unconscious and habit-based. If we want to live an intentional life, we must bring our gaze inward. Taking a few breaths helps us reconnect to ourselves and break that invisible barrier.

Stick to a Place

Have a designated time and place to mindlessly scroll. If you work from home, choose to always keep the phone and the charger in an area that's not your workspace. Place it in a cabinet in your living room or a drawer in your kitchen. When it's social media scrolling time, go to that place and catch up. Set a time limit and then carry on with your day.

Make Your Life More Interesting

Here's an uncomfortable truth: The main reason I hardly spend time on social media anymore is because I don't find social media very interesting. My life is more interesting than it looks on an app. My real life, my own creations, my daily activities, are far more entertaining to me than what everyone else is sharing. I don't scroll past a few swipes because I find social media rather boring. Sure, some Stoic philosophy accounts make me ponder on things, and there are some artists and photographers who inspire me, but aside from that, there's no *real* takeaway. Nothing I see on Instagram actively changes my life and benefits me in any real, tangible way. At the end of our lives, we are not going to remember the people we followed online. We won't remember the Instagram stories that made us laugh, the captions that inspired us, the influencers we wanted to emulate. What we *will* be thinking about at the end of our lives is the nourishing in-person relationships we had. When I realized how unimportant and boring social media really is, I stopped spending time on it. When you decide to make your *own* life more interesting than other people's curated highlight reels, you'll find social media rather boring. And you'll stop wasting your time on it. It's as simple as that: Make your own life more interesting than what you see online.

Now that I've shared some practical ways to slow our lives down, both in our routines and habits, it's time to take notice of the magic in life, *to notice the simple joys.*

"Love is not enough—intelligence is not enough—powerful strength is not enough. You may put everything on one side of the scale, but if you are missing gratitude, you shall lose."

—Yogi Bhajan

5

Simple Joys

Being in the present moment seems simple enough, but being happy, feeling *joy*, is far more complicated. Happiness and joy are different. Happiness is feeling satisfied with one's present circumstances and it's dependent on external factors, such as your living situation, current finances, health, relationships, and how you are succeeding in life.

But joy is different. Joy is deeper, richer, more nuanced. Happiness is not entirely dependent on presence, but joy always is. And one of the most undervalued pieces of living joyfully is *appreciation.*

As a collective, I believe people are starved for appreciation. Every time we watch commercials or read advertisements, we are sold the idea that we don't have enough of something. Don't like the fine wrinkles around your eyes? Here, buy this overpriced magic serum! Don't feel fully free and alive as your most radiant, authentic self? Opt for a wardrobe rehaul, and start your glow-up transformation with a Black Friday sale! We're constantly being told what we're missing, what we need, and what will magically cure our problems. Instead of looking and healing within, we slap a Band-Aid on it and hope for the best. Add to that the emergence of TikTok and Instagram highlight reels, and we're now comparing ourselves to celebrities, models, and influencers who have the lives we've always dreamed of—yet, never in the history of our lives have we had immediate and personal access to celebrities. Let that sink in for a second: never have we ever had immediate access to the wealthy and privileged few. We're comparing ourselves to those who live in radically different circumstances!

Within that spiral of comparison, we forget how blessed we are ourselves. We forget we have clean drinking water and access to reading material. We forget we can see and read from these pages you are holding (which, might I add, I'm so appreciative to you for reading, thank you)! We lose touch of the fact that we have a solid and sturdy roof over our head and food in the fridge. We become oblivious to our ability to hear and taste and smell and see. We forget our hearts are beating and how very much alive and fortunate we are to just be here. Simple things in the daily humdrum of our lives. Small things that are simple but bring us so much joy. This is what makes life worth celebrating.

If there is one simple act that can radically change your life, as it has my own, it's noticing the simple joys. This is otherwise known as "counting your blessings," as Bing Crosby so beautifully crooned in the comforting holiday film *White Christmas*.

Noticing the simple joys is being appreciative of what you have now—not what you're going to receive or what manifestation you're calling into your life in the future, but in the here and now. As the phrase suggests, it's rather simple: You express thanks for the things you have in your life. Appreciation is your most powerful tool. It is a sword we must continue to wield fiercely and gracefully. Without gratitude, you'll never have enough. Nothing you have, do, or get will ever feel good enough if you aren't appreciative of the simple blessings flowing to you always.

When you pour love and appreciation into all aspects of your life, your life flourishes. When you pour joy and appreciation into your work, your work flows. When you give thanks and actively tell your friends you appreciate them, your relationships strengthen. I believe we create our own luck in life. We are responsible for our own happiness, and everyone else is off the hook. Taking full ownership of your life is one of the most empowering belief systems you can cultivate. No one is responsible for your happiness but you.

The Simple Joys

To notice the simple joys, we must first be present enough to witness them. Noticing the small wonders in your life requires masterful levels of observation. You must look up at the sky often and survey your surroundings frequently. You must become a detective—look under rocks or explore the shadows. Listen to the sound of the wind, the rustling of the leaves, the tinkling of the spoon in your teacup. Allow yourself to be swept up by life, carried away by the romance of it all. You must start to see the beauty in, well, everything. And you must get good at it.

Once you start to see the beauty in all things, you start to view life as beautiful too. You notice the light in a stranger's eyes, the musical nature of your friend's laugh. You begin to see how similar we all are to one another: our dreams, our fears, our desires, and our shadows. When you start to see the beauty in others, you see how alike we are, how we aren't at all separate. Seeing the beauty in others, even those you've never met, is the antidote to bigotry. Noticing the simple delights and the small fragments of beauty in other people is how we strengthen humility and open-mindedness.

Expand Your Appreciation Practices

Write It Down!

Take note, on a sheet of paper or in your journal, of all the big and small moments you feel sweet appreciation for. List them out every night before you go to sleep. And don't go for the easy, low-hanging fruit—aim for specific things that aren't necessarily obvious! The more specific you can get and the more you can connect them with your senses, the better.

Go on a Gratitude Walk

Let the winds guide you on a stroll and begin to note and observe the things that are peaceful and beautiful to you. These could be simple things, like the way the light is dappled across a tree trunk or how a lone wildflower is sprouting up through the concrete. Just note them. Be mindful of your thoughts. The more you note, the more alive you'll feel.

Take Photos of Your Joys

Take photos of things that make you appreciative, and print them. Place them around your house. Get some twinkle lights or twine and clip your prints to it, decorating your home with your favorite moments in life! Put together a physical photo album, or explore the joys of scrapbooking (either online or by sliding them into the sleeves of an album, the old-fashioned way). Instagram can often be seen as a time-suck or a place where we compare ourselves to others. I challenge you to see Instagram and other social media outlets in a different light! What if, instead of scrolling, you playfully challenged yourself to post pictures of beautiful moments in your life that you're appreciative of. It could be as simple as a flower on your morning walk, or your cozy cup of tea and the book you're reading in your favorite armchair. Make Instagram fun again and start creatively documenting the beauty and blessings in your life!

Do you believe you are absolutely deserving of feeling appreciation without needing to *do* or *have* anything specific? Or does this idea trigger something within you?

Gratitude is not a transaction: you don't need to do or be anything to deserve it. You don't have to earn a life that is joyful. You don't need to work hard to *deserve* abundance and joy. You don't need to struggle. You don't need to tolerate anyone that is less than respectful.

Now, there will always be situations and experiences in our lives that are unfavorable. No one's life is perfect and endlessly sunny. Sometimes we get dealt a bad hand in life. Maybe you've been scammed or cheated on, or grew up in a situation that was deeply upsetting and unpreferable. But you can always choose to see the opportunity. There are lessons abundantly placed in all areas of our lives, whether we see them there or not. There are soul contracts energetically signed and dated. There are karmas and dharmas to be carried forth.

But from the pits of despair, we can empower ourselves to make profound changes in our lives. From the ground, we can vow to rise to the challenge and take life by the reins. When we take life in our own hands, we feel empowered. It's no one's job to see the light in the rubble but us.

How many of us ask ourselves, "Why me?" when challenging circumstances arise? *Why now? Why this?* These are all valid questions, worth acknowledging. We can't see the light without acknowledging the darkness. There is no compassion without witnessing pain. Both are necessary for the human experience—without duality, there is no life. But after sitting with that feeling for a while, you can decide to move on. You can decide to gather momentum. *Decide to rise* and ask yourself, "What can I receive from this?"

If you look for the opportunity in everything, you will find it. You can choose to see life this way. You must take responsibility for intentionally cultivating and carving your own life. Chisel away at that marble!

It seems more people are growing anxious and depressed with each passing year than ever before. And while there are many reasons for this (increased time on our phones, less in-person connection, a hectic pace of life, etc.), I do think it's still possible to cultivate more small appreciations in our daily lives. There is no good reason not to. If we had to choose between noticing the simple things that bring us happiness, or not, why wouldn't we choose to focus on the good? Our purpose in life isn't to waste time feeling sorry for ourselves. Self-pity can truly be one of the most destructive emotions, because it sinks us deep into an endless cycle of lack. There is no empowerment in self-pity.

But there is one group that thrives from your self-pity: corporations. Businesses thrive on people's defeatism. When you believe you are not enough, they profit. They tell you that this *one thing* will fix you! A magical cure! But they've forgotten the power you have.

You can redirect your thoughts and attention at any given moment. You have the power to turn away. You have the full capability to choose an intentional life—you can intentionally choose to observe and appreciate the simple joys. This isn't something that's reserved only for the privileged few. Everyone, no matter where they live or what hand they've been dealt, can choose to see this. Everyone can choose to see beauty in the mundane, just as children do.

Lightness of Being

"It is not uncommon for people to spend their whole life waiting to start living."

—Eckhart Tolle

Eckhart Tolle is a fascinating spiritual teacher. His deeply profound teachings are a strange contradiction to his playful and lighthearted persona. He's both childlike and wise, thoughtful with his words, a gentle knowing smile peering behind them, with a delightful trickle of a laugh floating out occasionally. The way he takes his life's work seriously, but is still playful, is *inspiring*.

Walt Disney is another who also inspires me. I mean what better way to spend your days off than building and riding your own miniature train in your backyard? Both inspire me by their embodiment of the dual energies that create a lightness of being.

Have you ever noticed that great things come when you aren't taking life too seriously? Every single time something wonderful happens to me—serendipitously crossing paths with a new friend, creating something that just clicks, a kismet blessing flowing in—I always notice it was ushered into my life when I was feeling most carefree. Being lighthearted unlocks resistance. Now, I'm not bashing on those who are more stoic and serious—the serious nature within us is valued and necessary for adulthood—but without that missing piece of childlike play, we miss the entire point of what it means to be alive. We forget that we are here on earth to have fun. If we don't enjoy the journey toward where we're going, we won't enjoy the destination. We must play and have fun along the way.

Let's take children as an example—they really are our greatest teachers, don't you think?

Children notice the joy in their lives so naturally. They find a way to have fun in even the most mundane chores. They infuse games into the simplest everyday tasks and even the most soulful and serious kids love to play.

Kids see wonder all around them. Every day is an adventure: a new flower to pick, a new insect to marvel at, a new illustration to color. Many of us have forgotten how to connect with that part of ourselves. We've lost touch with the joys of the mundane. Some of us have forgotten what we loved to do as children, how we felt when skipping to our favorite tune, or the joys of running barefoot and dancing in the rain. We don't want to get our feet dirty, we tell ourselves. We don't want to catch a cold.

There is so much beauty in the ordinary, and when we observe those small delights, it's easier to get excited about things: newly printed photographs from a disposable camera, candles on birthday cakes, a stray kitty in the neighborhood, bright pink nail polish, or all the animals floating visibly in the clouds. We forget how much fun Disneyland is, how exciting a carousel ride can be, or how easy it is to stop and smell the roses at the bodega on your walk to work.

When we forget these small, simple joys, we forget the magic of life. How wonderful are the gifts of rainbows, sunsets, and colorful flowers? What a miracle it is to have libraries and candles and books to escape into! As Oscar Wilde once said, "With freedom, books, flowers, and the moon, who could not be happy?"

When we aren't in touch with our childlike selves, we become our own worst enemies—we don't forgive easily, we close our hearts, we harden our shells, we make excuses, and we become defensive. In essence, we forget to see the good in others and in life. We stop trusting, and we start doubting. Cultivating that naturalness, that softness, is how we deepen our joy for living.

There's a little child at the core of everything you do.

What brought you to life before the structures and responsibilities life threw at you as you got older?

When you feel stuck, when you feel lost, when you doubt yourself, connect with your inner child. Connect with it by taking yourself out on a nine-year-old date! Make it a habit to regularly spend a day taking your inner child out on an adventure. Nothing is off the table! Set the judgment aside and, upon waking up in the morning, ask yourself what your inner child wants to do most that day. Allow yourself to flow with it. Let your intuition guide you. Allow spontaneity to take you somewhere new. The answers might surprise you. Maybe your nine-year-old self would love to go on a bike ride, pack a picnic, go to the lake or local swimming pool—preferably one with a waterslide! Perhaps your nine-year-old self would like to spend the whole afternoon in bed with a Harry Potter book. Whatever you do, gift yourself the enjoyment of play. Recently, I took myself out on a nine-year-old date and got out my old Gameboy Advance SP and played an old game from my nine-year-old days: *Sims Urbz in the City*. I put on a Spice Girls album and danced in a flowing dress in my living room, and I went skipping down the beach, collecting pretty shells and rocks along the way!

You may look silly, but at the end of the day, everyone needs time to play. Everyone needs a day every week with nothing on the calendar, no appointments, and no to-dos to check off. When you push aside your youthful nature and reject your inner-child's desires, slowly but surely, you start to believe that what you want and who you are isn't okay. That eats us alive from the inside out. We repress our innate desires, and we push aside our deliciously fanciful imaginations to fit in with the rest of the world—a world that is serious, fearful, and data-driven. We feel we need to constantly make the most of our time, do something big, or leave behind a legacy so we feel that we had importance during our time on earth. But in the process, we forget to play.

Our youthful nature is our most aligned state. When we laugh openly and love generously, our hearts are lifted, our energy expands! This energy is magnetic, and it attracts incredible people, experiences, and adventures when we connect with that essence. Like attracts like. We don't attract what we think about; we attract what we are. We don't manifest from our thoughts; we manifest from our subconscious beliefs. When we connect with our youthful selves, our eyes twinkle, our skin radiates, our nails are thicker, our hair is shinier! Everything in our lives benefits when we connect with our youthful selves. We like ourselves more, and other people want to be around us more. So look to your inner child, communicate with them often, and ask what feels like the most fun and exciting thing they could do today.

Look back and reflect on what you liked to do as a child. What were your hobbies? Look at old pictures of yourself—how did your personality shine through? Photos of our past selves remind us of who we are naturally, deep down. Were you a charismatic leader, organizing plays and dance parties in your garage? (Yes, hello! That was me.) Were you a thoughtful, quiet, and creative little spirit, feeling most at home with a sketch pad and a box of colored pencils? Or were you somewhere in the middle? Our childlike selves are an incredibly accurate indicator of who we are and what we enjoy now, but that doesn't mean everyone's childhood was all sunshine and daisies. Many repress their childhoods because of painful past memories. Our subconscious minds bury memories away to help us forget, to help us in growing up and moving forward. But even if we grew up in a household that wasn't ideal, we still liked to play. All children like to play.

Children can also teach us about stillness. They know instinctively how to slow down and have fun. As adults, it sometimes feels as if stillness is harder than action. Being a creative person myself, I need to intentionally give myself time to try new things, like hobbies that aren't associated with monetary gain and are more private. That privacy gives me time and space to play freely to my heart's content without thinking about what other people's reactions will be. Energetically, I feel like a hummingbird—I process, communicate, and learn quickly, and if I don't remind myself to slow down and connect with my childlike nature, my fluttering wings feel like they'll burn out. Stillness is necessary to regroup and recenter ourselves. Just as kids take naps and experience energy dips in their day, so do we.

But we force ourselves to "keep calm and carry on." We bow our heads down to the keyboard and tell ourselves to never quit, never stop. Breaks are healthy. Venturing outdoors in the sun, rolling in the grass, picking up some wildflowers to hand-press in your diary—these are all ways to break up the monotony in our days. Getting out the oil pastels and paintbrushes reminds us to add some color to our dark winters.

These acts remind us to stay open to gifts from the universe. Never quit looking out for those four-leaf clovers. Never shut down your imagination, your starry eyes, your thirst for knowledge and the Big Cosmic Quest. When did it become such a bad thing to have one's head in the clouds? When did dreaming become a bore?

Question everything you've been taught. Be the grownup your inner child would've been proud to know. Embody the spirit your younger self would've loved to have gone on adventures with. They haven't left you. Your inner child is always there and always patiently waiting for you to embrace that missing piece—the piece that is divinely and authentically you. The piece of ourselves we lost when the economy tanked and the world got hard. There's always a chance to reconnect.

Simple Ways to Connect with Your Inner Child

Get Curious

Children are innately curious, experimental, and playful. Ever notice how small children are always asking how or why things are made, done, or said? Take inspiration from a child and start asking "why" more often! When something unexpected or surprising happens, wonder to yourself. Ponder and remain open-minded and intrigued by life's mysteries. "Isn't that interesting?" Get curious with your shadow self. Our shadow selves illuminate the work that needs to be done. Dive deeply, get quiet, and see what discomfort wants to show you. Begin seeing life through a neutral lens, and remain open-minded to what comes your way.

Find the Humor

One of the best ways to cultivate a joyful spirit is to laugh regularly. The happiest, most fulfilled people in life have an ability to openly laugh—at anything and everything. Laugh loudly, boldly, and freely. Light and playfulness exist even in the most serious things, and when you can find humor, wit, and playfulness in your day-to-day, life will feel lighter.

Find It Easy to Love

Children find it easy to love and easy to trust. They have a natural way of loving life and loving others. It comes so easily to them because children are naturally open and trusting. When we see the unity that is within all of us, the link that connects us to one another, there is an emanation of compassion and love that flows through us, expanding to everyone around us.

Do What Brings You Joy

How you spend your days is how you spend your life. This life is a blip. It will fly by if you let it. Instead of doing what is expected of you, do what brings you immense joy, whether that's curling up in your favorite chair with a fairytale novel and a cup of cocoa, or practicing ten minutes of gentle yoga to the morning songbirds as the sun rises. Maybe it's committing to a 365-day photo challenge, where you take one photo every day, requiring you to slow down and intentionally compose, capture, and edit each one. It could look like taking lifestyle portraits of your children, candid street captures, or even the flowers in your back yard. Do the things that give your spirit a feeling of lightness. Fear is one of the greatest motivators in life, but refuse to allow it entry. Tell it to "settle down back there!" Don't allow your fear of regret to hold you back from living the life of your dreams. Don't *force* the work to *flow*. Instead, give yourself grace to step away from the computer for a few minutes to watch the birds outside your window. Let nature and your excitement inspire you. Spend your limited time on earth doing what you want, and not what others want of you. At the end of your life, you'll be so glad you did.

Stop Being Judgmental

So many of us judge other people and situations all the time. We judge so often, we don't even realize how much we do it. This is one of the most transformative practices I've incorporated in my life. It's easier to say than do, but letting go of judgment can immensely lighten our load. It's the best way to spring-clean our heavy hearts. Let go of judgment—of yourself, of others, and especially of those who judge you. Judgment doesn't welcome conversation; it shuts yourself and others down. When we shut ourselves down, we are less open-minded and curious toward new circumstances, environments, and people.

Celebrate people for living out their truth—their own values and beliefs. Live and let live. Let others be where they are, and celebrate them for being true to their own hearts. When we are less judgmental, we become more compassionate and understanding of other people. As a result, we don't take life so seriously. I encourage you to take a pause before automatically assuming what someone is trying to say. Before responding to people or situations, take a few seconds to look within at the energy you're projecting, and inquire deeper.

Connect with Your Heart

Adults live in the mind, but children live in the heart. Bring back the wonder, play, fun, innocence, imagination, make-believe, and leaps of faith. Give yourself space and time—a child needs those things to grow and evolve, to be on their own in the sandbox making a sandcastle. Don't put pressure on yourself to be a certain way by a certain time. Know that you are already on time and exactly where you are meant to be.

Put a Daily Limit on Self-Pity

Allow yourself to cry for a bit. Have a meltdown for a few minutes. Call a friend. Go wild. Then, it's time to buckle up and move on. Choose to see the good. Actively make a choice of noticing good things in your life, and put a strict daily limit on self-pity.

Follow Your Excitement

Be adventurous and seek out new hobbies and ways of doing things. Follow your gut responses and allow your heart to guide you. Try wandering down a new path in your neighborhood, pick up a silly hobby your partner will roll their eyes at, go back to school and enroll in the creative major you considered studying before your practically minded dad told you to study law. Follow your excitement. Allow yourself to play and experiment with something new, different, and unknown! Follow what lights you up and sets your blood pumpin' with eagerness!

Ways to Find Your Excitement

Begin Data-Collecting

When it comes to figuring out what you love or what career to pursue, you must first test the waters. Gather all the data! Pull out your journal and scribble "Data" at the top of the page. Then, begin exploring and experimenting all the hobbies, projects, and interests that catch your eye.

Don't Label Just Yet

Don't judge or label the experience right away! Focus on collecting information. Notice how you feel when doing things: Are you enjoying the process? Reveling in the journey is an essential point to consider when eliminating your options. If you enjoy doing something, day in and day out, the pressure and stress of the result won't matter, and you'll be more fulfilled in the long run.

Note the Similarities

After you've collected data, look back at your list and note if there's a similar theme or essence those activities, internships, or jobs you really loved all share. What do they have in common? Perhaps you'll find the jobs you most enjoyed were more creative and playful in nature. Or did you thrive in jobs with structure that catered to routine? Do you like meeting in person and collaborating with others? Or did you find you came alive most when working solo in your pajamas from home? Note the things that made you most excited, and see how they are all similar.

Go Back to Your Values

Lastly, when you've narrowed it down to a few, it's time to reflect on your values. Do these projects align with your core authentic self? Are they a reflection of your innermost desires and needs? Or do they simply satisfy a short-term fix? Remember the big picture of your life and what's most important to you, and cut out the nonessential. Let your core values guide every action going forward. Any career or job that isn't aligned with who you are and what you need on a deep, integral level is a waste of time.

The Big Picture

It's easy to get bogged down in the nitty-gritty of our everyday. The errands are never-ending, obligations fill our days, appointments flood our calendars, and it often feels like a large portion of our time as adults is spent just filling out paperwork. If I don't stop to look up and periodically reflect upon my life and how I'm spending it, the months start to bleed together. Pretty soon it's a new year, and I have no idea how I ever felt about it. This happens when we live life by default, rather than consciously creating our existence.

As I mentioned in the beginning of this chapter, I believe the simple aspects of life are the things we remember the most. The daily humdrum of our lives contains the things worth celebrating: sleepy mornings in bed, drinking coffee on the porch, listening to our favorite music on the way to work. Those things, while ordinary, make up the majority of everyone's lives. We should honor them, because that's where most of our life's time goes. But while the simple day-to-day is important, we must also remember to zoom out. Periodically, we need to step back and see the big picture of our existence. In these moments, our lives become clear. We remember what's most important to us and what's not. We realize that freaking out and stressing over missing tax deadlines isn't all that important in the grand scheme of our lives, and getting annoyed with your partner for forgetting to fold and put their laundry away isn't really that big a deal. Erupting into a fit of road rage just isn't worth it. Our days matter, and how we spend our time is valuable. With every tick of the clock, your life is one second closer to your death. While this is dramatically morbid, it's reality. The sooner we own it as fact, the sooner we start living our lives with radical honesty and courage. The sooner we accept it, the sooner we can have fun—*lots of it.*

This requires us to be radically honest with ourselves. No more bypassing. No more setting aside your values for a quick dopamine hit on Instagram. No more spending another night on the couch binge-watching yet another show to take you away from your current reality. It's time to celebrate your life.

There is a famous stock photo, a picture of the Milky Way galaxy with a little arrow in the middle with some text that reads, "You Are Here." You may have seen it. It's pretty popular. Most people ignore it or don't look at it closely. Some give it a smug eyeroll and think, *What pretentious, holier-than-thou, dramatic preacher of a person would make a poster of this and put it in so many schools, and doctors' and therapists' offices? What's the point?*

It's quite brilliant, really. It reminds us of the big picture: We're floating around on a speck of dust, whirling through infinite space. Photographs of outer space inspire my everyday choices. It's why I love following NASA on Instagram and why I have a screensaver of the Milky Way on my MacBook. It's a reminder that nothing is worth stressing about. In the grand scheme of existence, I'm rather small. And that's a beautiful thought.

I'll never forget the day my life took a drastic turn for the better. I was twenty-one and living in a dingy apartment in Harlem. My dad had died suddenly a week earlier. I had just gotten fired from my job (which I hated) and then promptly fired from an internship (which I also hated). With my dad's sudden passing, I couldn't stop thinking about where life was leading me. How were my life choices affecting the big picture of my life? Why was I spending my days working at a job I despised, surrounded by negative people who made me sick to my stomach, for eight hours a day? Why was I spending all my little-to-no money on cheap tulle dresses and silly trinkets that brought no value to my life? Why was I still chasing a "dream" from my childhood in a city that took more away from me than it gave? *What was I doing with my life?*

Death is a strange thing. It can make the most joyful souls crumble. It can make the sweetest souls hard. But challenge brings wisdom. Hard experiences can cultivate insight. Death makes an impact that hits so hard it knocks the wind out of you, and you're left looking at your reflection, your own mortality, and all the choices you've made up to that point. There are no words.

It's a real shaker-upper, that death is. But it needs to be reflected upon at one time or another.

How to See the Big Picture

These are a few of my favorite ways to zoom out to see the big picture of my life. May they inspire you to examine your own existence.

Visualize a Bird's-Eye Perspective

In this moment right now, as you're reading these words, I want you to imagine looking at yourself from above. What do you look like? Where are you located? Step outside of yourself and simply watch yourself reading. Now, take another step back and see yourself reading in your home, in your neighborhood. Then look at the path your life has taken to lead you to where you are now. How did you get here? Where did you come from? What did you encounter along the way? Take fifteen minutes every week to sit down in meditation and visualize your life zoomed out. You can do this by simply allowing your imagination to guide you. With each inhale and exhale, take a step back and zoom out again. See your entire life path before you—the detours you took along the way, the sidesteps and mistakes, the mini inner transformations and experiences that led to your becoming. Watch your life unfold before you; be in awe of how you got to be here, now.

Question Your Actions

Be honest with yourself: Will what you're doing for work right now *truly* matter one year from now, five years from now, or ten? If not, cut it out. It's not worth your time. It's time to think big-picture. Ruthlessly eliminate the unnecessary. Cut out the things draining your time, energy, and resources. Life is too fleeting not to.

Venture to Outer Space

One of my favorite ways to remember what's important in my life is by taking myself to outer space. I sit down in meditation and imagine myself observing Planet Earth from afar. I visualize myself sitting cross-legged in a beautiful room, with floor-to-ceiling glass windows, a spectacular view of Earth in front of me, galaxies swirling on either side, and I just observe. And breathe. In this experience, I am reminded of how silly all of this really is. We're sitting on a floating blue ball of dust in the middle of space. Imagine that!

This little exercise is one that immediately takes me out of whatever stressful situation I'm in, and it helps me remember where I am and what I'm here on Earth to do: simply be. It reminds me to slow down and see my life's big picture. Guided audio meditations are great for this, but you can also do this little practice on your own by slowing down your breath and imagining yourself taking a glass elevator to your special place, looking out at this big, swirling blue ball we live on. Have fun with it! I guarantee, you'll feel more peaceful when you come out of it.

To live more slowly and intuitively, we must listen to the childlike nature in us that just wants to have a good time. Children are so easily excited by the small wonders and the simple things in life. Children get excited by just about anything: a piece of candy at the doctor's office, a sparkly sticker, new neighborhood friends to play with, a freshly plucked dandelion to make a wish. Everything is so exciting, and they act on their excitement! When a child has an idea for a play, they put on the performance right then and there. When they see a freshly opened box of crayons or markers, they eagerly start drawing a masterpiece! They don't worry about what the kid sitting next to them thinks of them doing it. They don't wonder if their drawing, play, or Lego amusement park is any good, or whether they are well-equipped to pull off such a creation! They just create. *They just do.* They follow their excitement. They put their head down and let their intuition guide them, even if that looks like changing their outfit ten times in a single day because they got "bored." They experiment, play, knock things over, scribble things out, and start over again—their excitement leading them through life.

We too have this ability. We still have this connection to the inner childlike selves within us. It's just a matter of remembering what it *feels* like. This sacred connection doesn't leave us, but it certainly softens with time. By actively choosing to make time for the things that bring you joy, by noticing the beauty in the small moments around you, you re-enhance that connection.

"You are not your thoughts. You are simply aware of your thoughts."

—Michael A. Singer

6
—

Your Intuition

Have you ever noticed that, right before you take a big leap into the unknown, right before you bust through fear, venture outside your comfort zone, or break through an internal barrier, a feeling of fear accompanies it? Know that that isn't your true self. That's fear talking. Or, more accurately, your *ego*.

The next time you have a big decision to make, notice how your mind tells you to do one thing and your heart tells you to do another. Movies, songs, operas, and books have been written about the two distinct parts of ourselves. It's so common, you might even witness the two energies playing out within you right now.

Take a moment to pause and listen to what's playing out in your mind. Pay careful attention to their difference in tone. One voice is risk-averse, fearful, and unsure. This is the shell that contains the essence of your spirit. It's a chatterbox, and it never stops worrying. It can feel almost like a dog's chew toy that you just can't let go of, or a fire hydrant spewing messages that you "should" do something and if you don't, you're unproductive or not "enough." The ego can be fierce. It's certainly demanding of our time and energy. It has preferences, opinions, insecurities, and objections. It doesn't want to slow down because it feels it'll be left behind. And it never wants to go against what everyone else is doing, because it wants to be accepted and loved by others. Safety is always its main concern. In the past, this voice has been referred to as "the monkey mind," "the ego," and "the lizard brain," but the most important thing to remember is that it's there and it's always seeking to gain control over you. Now, there's no need to ever fear the ego, or as I like to call it, "the mind." It has a job to do, and a helpful one at that: it keeps us alive.

You'll feel the ego as *fear*. It may even seem insistent that this voice within us is our own. It's a constant companion, always letting us know how it feels, what it wants, and what its preferences are, so much so that it really feels like us. We inevitably start to *identify* with it. It's our personality, our mind. We're so used to hearing this voice and seeing this personality play out, both inside our heads and interacting with others, that this voice starts to feel like the only voice we know.

Over time, the other voice we have within us starts to feel hidden. It's a whisper so soft we can't seem to hear it above the chatter of the other.

This is where we get to the *heart* of who we are. Our true self, our actual best friend, is the second voice—the one buried deep within us. This voice is our intuition. Perhaps you call it your higher self, your inner being, your inner voice, God, Source, the universe. Call it what you want, the name doesn't matter. The most important thing to know about this second voice Is thul il's always peaceful and present-focused. With our inner being, there is no future and there is no past. It never worries about a *thing*.

This is an energy of pure love.

It has a different feeling from the first voice in that the intuition always feels accepting, calm, loving, all-knowing, and certain. It doesn't pass judgment, and it doesn't make assumptions. There are no doubts or what-ifs—only complete trust. Our inner voice, this *knowingness* we have within us, is constant. It never wavers. Like a steady flame, it burns bright. And it's often buried so deep within us, we've forgotten it's there.

We feel intuition guiding us when we experience sudden gut feelings. It may activate when we have a knowing feeling about something and don't understand why. It's expressed as, "I don't know how I know. I just know." Intuition emerges from the depths when we feel a sense of total and complete trust in life. Even when your life is in shambles and falling apart at the seams, you know your intuition is guiding you when you hear yourself saying, "Everything is going to be okay."

Intuition is never explained, only revealed. We *witness* the inner voice; we never need to search for it. We may hear from intuition directly—a word or phrase or a direct action that seems to come from out of nowhere. My own intuition doesn't speak to me in spoken words, but in sudden gut feelings. In a split second, the entire message is downloaded and received, and I know exactly what to do. I don't hesitate and I don't doubt, for the message is always clear. Sometimes the message drops down like rainwater atop my crown, and I receive it in my stomach. You may feel your intuition communicating to you through your heart (chest), gut (stomach), the back of your neck, the crown of your head, or even in the tips of your fingers.

The messages from our intuition are always delivered quite clearly, and they're received instantaneously.

Your mind might rationalize that it isn't worth taking a leap of faith toward your dream, out of fear that your actions won't work out as a result. But your inner voice encourages you to do what you love, in the present moment, even if it seems risky.

Here's an example of how the two voices might sound regarding a dream in your heart.

The Ego:

"If I speak about this passion of mine, I might make others uncomfortable. My family will totally make fun of me. What if no one cares? My spouse doesn't understand why I love this, so what makes me think anyone else will? What if I trigger people by sharing this? What if people get turned off by my enthusiasm? Or make fun of me for it? I'm just not likable enough. Honestly, I'm just wasting my time. I could be doing something that will actually make me money."

Intuition:

"Share your voice."
"Express freely."
"Go do."
"Speak your truth with love."
"What is meant to be will be."
"All is well."
"What's for you will not go past you."
"Yes. Yes. Yes. Yes. Yes!"

The ego is often long-winded. It's fear-driven and has plenty of justifications, disclaimers, reasoning, and "what-if" thoughts. On the other hand, the inner voice is simple but quite profound in its messages. It always comes from a loving, peaceful, and present place. Often, it might feel or sound like one-word answers. It may also just be a gut feeling we sense deep down, without knowing where it originates from.

So why don't we always follow it? What stops us?

Fear.

At some point in life, we get stuck. We forget what it feels like to be fully connected to ourselves—our bodies, our hearts, our souls. We lose that connection. We cut off communication. Life speeds up. There are job promotions and cross-country moves, not to mention giving birth to new life and adapting to new milestones that completely shake up our existence! We change, and our interests fade. We make new friends and outgrow old ones. We move and travel more now than ever before. Life moves so fast, we forget to check in. As we consume more externally (media, other people's opinions, etc.), we rely less on our own instincts and gut feelings. But the great thing about our intuition is that it never leaves. It never decides to give up on us. Our intuition wants to connect with us because it's who we are, and it wants to *remind* us of that. It wants us to remember our gifts, our abilities, our infinite capacity to *love*. It's not some mystical god or angel or spirit guide. It's us—the purest, most loving form of us. And it's always here to help. It's always present, lurking in the background, whispering, begging us to call out to it. It only takes one call to retrieve it.

Feel the Energy of You

1. Place one hand on your chest and one hand on your stomach. Slow your breathing and quiet your mind. With each inhale, watch your stomach expand. On the exhale, place your full focus on your hands, the feeling beneath them. This action activates a little thing called "heart-brain coherence." In essence, you're connecting the heart and the mind. Feel that energy pulsing through you. Sit with it for a moment.

2. Place your hands in front of you, opening your palms toward one another. Set them about a foot apart. Take a deep breath in, and then allow your eyes to flutter closed. Feel the energy radiating between your hands. You may feel your fingertips buzzing or a warmth emanating from your palms. Feel the power within you!

Keep an Open Mind and Test It Out

If you feel skeptical or hesitant about connecting with your intuition, adopt a scientific perspective and test it out. Data cannot be judged without first testing it. Observe the feelings that rise within you. Keep track of your gut feelings. Record the data and jot down your hunches before outcomes or situations are presented. Train your intuitive muscle and simply practice making intuitive predictions. Don't cast judgment—remain curious. Remain a scientist, an explorer of life's mysteries that have yet to be unraveled.

Whether you've lost connection or you're looking to deepen the connection with your inner being, here are some tips to get you back in communion with it. Trust me, you'll be ecstatic to hear from you!

·

How to Connect with Your Intuition

Make Quick Gut Decisions

Begin to train your mind to make decisions on minor matters very quickly. Like within ten seconds. When you are presented with choices in your life, exhale and decide quickly. Don't second-guess yourself. Go with your first impulse, as it's usually the one to listen to. This might move you outside of your comfort zone, but that is a good thing! If you feel a tiny bit more excited by one option than another, go for it. Jump right in and make the decision to move forward with the option that compels you.

Notice the Two Voices Every Day

Start taking notice of the two voices within you. The one that is more anxious, worry-prone, logical, skeptical, unsure, fearful, and nervous is likely your ego. The other voice that is more peaceful, loving, certain, spontaneous, playful, humorous, encouraging, and kind is likely your intuition. One feels like a fire hydrant of thoughts, while the other is a bottomless pool of calm water. When a voice or feeling pops in that feels connected to one of the two, notice it and observe the feeling. How are they different? Is there one you'd rather listen to and commune with? Just notice it.

Find Moments to Breathe

Actively take deep breaths throughout your day—on the train, when you're about to brush your teeth, while you're cutting up vegetables for dinner, when you're in bed about to go to sleep. Make a habit of deep breathing, because it's the easiest way to tap into your intuition.

Notice the *Gap* Between Thoughts

Try this for me: Take a deep breath in, hold it at the top, and exhale. Now do this a few times. Watch your thoughts roll around in your brain. Observe the randomness of it all, moving in, moving out. Once you feel relaxed, ask your intuition a question. On the next exhale, listen. Don't think. Don't reach for an answer or try to reach out for some easy, low-hanging fruit. Just notice.

In that tiny space, that small gap between the end of the exhale and the start of the next inhale, is where presence lies. That presence, when tapped into, can feel limitless and like it ventures on forever, gliding into the ethers. In that small gap, there is not fear but peace. Sit in that and let it wash over you. The more you spend time in that gap, the longer it will feel.

Allow the Message to Rise

Don't try to understand it; *feel* it. Don't pull an answer down; allow it to float up. Let the answer rise and bubble up from within you. When we feel stressed out, angry, or overwhelmed by our emotions, it's difficult to connect with our intuition. Our minds will start trying to create answers using our past experiences, but our inner being always lives in peace, presence, and a state of total surrender. It doesn't worry about receiving answers, it just *has* answers. And you can't receive truth if you're in a state of panic. Desperation is an instant blocker. So don't search for your truth. Instead, have patience and practice breathing exercises first before asking any questions. When you start to notice that gap, wait for the answer.

Wait for Gut Feelings

You may feel those *knowing* feelings in the pit of your stomach (gut) or a swelling in the heart (chest). Your intuition doesn't live in the mind. It lives in the body. Connecting with your physical body and your senses is an easy way to tap into your intuition, because that's where your wisdom lies. When you ask your intuition a question, direct the question down to your stomach or chest and wait for the answer.

Keep It Simple in the Beginning

If you've been living in the mind all day, as we all often do, start with some simple questions to open your intuitive channel. Begin with simple yes/no questions. Ask yourself, "Inner Being, am I safe? Intuition, am I loved? Higher Self, is everything going to be okay?" Breathe and allow the answers to come forward, peacefully and calmly.

Inquire Deeper and Ask Again

So often, if we don't hear or receive an answer from our intuition, we give up, thinking maybe we just don't have a good connection or we aren't naturally "gifted" in our intuitive ability. Rubbish! Just ask again. Or better yet, ask the question a different way. Don't quit, dig a little deeper instead. If no answers appear, rephrase the question. Ask your inner being to show you the answer visually, rather than through words. Always take your question a step further by asking, "Why"?

Write to Your Intuition

You don't have to have conversations out loud with your intuition if it makes you feel silly! If you're more of a verbal processor and enjoy speaking as opposed to writing, speak to it aloud. But if you'd rather quietly engage with your intuition through writing, this is a practice you'll love! Anytime you feel stressed, anxious, or worried, write to it. Pull out your journal. Connect with a pen and a piece of paper. If you're on the go, pull out the notes app on your phone and start asking it questions. Just opening that channel every day strengthens your connection.

Access the Power of Your Daydreams

Pay attention to your yearnings whenever you find a thought crossing your mind that starts with something like, "I wish I could…" or "I hope someday I'll be able to…" or "Someday I want to…." These are small nudges from your soul. This is your intuition speaking to you. Follow the clues of what brings you joy, the hopes and dreams of your wildest fantasies. Start with those and keep going, one small action step at a time.

Trust Yourself

Listening to our intuition requires a certain degree of trust. We must trust ourselves enough to listen and follow the guidance of our inner voice. Many of us are looking outside ourselves for approval, acceptance, and recognition. We feel we need to be loved by others to fully feel love within ourselves. We feel we need to be people of service before we can cater to our own needs and desires. The opposite is true. To take aligned action from our intuition, we first need to trust ourselves.

Life is full of choices. In every single moment in our lives, we are confronted with two options: we can choose to surrender to love, or we can bow down to fear. We can trust ourselves and the tiny voice within us, whispering for us to follow peace, joy, freedom, and the wildest dreams of our hearts, or we can remain in the comforts of what is, sitting idly on this plateau. We can choose to settle for small things, or we can choose to live in unabashed integrity.

We see fear overriding intuition all the time: Polly, who's enrolled in pre-med because it's what her parents want, secretly dreams of enrolling in art school. Sam in accounting dreams of a life as a creative designer, not knowing where to start but afraid to take the financial risk and leap. Karen, crushing it hard as a CFO, secretly dreams of leaving the corporate world so she can become a stay-at-home mom and spend more time with her kids. It doesn't matter what the dream is or what life is being called to us. It matters that we listen and pursue it.

Life asks us to take the risk, to make the leap, to trust in our inner wisdom. But we are all programmed to follow the safe route, to do what has always been done, and to accept mediocrity. We keep our life small because we're afraid of taking risks. We want approval from the establishment on things we've done before we feel we are worth something.

I experienced this feeling recently. A lot of my income as a freelancer writer depends on people liking my ideas. My thoughts need to be captivating enough to receive compensation. Recently, after a three-month period of constantly pitching ideas to magazines and videos topics to brands, I felt drained not hearing a single reply. My articles, essays, video topics, and travel photography submissions were being rejected one after the other. For months, my emails went without a reply. I felt like the work I was doing was not good enough, or that my writing wasn't intelligent enough. Eventually, the work merged with my identity: Maybe *I* wasn't good enough. Maybe *I* wasn't likable enough or talented enough. Maybe *that's* why I was rejected: I just wasn't good enough.

This is where we fall down a slippery slope. Our intuition doesn't need validation or approval. Our inner being doesn't demand a response. It doesn't ask to be praised or acknowledged. That's all ego. That's the part of us that just wants to be seen, heard, and loved. Our inner being merely wants us to act on the things that light up our heart. Intuition wants us to do what makes us happy—and not the egoic, shiny-penny kind of happy, but the emotionally fulfilled and fully engaging-in-the-process happy.

Can you take the risk, without the end in mind?
Can you take the leap and try again, despite the rejection, listening to the whispers from within?
Can you love yourself despite the results?

You may learn all this, master it, and embody your higher self. But even if you live in alignment with your inner voice 95 percent of the time, you may still notice that the ego comes crawling back in, wanting to be accepted by the outside world. This is natural. This is what makes us human.

The shiny pennies will tempt you. The promise of security and safety will comfort you. But is it worth it? Never. Not if it's not based in love. If your decisions, actions, and emotions are plagued by fear, you can be assured it is not your inner being leading you.

So what do we do? How do we live in integrity with our highest self?

We listen. Then we take courageous action.

Following our intuition requires us to break the cycle of what we've been told. If we yearn for a slower life of peace and simplicity, that goes against where society is now. In today's modern world, achievement is king. Accomplishment and wealth are to be envied. Corporations value individuals who are ambitious, achievement-driven, and who steadily produce. But we are not cogs in a machine. We are not meant to live our lives constantly churning out content and proving our worth to others. Our worth is not determined by what we've done or how much we have. Living slowly and in divine harmony with your intuition means being gentle with yourself, having compassion for yourself, for where you are now and where you are going.

Slow Living Is Intuitive Living

To live a life of peace, ease, joy, and fun, we must look to our intuition to guide our next steps. We must ask *ourselves* questions. We must look to ourselves for advice, not to anyone else. Not to any social media influencer or spiritual teacher, guru, or friend. You are your own guide. The wisdom you seek is already within you. *The answers you seek, you already know.* You must simply peel back what is blocking you from that awareness.

Just as Michelangelo described making his *David*, everything you need to know, you have. All you need to do is remove that which is covering it up. Remove the excess—the fear, the insecurities, the desire for approval—and discover the core: the radiance you already are.

Slow living is self-sovereignty. Instead of comparing yourself to other people's speed or caring what other people are doing, look up to your higher self, the part of you that is growing and evolving into its best and highest good. This is self-trust. To trust in yourself is a radical act of self-love, and that love is needed now more than ever.

Be Your Own Influence

This is the beginning of the end of an era: the influencer era. It's the beginning of the end of the "guru" days. This is a time of discernment. It's the time to question all you see, to take what works and toss what doesn't.

I often find it interesting when I watch creators getting canceled online. I read the comments and see a lot of the same thing: "I trusted you," or "Everything I learned from you was a lie. I feel lied to!"

In these stoic moments of observation, I wonder how these loyal followers and subscribers arrived at their conclusions. Why aren't they more discerning with their energy? Why did they give their power away to some creator *they don't even know?*

The truth is that celebrities, influencers, creators, writers, and TikTokers are all just living their lives and speaking their truths to the best of their abilities, to the best of their present-moment awareness. Sometimes, the reason they're being called out is valid. And sometimes, it's not. It's a shame to witness the defamation of innocent people. Slander kills more livelihoods than anything else.

But despite that, the amount of power being thrown at people is always fascinating to me. Instead of honoring their own energy, these followers give it away freely. They forget to have their own perspectives and nuanced ways of viewing things. We idolize creators and forget about the power within ourselves. We forget we are just as worthy and valuable as the people we look up to. We hand over our trust, giving it to strangers. We should be careful and cautious toward these people. We can follow them and like them, sure. But to freely trust them? That's not honoring ourselves. We aren't listening to ourselves when we give our complete trust to people we've never met.

When we don't listen and trust ourselves first, we start to attach ourselves to outside people, ideas, and belief systems. This is how cults and some religious groups become so powerful. We can easily lose ourselves to them. We can fall into a pit of addiction and desperation. We can find ourselves obsessing over insatiable desires to be wanted, desired, and loved by other people. It starts out small, by not seeing the beauty and wisdom within ourselves first. It starts with a quiet admiration of someone else. We often wonder how we can be like them. We study their favorite books. We observe their habits, their morning routines, their daily rituals. We wonder how they got to where they did. We memorize their origin stories, and we buy the products they use. Perhaps we copy. Perhaps we steal. Perhaps we even start thinking *just* like them. It can just as easily turn into an obsession. And then, just like that, we find ourselves manipulated. Suddenly, we feel "lied to."

Life can take an unhealthy shift when we don't honor and value ourselves first, when we don't know ourselves well enough to trust our inner guidance system.

The reason you are intrigued by, interested in, or attracted to anyone is because you see in them a fragment of what you already have within you. They are simply a mirror reflecting your potential in true form. As humans, we like people who like us. Similarly, we also like people who *are* like us. There's a saying that goes, "You are who you hang with," but it may be more accurate to say we hang with people who reflect who *we* are.

Anytime you are intrigued by, attracted to, or inspired by someone, I want you to turn it back to yourself. This isn't narcissistic; this is awareness and observation.

I implore you to dig deeper, inquire more, and ask yourself:

> *Why this person?*
> *Why am I so interested in this person's life, and what does that have to say about me?*
> *Are they reflecting my core values back to me?*
> *Are they an inspiration to me because they are doing or living the lifestyle I dream of living?*
> *What does this say about my own aspirations? My own potential?*

It's time to take your power back. It's time to be your own influence. You are your true healer. No one can heal or guide you more than the inner voice that is always within you. Be your own teacher; be your own guide. Let the wisdom you have shine brighter than any teacher, coach, or so-called guru on the internet. Look within, because *the answers are there.*

The other wonderful thing about listening to yourself first is that everything you say, do, or think is entirely original. It cannot be replicated. It is an accurate, authentic representation of who you truly are, on a deep, soul level. By igniting your own light, others will get curious enough to find the treasure that uniquely belongs to *them.*

That is how we lift humanity. We show up, do the work, and make life on this swirling blue planet a lot happier by going within ourselves first.

I imagine this as tiny raindrops—droplets of pure, golden light falling to the earth, igniting and scattering light into the homes down below. This is true inspiration, and it is how others can shine and share their own unique light. We need more truth-tellers and embodiments of light in these dark times. Communicating with and trusting your inner voice is the way to become that. By shining your joy, unique energy, perspective, and light, you can inspire others to do the same for themselves. As cliché as it sounds, no one is like you. No one can do what you do in the exact way you do it. No one can embody your unique energy in the way you can.

Having the self-sovereignty to live your truth, according to your intuition, is your greatest superpower. Be entertained by others, feel expanded by other kindred spirits, but don't lose yourself. Don't give away your power by seeking outside of yourself for answers. They don't have your key. Only you do.

Be inspired by others, but always reflect and ponder on *why* you're inspired. You'll find these people are showing you how you can be an inspiring light to others as well.

And if someone changes (and not to your liking), leave. If someone you follow has changed (and not to your liking), unfollow. It is time for self-sovereignty. It is the age of discernment. It is time to question all you see, to ask if it rings true for *you* and to go deeper within yourself for guidance. You were born with the ability to find stillness anywhere, so listen. You don't need to be taught this. It is simply my hope to inspire you to look within yourself for answers, to seek the light that shines deep within your core, and to bring it to the surface, so the people around you can shine too.

We have been looking to outside influence for far too long. You are your own influence. So allow your inner voice to lead the way.

The Poison in People-Pleasing

People-pleasing is one thing that can easily get in your way.

Our human collective tends to do things to please other people. How many students are enrolled in university, studying things they don't want to learn because it's what their parents want for them? How many people are chasing success in their careers to prove to others their worth and value? How many women are having children because society pressures them to want to be mothers? The people-pleasing is constant. The need to be accepted by the group is rampant. It's biologically ingrained within us to want social inclusion, to feel like we are part of the pack. It's not just yo— *we* are hardwired on a primal level to desire this, to feel part of a community. Just as we all desire to be accepted and appreciated and to feel seen and heard by others, we equally fear being rejected, ostracized, and ignored. Perhaps this is why our early teenage years often take such a hard toll on our mental health, and we spend the rest of our adult lives trying to heal those wounds.

To a certain extent, wanting to be accepted by others is helpful. In some ways, we *should* care what people think. If our friends or loved ones are unhappy with how we are behaving, we should *want* to better ourselves, simply because we love them and want to have a positive relationship with them. Having healthy relationships with the people we care about is important. But there comes a point where not being authentically true to yourself is more painful than pleasing others.

Knowledge is power. The more data you have on something, the greater the chance you have of defeating it. It's important to know why our people-pleasing tendencies kick in. The reason why we want validation is because we are seeking love, approval, and acceptance from others. The only reason we are affected by negative reactions from other people is because we want them to like us.

If you like yourself already—if you love, accept, and approve of yourself as you are right now, regardless of circumstance, accomplishment, or merit—you will not give a hoot what someone says.

If you love yourself fully, you'll get your approval from within. When you trust yourself and your decisions enough, the external noise is muffled.

This matters because, when you decide to slow your life down, people in your life will question you. It happens to me all the time in private messages, emails, and comments from lovely souls on YouTube. People share with me how they yearn to live slower, to say no to more job responsibilities, to tell their family they don't really want to get a master's degree, but they don't know *how*. They're afraid to say what they want. They fear rejection or condemnation, and they fear what others will think of them.

When we prioritize the needs and desires of others, we ignore our trusting relationship with our own intuition. When we stop listening to ourselves, we lose integrity. When we follow other people's values over our own, it spares *them* suffering, but it puts all the suffering on us. For example: If our parents encourage us to pursue a line of steady work or formal education that doesn't peacefully align with our heart and values, we end up willingly taking their own fears as our own because we love our parents so much and we just want to please them. But just know this: By sparing their suffering and putting the suffering on yourself, you instantly lose that integrity with yourself. You lose connection with your inner voice, the most important relationship you have. This misalignment inevitably leads to stress, unhappiness, resentment, and eventually poor sleep patterns, potentially body reactions, and even illness.

We've been taught that loving ourselves is selfish. But ask yourself this: Who is the more selfish person? Is it *you*, living your life peacefully, quietly, doing your own thing according to your values and being nice to people along the way? Or is it the person telling you what to do and how to do it all in the name of "love" and "concern"?

I'm sure you can guess. The selfish person is most certainly not you. What they are doing is selfishly asking you to do what you don't want to so *they* can be happy, because it aligns with *their* values and belief systems. They are assuming what is the best and highest good for your life, for your unique soul's evolution. In essence, these are people telling you that you don't have an internal compass of your own, an intuition to guide you.

People may sprinkle this on you in myriad ways, like, "I'm telling you this because I love you," or, "I just want the best for you." But at the end of the day, it's all very simple: They want you to live your life in the way that best suits and reflects their own life.

People most certainly do not agree on values or how to live life—everyone's opinions are different. But that's on them. Their criticism reflects themselves. It has nothing to do with you. Your only job is to live your life in genuine integrity with your values and to be kind to others along the way.

So often in my life, I've had family, friends, coworkers, and even employers tell me how I should live my life. They've told me I should want more, that if I had any ambition, I would aim higher or dream bigger. I had family members disown me and shut me out of their lives when I left college to work as an actress. I've had people question my decisions to work for myself, to get married young, to live abroad. I was given worried glances when I mentioned I was closing my business to accompany my husband to France for his job. So many times in my life, I've felt tested by life and others, and I've had to ask myself: Do I really trust you, intuition? Do I have the faith to follow your inner whispers? Am I willing to give this up in the hopes that you'll catch me?

Yes. A thousand times, yes.

Never once did I ever doubt my intuition. I've questioned myself and my abilities endlessly, sure. But never have I doubted my inner voice. Time and time again, my inner voice guides me to an even better path my mind can't yet see. Every single time I listened to my inner voice and ignored the looks cast and criticisms thrown at me, I was gifted an opportunity even better than the previous one. Listening to my inner voice took me to New York, it brought me my husband, it brought me to France. Listening to that soft, gentle pull led me to pick up a camera and learn photography, and then videography. It told me very peacefully to start a blog in a little café in Bali. While in meditation, I downloaded the message to "Speak online, speak what you know" at the beginning of the pandemic. It's led me to a life I couldn't have imagined before: a life of freedom, fun, and so much personal fulfillment in my creative expression.

Our higher selves will send us gut messages and knowing feelings, but we must trust that the dark path ahead will illuminate each step along the way. People will question your lifestyle changes. Your loved ones may object to your heart's wishes. At the end of the day, you have to listen to yourself. *You must.*

The hard truth of the matter is that this life is short, and it will end. People will go on living, and future generations will not remember you. You must live this life for yourself. You must follow the dreamy urges of your soul because you came here to this planet to live a life you are proud of. You don't owe this to anyone else but yourself. It's your life. Live it full-out and with authentic integrity.

Only you can give yourself the love and acceptance you are seeking. When your cup is full and your high degree of self-worth is cemented in appreciation and acceptance for who you are now, other people's dreams for you won't matter. Like water off a duck's back, it won't affect you. Their criticisms will no longer cut you like a knife, and their words will no longer be a trigger.

When you're comfortable with yourself, start expressing yourself. *Boldly*. Be brazen, be vulnerable, be raw. People can always sense when someone is living in alignment with themselves , and in turn, it inspires them to do the same.

Tips for People-Pleasers

Ask Yourself First

As social beings, we naturally feel inclined to ask other people for advice before asking ourselves. Stop asking people for their input. Start asking yourself.

Honor Your Values

Recognize that if someone is pushing their values onto you, it is because those values give *them* meaning, fulfillment, and personal satisfaction. Don't get pulled into their narrative; their soul path is different from your own. Decide what gives you meaning, fulfillment, and personal satisfaction, and go do *that*. And celebrate others for living their lives true to *their* values. Acknowledge them. Give them words of affirmation. Tell them how refreshing and nice it is to see them living their truth! Simply recognize them. That's really all people want: they just want to feel seen and accepted.

Don't Explain Yourself

You don't need to explain your lifestyle or personal dreams to everyone. Less communication sometimes allows for more harmony with family members. Stay quiet, at least in the beginning. True confidence is quiet. Let your outcomes speak for themselves.

Or Don't Tell Them at All

At least, not at first. Don't utter a word to anyone in your life that you think may judge you while you're trying something new. Whether a simple lifestyle change or a dream to move abroad, you name it, just don't say it. This will feel difficult to do at first, especially for those who feel closely connected to their family, but trust me, it'll be worth it. When data-collecting and experimenting with a new lifestyle, career prospect, or project, people may judge you or think you're making the wrong decision. They may call you "flakey" or "distracted" or criticize you for not sticking to one thing. You probably won't feel certain about the things you're testing out. Knowledge is power, so wait until you feel confident in your decision. When you decide to move forward with certainty, you won't feel triggered when your family or friends question you because you'll feel confident in what you now know.

Do Not Respond to Negativity

If you put all your energy toward responding to negative comments or feedback and try to reason with them or convince them of your worth, you're going to have nothing left to give to the people who support you. Speaking from personal experience, responding to negative feedback will completely drain you of energy. And it's a shame for the people that support you.

Let Others Be

Accept that this is where they are right now. Accept that that is how they perceive life. Allow them to live their truth. Easier said than done, I know, but acceptance is the only true gateway to peace.

Observe Their Values, Not Their Reactions

Look at them through a lens of neutrality and observe the values underneath the reaction. Get to the root. Seek to understand what they value. How has that played out in their lives? How have their values manifested? How do they express those cherished values in their day-to-day? Seek to understand them, for you can disagree with someone yet not be disagreeable. You may not agree with someone's point of view and still get along with them. Don't hit them back with a verbal attack. Don't poke at them; just observe their values.

Lastly, remember we will never completely stop caring what people think. We are pack animals, and it's honestly *healthy* to care about what others think. In terms of asking for advice, it's best to have a safe place: Keep a few very trusted friends or "consultants"—kind people you respect who will honestly share the truth and give you constructive feedback from a place of love and compassion. These people love you! Remember to cultivate deeper friendships and relationships with people who have your back and will support you in an honest way.

You owe it to yourself to live fully, shamelessly, vibrantly, and unabashedly true. You owe it to yourself to listen to your intuition first. Mean comments are not a reflection of you. They're a reflection of them. Even in positive words, everyone reflects the energy they are currently holding within them.

How to Develop Confidence in Your Intuition

Actively Be Proud of Yourself

Reflect on what makes you proud of yourself. We do not reflect enough on the things we did *right*. If you're like me, you probably overthink your actions, worry about the things you said that one time, or are just generally hard on yourself. It's the perfectionist's curse. But you know what's sort of radical? Being genuinely proud of yourself for all the small things you do each day—like making the bed in the morning, or taking the time to show yourself some self-love by tending to your morning rituals before the kids wake up. Being proud of yourself for actively listening to your partner talk about their workday at dinner, being the thoughtful parent you are and making your child's lunch each day for school, showing up for other people in your community, being a kind neighbor, showing up for and honoring your creative heart each day by taking the time to paint in the evening. We don't reflect on these things enough. Do yourself a favor and take some time each night before you go to sleep to jot down and reflect upon what you did that day that made you feel proud of the person you are now, the person you are becoming. I assure you, you have a lot more to be proud of than you think.

Ask Yourself What You Have to Lose

The writer and philosopher Elbert Hubbard said, in *Little Journeys to the Homes of the Great Vol. 3: American Statesmen*, "To avoid criticism, say nothing, do nothing, and be nothing." People will always project their own pain, shortcomings, and fears onto you, so you might as well exist loudly. You might as well exist in full integrity with who you are. You might as well go after what you want. Life will be full of disappointments. At the end of the day, at the end of your life, what have you got to lose? You may as well go for it. There's more to lose by not living your life fully than there is to gain living it for others.

Do Esteemable Things

To have high self-esteem, you must do esteemable things. Confident people are service-oriented people. They give back, and they give plenty. Confident people are generous with what they know—their talent, their voice, their time. One of the easiest ways to develop confidence is to take the focus off yourself and put it on other people. So often, social anxiety is attributed to being intensely focused on ourselves. How do we look? What do other people think of us? Did I say something wrong? Let go of self-absorption and give value to others.

Know What You're Good at and Then Improve

Confident people are passionate people. One thing confident people all have in common is a talent or skill they've honed. This may look like discovering a hobby, talent, or interest that captivates them and dedicating years to improving it. Figure out what you're naturally good at. It could be a specific skill, or it could be that you're a great listener. Know your strengths and remind yourself of them often. In fact, keep a list going! Note those specific traits and abilities when they arise. When a friend tells you they're inspired by your courage, write that down in the back of your notebook. This list will keep you confident when you forget about the wonderful qualities you possess!

Take Small, Consistent Steps

One of the best ways to increase confidence is to consistently show up for yourself by taking small steps daily. It's not about doing what you want, but what you *need* to do. Good habits make the insecure days bearable. We all have those days when we feel less than ideal, but when we have automatic good habits in place—like drinking lots of water, eating lots of greens, moving our body, meditating, etc.— they make us feel a little bit better, which gets us through whatever confidence spiral we're in.

Allow Others to Freely Misunderstand You

Confident people don't feel the need to defend or justify their choices to everyone. They pick their battles wisely. Allow yourself to be free of what others think by allowing others to misunderstand you freely. The more sacred an idea is to us, the more closely connected it is to our identity. Thus, the more we will defend it against criticism, closing us off from growth. The sad reality is we *all* project our own confirmation bias. We see life and the lives of others through our own filter because our beliefs and personal experiences color our world. We assume we know what someone else is thinking or experiencing, when we are just seeing it through our own lens of perception. By adopting a lens of neutrality, we can bring more clarity and compassion to our relationships with others. By remaining open to others inevitably misunderstanding you, you spare yourself the insecurities that arise from needing to constantly explain yourself.

Try the Power of Affirmations

The love you are seeking is the love within yourself. Tell yourself aloud, "I love, approve, and trust you, (name)." This is a powerful practice, and one that seems to ground and bring confidence to the biggest people-pleasers. We have a choice to seek out where we receive love and approval from. Allow the love for yourself to stem from your intuition. Make this a daily part of your morning or evening routine. Place your hands on your chest and tell yourself you love and approve of you. Don't let yourself down; be consistent.

From birth, we are conditioned to believe we need approval from others because it was our chance at survival. We always had to assess if something was "okay" or "not okay" based on reactions from our parents and teachers. As we age, we realize how well we can thrive on our own self-reliance—how liberating it feels! The more you love and trust yourself, the more you listen to yourself. Trusting yourself enough to listen to your divine wisdom is essential to living a slow life in harmony with your natural energies.

Slow living isn't an aesthetic or a cosplay hobby; it's a deeply intuitive lifestyle. To live slowly means to honor yourself and honor your energy. To live slowly means to live life at your own speed, and go about living your dreams at a pace that aligns with you. You are not conceited for choosing to respect and honor yourself. You are not a narcissistic self-involved prima donna for feeling loved from within. Self-love isn't selfish. You can be the most service-oriented contributor in the world and still honor your inner voice.

If you take one thing away from this book, it is to *listen to yourself*. Honor the whispers of your heart. By living intuitively, you will naturally start to live slowly, because you're honoring the magical energy that is within you.

"Don't hope that events will turn out the way you want, welcome events in whichever way they happen: This is the path to peace."

—Greek Stoic philosopher Epictetus

7

Presence & Surrender

Slow living is more than just finding stillness in your days to enjoy the quiet moments. Much of what I've shared in this book so far are simple things to enjoy a simple life. But let's go *deeper*. When we live slowly and in total awareness, we have a greater advantage in accessing presence. And experiencing presence—deep, profound peace in the moment—is only enjoyed when we venture *beyond* the comforts of the material.

Acceptance

Having acceptance for ourselves and for life is one of the most poignant ways we can exude gentleness. To many, cultivating acceptance within ourselves is often seen as a more passive way to live life, but acceptance is simply remaining present. Accepting your life does not mean staying in a situation that's unhealthy or dangerous, or one that doesn't make you happy. Rather, acceptance is acknowledging your present reality as the only reality that exists in the current moment, given the circumstances. Your life isn't any other way: the only existence available to you in this moment is the existence of here and now.

When you argue with your present reality, you have already lost. Instead of arguing or fighting against life, recognize the value and lesson in every moment, in every situation. Adjust your sails and change your course, but first acknowledge and accept that this is the present-moment reality. There exists no other. This is the hand life has dealt you. The first step toward forward action momentum is acknowledgment and acceptance. Without acceptance, we cannot see the big picture and the buried lessons.

There's an idea in Buddhism that attachment is the root cause of all suffering. We suffer because we are too attached to this life experience. We identify ourselves based on the physical items we hold dear to us, the relationships we share, the talents and skills we've cultivated. But what if that all disappeared? What if, overnight, your spouse decided to leave you? What if a fire erupted in your home or you were physically harmed in an accident and—worst-case scenario—you don't have disability insurance:

Would you be okay? Is your happiness tied to that to which you are attached? Do you suffer internally for the things you cannot control?

It's the same way with beliefs. If you identify yourself and your personality with a specific belief system, you may suffer if someone disagrees with or challenges your belief. If someone questions what you hold to be true, you may feel compelled to defend yourself, to justify why your beliefs are valid. But what is the purpose in this? What is the purpose in fighting, defending, or justifying when all it seems to do is cause separation between people?

The reason you suffer is because you won't allow yourself to let something go. Oftentimes, that something is sinking its claws into you, dragging you down. Whether it's not being able to let go of the critical remarks from your mother, your first love, or the mistakes of your past, you must remember to have compassion for yourself. Gentleness and compassion are qualities that, as a society, we have not cultivated enough. The modern world is obsessed with grinding, hustling, and getting back on our feet after setbacks, but we also need to make time to heal and look inward. That introspection requires us to slow down and pay attention to how we are *really* doing.

We must forgive our tender hearts and make peace with the past. It is only when we accept what has been given and heal the wounds within us that we create the space to expand. This time of reflection can come by way of journaling, grounding in nature, or even in solo walks. It can look like writing a letter to someone you're having trouble letting go of and then burning it, forgiving yourself and them in the process. It can be as simple as gazing at the full moon and allowing your emotions to bubble up to the surface. It's allowing yourself to cry deeply.

In that process of reflection, we must remember to forgive ourselves. Hence my love for EFT tapping.

EFT, also known as Emotional Freedom Technique, is a simple practice where you physically tap on the meridian and pressure points on the body to clear emotional blockages. It's an energetic healing technique, like acupressure, and best of all, it's free, easy, and only takes a few minutes to do. Essentially, you press on various points on the body while expressing aloud what it is that's bothering you and what you want to let go of. I sometimes tap on the points in the morning to get me jazzed for a fun day, as well as when I'm in need of release. Vocalizing our feelings aloud while admitting our suffering and choosing to forgive and accept ourselves is infinitely more powerful than just thinking about it. Speaking it out into existence and stepping fully into your voice is your way of taking ownership of the present reality. I love to end every tapping session with, "And even though I am feeling this way now, I love and accept and forgive myself anyway." Speak your truth, for that is how you step toward acceptance and forgiveness for yourself and others.

To feel greater joy and peace within ourselves, we must find a way to accept our past. You wouldn't be here today without your past. The challenges, the growing pains—this is all your becoming. Your past made you the resilient, intuitive, powerful, and discerning person you are today. It is through mistakes that we better understand our world. It is in solving problems that we find great personal fulfillment. It's as simple as this: If your life were supposed to be different, it would be.

Embrace That Life Is Fluid

Be accepting of life's fluctuations. They are inevitable; it's not a matter of *if*, but a matter of *when*. Your career will fluctuate: You'll go through periods of success and periods of stagnation. Same with your weight. Same with your friendships. Same goes for your self-confidence. Life is not about controlling any of that, but rather about recognizing that this experience is what life is all about. Life is an adventure, and it's one we signed up for. We all signed up for an unknowable adventure, and that's what we're given. Since life is always in motion, life will continue to change. Allowing and accepting the impermanence of life is one of the secrets to inner peace. There is one thing certain in life, and it is that all things in life are uncertain. There's no need to attach your emotional state to that which you can't control. In my own path to sustaining inner peace, I have found that remaining flexible and adaptable to life's changes is what keeps me joyous. When a wave appears, adjust your sail.

Seek the Middle Way

Life is full of polarities and extremes. Circumstances can make us feel more positive or negative. By default, we react to whatever life hands us. But can you challenge yourself to seek neutrality? Can you live in the middle way, where positive experiences don't overwhelm you with joyous ecstasy and negative experiences don't severely disappoint you?

The Stoic notion says things are neither good nor bad in life, but rather preferable and unpreferable, which is certainly a more peaceful way to look at it. Peace only resides in neutrality. The middle way is calm, observant, and *quietly* appreciative. So how can we stay neutral and remain in the middle space between joy and grief? By observing our thoughts, without being *in* the thoughts themselves, as we learn in meditation. Through our carefully cultivated mindful slow-living habits, we can resume a neutral stance, sustaining clarity and peace of mind. I also find it's important to remain curious in the good and hard times. Be happy with what is *and* eager for more. Remain appreciative of the joyful experiences while *also* remaining focused on unearthing the lessons the harder ones teach. When we gain access to this place of neutrality, the middle way, the stormy highs and lows of life don't shake us and rock the boat as much. Rather, a light wind ensues, advising us to chart our course in a new direction.

Release the Need to Assume

Whether it's about people, places, or situations in life, without a doubt, making assumptions is a dangerous habit—and an easy one to develop, too. We all judge and assume things about what we don't know; it's a fool's errand.

Movies exhibit tales of good vs. evil, always glorifying the hero. But in life, villains are often more complicated: There are simply people who have been shaped by their environment. We forget nuance and lack empathy. We forget to dig deeper, to question what is being shown.

When we assume and cast judgment on things we haven't collected enough data on, we block the truth from being shared. Honesty cannot be heard when connection is severed. This can look as simple as putting words in people's mouths and assuming what someone is saying without taking time to *listen* and ask questions. It can look like having an automatic, knee-jerk response as you form an opinion about someone without ever knowing them personally. It's acting as a mind reader when no logical evidence is provided. Assumptions create ignorance, and ignorance creates bigotry. It's one of the reasons I'm passionate about traveling, meeting new people, and asking them questions about their lives and perspectives. It's why I love befriending people whose political beliefs and cultural backgrounds are different than mine: I seek to learn and understand. I always look for similarities, not the ways we are divided and separate. Constantly making a mental note of what makes people different from you is a surefire way to stay closed-off, resentful, and ignorant. That's how we isolate ourselves, and it's near impossible to understand where another person is coming from when we're so deeply entrenched in our own emotional turmoil. So often we interpret another person's perceptions from our own biases and past experiences. Where is the open neutrality in that?

It is only when we disidentify our own self-attachment that we are readily able to see our interconnectedness, and thus have kinder and more compassionate relationships with others.

Silencing our assumptions and considering the unknown is the only way to truly understand what we do not know. As students of life, open-mindedness is crucial. Honor your self-sovereignty just as you honor the sovereignty of others. Release the desire to assume. Let go of judgment. It will open your life and lighten your load in more ways than one.

Reclaim Your Peace

When we encounter conflict or difficulty, there are two ways we tend to go about it, depending on our personality: We either embrace the peace, or we embrace the process. If you're a more process-oriented personality, you want to fully experience *all* the feelings—including the negative ones. Within the experience, you want to find a way to learn from it and, ultimately, control it. You may feel the desire to fight back and do whatever it takes to get yourself out of it. But if you're on Team Peaceful, there's a sense of detachment. The emotion is just there. The circumstance played out as intended, and in this peaceful stance, you accept all life as the present-moment reality. It's the natural ebb and flow of life. It has nothing to do with you personally, and you know tomorrow is another opportunity to start again. While experiencing that negative emotional state, you remind yourself that tomorrow is a new day, and you're going to make it a good one. There is no fighting it. There is a lack of resistance, with no need to justify, defend, or challenge. Always trying to get the last word wastes energy unnecessarily. There is far more peace in detaching yourself, and this is something I am learning every day.

Stand Up for What You Believe In

When talking about acceptance, arguably you might think acceptance also means remaining indifferent, adopting a neutral stance on the difficulties and hardships of life. Earth can be a painful place to live: humans commit acts of evil, and more of our present-day leaders seem to care less about climate change, social justice matters, and criminal justice reform. The list goes on. When we remain calm and peaceful from within, this does not mean we are complacent or accepting of those who are unkind and unfair, but that we must adopt an inside-out approach.

Most people are completely unaware of the effect emotions have on the physical body. We're so busy acting and reacting to others, we aren't aware that our stress is causing more harm to ourselves long-term.

Here's something to note: The body can only ever be well through *well*ness, not illness. Just because others express anger and hate and are not well internally, that doesn't mean it's better off for you to feel the same. Adopting their energetic setpoint does nothing but bring you down closer to their level. It is only when we have adopted a calm, peacefully steadfast inner life energy (essentially, one that is *well*) can we truly do the work and stand up for what we believe in. It is when we are well that we can generously donate, protest, sign petitions, and go about taking fierce action for positive change. In your wellness, you have resources to share. But in your pain, you have nothing to offer. Anger invites more anger. Hate only empowers hate. You can only create long-standing radical change when you are well and strong from the inside out. A quiet inner strength, a steadfast, resilient, pure heart, is infinitely more powerful in creating change than many who are emotionally reactive and unwell.

Nonattachment

We obsess over how our lives should look—today, a month from now, a year from now—and we completely miss the beauty in front of us. We get all caught up in our minds: worrying about the things we wish we'd said, the things we want to say but don't. We get anxious over the idea of time passing, running out. We fret over the notion of enough: there isn't enough time, enough money, enough love.

The self-help world glorifies productivity, glowing up, and before-and-after transformations. But upon closer inspection, these things don't help us. They make us believe we *need* our lives to be infinitely better to be satisfied with the present. We believe we need to embark on our own glow-up journey, transform our identity and daily habits, and reach "peak performance" to be the best version of ourselves. We're constantly fed the idea we need to change, to improve, to be *better*.

Those who have experienced this hunger and seeking of external validation know all it does is lead to inevitable suffering. After enduring that suffering—whether as disappointment, a feeling of failure, or straight-up burnout—there comes a point where we develop a soft and quiet courage, a strength to dive deeper within to find joy. It's true that achieving all we desire might be nice for a while. Having desires is what makes us human. Having dreams—whether big or small—is valid. Please don't mistake living slowly for a life of toned-down dreams. By all means, follow your heart! But the real awakening happens when you realize you don't *need* things. Letting go of the insatiable need is how we free ourselves from attachment. It's freedom from the ego—the chew toy of the mind.

Nonattachment is letting every situation be as it is instead of as you think it needs to be. It is choosing to make the best of what you have in your present-moment reality, given the circumstances.

What if, instead of feeling desperate for your life to be a certain way, you allowed life to guide you?

If you chase something and feel thirsty for it while pursuing it, you won't feel satisfied once you get it. What you feel in the middle of the journey is what you will feel at the finish line. No matter how many times you reach the destination, you'll eventually feel thirst again.

When your emotional wellness comes from within and you live according to your values and not the results, the things that are meant for you come as they may. You no longer wish for an outcome to give you joy because you're already feeling joy from within. You can *enjoy* the fun, pretty things, experiences, and outcomes *without being attached to them*. Detach your emotions from the circumstance itself, and instead experience your reality so fully, *so deliciously,* that you allow experiences to move *through* you. Instead of clinging tightly to the present, move *with* it.

It's been said that we are in the world but not of it. You can have a gorgeous apartment, but you aren't *attached* to the gorgeous apartment. You can adore your sparkling eyes, your long hair, and all the personal preferences that make you who you are without *believing* so intensely that you are attached to them. The seriousness of it all dissipates. This poses the question: *If something about me were taken away, would I still feel whole? Or I am relying on this to feel good about myself?*

Close your eyes and imagine your life without what you identify yourself with. Imagine those things gone: the relationships, the clothes, the car, the house, the job, the reputation, the talents, the skill sets, the college degree, all of it. With nothing left, who would you be? What energetic qualities do you radiate? How does your energy *feel?*

Feel Good First

First, it's important to get good at not emoting on the basis of circumstances. Your only job is to feel good. No matter the circumstance, stay rooted in that *feel good* place—feelings of peace, connection, joy, playfulness, hope, curiosity, openheartedness, love. Feeling good is your only job. In that place of *nonattached* alignment, you'll have an easier time receiving and acting on the wisdom of your intuition.

> **Feel good, know what you value in life, and follow your hunches—those are the three key things to remember.**

Meditation

Only through meditation can we acquire true equanimity, because it is a place where the ego cannot interfere with our thoughts and emotions. In the state of present-moment awareness, it feels as if we've attained a level of neutrality. When something happens to us in life, we neither object to it nor support it. We manage the situations we are given in life without ego involvement, without the chaos, stress, worry, and fears that plague *all* minds. With enough practice, we realize we don't, in fact, need to *control* the ego. Instead, the ego is simply no longer there, or is small enough that it doesn't affect our connection with our inner voice. While I don't believe we can let go of the ego entirely, unless we've achieved enlightenment, I do know we *can* harness the ego to create space for more emptiness in the mind.

The ego is like a wild horse that needs to be tamed to accept the saddle one gives it. Transformed from wild to wise, it becomes quieter, more grounded, and ultimately develops a peaceful, symbiotic relationship with its master: the soul.

When our ego quiets down, we no longer take offense and are no longer reactive. When affronted or complimented by others, we remain neutral and impartial. We don't attach ourselves and our identity to what we are told. There is inner peace, a calmness. This is obviously an advanced level of presence, and one person I am greatly inspired by in my own quest for more presence and stillness is Tenzin Palmo.

Tenzin Palmo is a woman who lived in a cave in the Himalayas for twelve years to reach enlightenment. For three years, she lived in an intense retreat where she didn't speak to a single soul and spent the majority of her time in meditation, even sitting upon her meditation box to "sleep." While I have no interest in living in a cave myself, I find her inner stillness and imperturbable nature fascinating. After living in the cave, she said, "I have the kind of mind that wherever I am, that's where I am."

This simple sentence is exactly the level of nonattachment and peace of mind we can all reach in our daily lives. We can have desires, but can we also be content with what we have now? You may have a dream to move to a new city, land a better job, marry your soulmate, but can you find peace in the *now*? When we find joy in what is present today, and when we accept the given moment as valid and true, only then do we find true peace. With the ego flareups abated, we're able to live in a perpetual state of calm.

Our thoughts always want to keep us safe where we are. Our ego wants to keep us from taking chances. Meditation is a practice that helps me turn off that fearful chatter of the mind. Meditation is one of those things that make some people scoff and roll their eyes. And it makes sense: we feel uncomfortable about meditation because we know it's much harder to do than it seems. It's difficult to tune out thoughts when we've spent our entire lives catering to them! Focusing on your breath and listening to silence is much easier said than done.

For me, meditation was like a gold star to be earned. Another item to mark on my spiritual checklist. More brownie points for how well I've been sticking to my morning healthy habits. When it came to meditation, for years, I felt like a not-yet-ripened banana. But some breakthroughs take a little more time to ripen.

One important thing to know, that many people don't seem to talk about, is that the mind loves vision boards. It loves ownership and goal-setting, acquiring more money and more recognition to satisfy the never-ending thirst of its insecurities. Our mind will always want more to bury its fear of not being enough.

But this place, this feeling I've experienced in meditation this last year is going beyond the mind. In meditation, you stop caring about any of it. The heart of us doesn't care about shiny pennies because there is no fear within us. There is no concern over what it cannot control. *It's fully content with what is here.* It's a feeling of quiet appreciation, groundedness, and unity with all that is. Meditation is a tool to help us learn how to quiet the constant hum of our thoughts so we can appreciate the simple joys.

Meditation is a place where we can access the eternal *now.* While in it, you feel a deep sense of connection and presence with the world around you. It's a place where nothing exists but the present. Meditation is not about escaping life, but about gaining a deeper awareness of it.

Meditation, in the beginning, feels as if you've entered a dream-like state. You may see colors, symbols, visuals, or movie clips play out before you. But there comes a point in one's practice where one enters a state of deep inner presence. It feels steady, calm, and loving. You feel interconnected with all of life.

As you adopt a meditative practice, you can see the illusory nature of life. Instead of being in the center of it, it's happening all around. Rather than being in the middle of the experience, you observe it from the outside. The longer you meditate, the more you begin to see how pained people are and how much people are suffering, and it's because the chaos of the mind has caused the self to identify with its environment and with what it's *created.* We suffer because we are wedded to our identity. We pain ourselves by becoming attached. There is no space to simply *be* when we have this impassioned conviction of our identity, when our worth and sense of self is dependent on the creations we've curated and cultivated. We must learn to be satiated with the mere breaths in our lungs, the remaining beats of our hearts. This is enough for us to thrive and find peace of mind.

Practicing nonattachment to all things, people, and circumstances in our lives is not a heartless act. On the contrary, when you feel this internal presence, a stoic vibration, it's a feeling of interconnectedness with all living beings. Most people believe that, if you don't react with emotional fervor and passion, you are cold. But when we don't react to these ephemeral emotions—many of which are up and down and dictated entirely by external circumstances—we create spaciousness in our minds. This is not cold, it's *unwavering* warmth. A warmth that doesn't leave when we are disappointed by another, a flame that doesn't suddenly burn out because we're upset. This is eternal warmth and *eternal* love—a feeling that can be felt more clearly the more we spend time meditating and questioning the thoughts playing out in our minds.

Much of society will not be able to fully understand or contemplate this state without doing meditative work. Without a meditation practice, we are at the whims of thought—the trials and tribulations of life and the suffering of all of those around us. Thoughts are undependable and reactive. Without meditation, peace is a fruitless pursuit, and life will drive us insane. Without meditation, there is no finding this source of oneness.

Tips to Make Meditation Easier

Start with One Minute

There's no right way to meditate. You don't have to meditate for ten minutes a day. Heck, you don't even have to meditate for *five minutes* a day! Start with one minute. Slowly inch your way up, and add twenty seconds with each passing day. That's it! Over time, it'll get easier, and soon you'll be meditating for five minutes or more. When I struggle with getting into a new routine or feel lazy or unproductive, I tell myself, "I only have to do this for five minutes. That's it!" You don't ever have to set a high bar for yourself if it feels unaligned. Unless you're a go-getting, challenge-loving personality, if you repeatedly set a high bar for yourself and it doesn't feel quite right, you'll eventually burn out. Meditating used to be really hard for me in the beginning; even just a few minutes felt like a huge hurdle to overcome. But make it a habit: Start with one minute a day and work upward from there.

Be *in* Your Body

When you begin meditating, feel what it's like to be in your skin, connected with your physical body. Pay attention to any tension you might be holding. Slowly observe the sensations as you work your way from the crown of your head, down through each muscle, to your feet. Notice what feels open and what feels closed and cramped. The simplest way to practice mindfulness is to pay attention to the way your body feels. There is so much our bodies know that our minds do not. What can you learn from your body in your meditation today? What is your vessel softly whispering to you?

Focus on Your Breath

Connecting with your physical container is the ideal time to focus on your breath. Its rise and fall. The inhale and exhale. Notice how your lungs expand and release. Don't think about how quickly or slowly you're breathing. Don't worry if you're breathing deeply or not breathing deeply enough. You know how to breathe—your body will do it for you naturally without thinking. You don't have to remember to breathe, just *notice* it. Observe the breath. That's where the real practice begins—in noticing it. Becoming a watcher of the steady inhales and steady exhales, one breath at a time. If you find yourself falling asleep when you meditate, sit up in a chair or lean your back against a wall, and/or meditate at an earlier time when you're not sleepy.

Meditate While in Activity

You don't need to sit straight up, cross-legged, or in total silence to meditate. You can also practice meditating while *in* activity, like stirring a boiling pot of pasta, lighting candles, or folding laundry. No matter how busy or chaotic our days may be, we can still cultivate moments of awareness. While engaged in a task, take a deep breath and shift your focus to the task in front of you, preferably with no music or sounds playing in the background. Pay close attention to the current task, the textures in your hands.

Find pockets of space in the busy moments to bring your awareness back to the breath; I promise life will feel slower. I have found meditating while in activity to be infinitely more powerful than meditating in total stillness.

Don't Give Up

If you get distracted, that's okay! In fact, that's *normal.* If you don't *ever* get distracted while in meditation, you *must* have a few past lives as a monk under your belt. Seriously, everyone gets distracted. Everyone loses focus and finds their mind drifting and wandering around. Sometimes several minutes pass before you realize you've been lost in a spiral of thoughts. *This is okay.* What's important is that you're not hard on yourself, and that you remember to go back to focusing on your breath. When you notice you're thinking, *gently* pull your attention back to your body, your breath. The inhale, the exhale. The rise, the fall. In, out, in, out. When you find your attention wandering again, gently bring

yourself back to the sensations in your body, the way your muscles feel. Again, there's no right or wrong way to meditate.

Note It

Carefully note what crosses your mind. We don't want our minds to become unresponsive. We simply want them to be less reactive. We want to react less and *be* more. While in meditation, the ego or the thinking mind is quieted and released at some point. With careful observation, the thoughts and emotional responses we feel in the beginning grow smaller and smaller, until the reaction dissipates. In this quiet steadiness, we start to feel a poignant connection, a *release.* In meditation, we learn how to separate the emotional reaction we feel from the sensory experience currently being had. The next time you're emotionally wound up, refrain from banishing all the thoughts whirring around in your mind. Simply note them and move on.

Simple Ways to Meditate (that aren't what you expect)

- Take a solo walk and let nature guide you
- Gaze at a candle
- Sit by the shore and watch the waves
- Look out the window at nothing in particular
- While walking, watch your footsteps, the soft blur of your surroundings, and allow your thoughts to dissipate
- Listen to gentle music and pay careful attention to each note
- Ask yourself where a thought came from; venture deeper and ask again
- Watercolor paint with no design in mind, just observe the colors bleeding together

Surrender

Living abroad has taught me its own lessons in nonattachment and surrender. When we are constantly moving and transitioning into new jobs, it's hard to form community. It's hard to always be saying goodbye to the people you love. When you're regularly packing, moving, and creating a new home for yourself, you can't take much with you, so you don't own much of anything, leading to a feeling of weightlessness and freedom to roam. Moving abroad has liberated me because I've learned the precious gift of nonattachment to objects, sentimental items, and journals, as well as to money. Moving has taught me that money comes and goes. Living abroad has taught me that money always comes at the exact time you need it, in the exact amount you need, and *more money* is not often needed or even better. Frequently packing up and saying goodbye has imparted a nonattachment to people as well. For years, I remained loyal to a fault, dutifully keeping in touch through regular phone calls and handwritten letters to friends back home, fearing the ticking of time would disrupt the bonds we forged. As I've lived abroad and said goodbye to countless people, I realize not all cultivated relationships are meant to stand the test of time.

Some friendships are cultivated for a sliver of time and leave everlasting footprints on our hearts, imparting wisdom that would have never been gained otherwise. The love doesn't leave; it just changes shape. I'm now more open to accepting change, especially the kind I can't control, and I've learned to deeply appreciate the relationships I have in the present moment because these moments only exist in a single drop in time. Years from now, a singular moment will only be a memory, so it must be carefully cherished in the time it is presented.

Living in France has its joys and challenges, but this is the life I chose and continue to choose with passion and fervor. I live slowly, but I am also a wanderer, in search of adventure and truth. In my life, I seek simplicity—in my relationships, obligations, responsibilities, and possessions—because I value a life of freedom and travel. Not all who wander are aimless, without a sense of direction; some choose it consciously. When you know your values, there is not much else to do except surrender to the unfolding.

Here are some ways to practice surrender and nonattachment, no matter the circumstance.

Wait Patiently

Timing is more important than we realize. We won't always be in a peak period in life, or even experience the more positive periods. A season of waiting is crucial for everyone, and this incubation period is just as important. Just as a green banana shouldn't be eaten before it's ready, we too need to mature and ripen. I encourage you to remain still until you feel inspiration. Practice patience until you feel clarity. When you feel the need to rush or act immediately, even when you don't feel divinely guided by your inner voice to do so, say aloud, "Stillness." Allow the energy of the word to melt you into this present moment.

Remaining nonattached to the comings and goings of life is about being comfortable in the seasons of waiting. Just as with silence, we need the contrast between doing and not doing. We all experience foggy periods in life, so we might as well learn to be content in them. This doesn't have to be hard. Just practice. Get into alignment, pick up a hobby for fun, watch a show that brings you comfort, do the things that make you feel good. Allow yourself to be nonattached, to not need to know everything before it happens. Learn to be okay with not knowing. Stay open to the possibility that what you think is the way forward may just be the beginning of a much larger picture, a much larger mountain you can't yet see.

With enough practice, you'll feel more and more comfortable sitting in the unknown. This state of surrender allows life to open to you. Blessings shower over those who are patient and open to receive.

Thank Your Ego

While the mind can conjure a lot of problems for us (emotional reactivity, obsessive thoughts, paranoia, fear, worry, stress of the unknown future), this doesn't make the mind malicious in intent. The ego is here to help us. Our ego wants to keep us safe, to survive and stay alive! Our mind has evolved with us since the beginning of time. It's helped us fend off saber-toothed tigers! The mind wants to protect us and make sure we keep on keepin' on! So I encourage you to thank your ego when it arises. Actively note its presence. When you find yourself afraid or in fight-or-flight mode, take a deep exhale. Breathe out the fear quickly and sharply (*Whoosh!*) and close your eyes when you do so. Steady your heartbeat, one hand on your chest and one hand on your stomach. Acknowledge the ego's presence, the worrying part of your mind that wants to keep you safe, healthy, and so very alive. Thank it for showing up today. Remind yourself that you no longer need to listen to it. You can acknowledge the chattering of the mind without listening to it. Simply acknowledge its presence and thank it for trying to help. There's no good guy or bad guy—there are just two distinctive energies.

Surrender to Life's Changing Plans

While I think it's lovely to go through life without a plan or dream, I also think it's unrealistic. As ever-evolving beings, we will always have desires. Further, our desires will frequently change into new ones. Having direction in life is enormously helpful, but there needs to be a balance. There is a saying that "The best way to make God laugh is to proclaim your five-year plan." As someone who grew up with an insane level of ambition and direction, I know firsthand that not allowing some wiggle room for life to guide you can lead to resentment and frustration in the long run. Go ahead and tell yourself, "This is what I want my life to look like," and proclaim away! Write it down, send a voice memo to a friend, exclaim it to the universe as if it's *already* happened! Have fun with it. Exist loudly. Take up all the space! Doesn't it feel wonderful to stand firmly and fully in your truth, singing your desires out for the world to hear? But also be open to the potentiality of something else, something *better*. Bask in the glow of your dreams, but don't forget to surrender to them. This requires us to have humility, to be open to possibility. Cultivate more space in your dreamy visions. If life has other plans, learn to be content with what comes. *It is what it is.*

Let It Go

To remain nonattached and fully present in our lives, we must let go. *Often.* When you feel the need to eliminate and remove something from your life, do so without hesitation or a second thought. Ask your inner voice regularly if something is worth keeping, if a memory is worth revisiting, if a thought is worth thinking.

When you desire to let go of a person in your life or a haunting memory from years ago, write it all down. On a piece of paper, write down everything you wish to let go of—beliefs, things, memories, people, you name it! Write that letter to the person you think about and can't quite forgive. Express the torrid flames of your heart. Cry so much your vision blurs and you can't even see the paper and pen in front of you! Then, I want you to forgive yourself and forgive them. Then, burn it. Take a hot shower, scrub all the thoughts and emotions off your body. Then, light some palo santo and go to sleep. Do this often, because the more you let go and release what is clouding your vision and dragging you down in life, the sooner you can do what you're meant to be doing here on earth: having fun.

Navigating the Darkness

"Nothing ever goes away until it has taught us what we need to know."

—Pema Chodron

Here's the truth: We didn't sign up to enter these human bodies just to experience joy and happiness. We also came here for soul growth and development. We also chose to come here to experience challenge and struggle—yes, pain and negativity are included in this buffet of life! We're here to get stretched. Like coal, we need to experience pressure to transform and alchemize into another level and become diamond. This human experience we're having right now? It's like school, and we're on the fast track to learning our individual soul lessons. Yes, there's recess and playtime and summer break and holidays and fun! We get to play here. But we *also* have difficulties to face.

Here are some ways to navigate the darkness.

Coexist

In life, dualities coexist. Light cannot exist without darkness. We cannot fully understand joy without experiencing suffering. Encourage the chattering mind of your ego and the calm, patient wisdom of your inner voice to be together. Allow them both to sit together at the table.

All of it has validity. All emotions on the spectrum are valid and worthy. Instead of beating yourself up over not doing enough, not being appreciative enough, not being *healed* enough, show yourself compassion and grace. Be patient with your tender heart. Allow both emotions, both human experiences, to be present together. Before we can get to work on *anything* in life, we first need to acknowledge, accept, and own our dual natures, our multifaceted parts.

Adopt a Lens of Neutrality

Neutrality doesn't mean you have no emotion or attachment. It doesn't mean you don't care. It means seeing your life, actions, patterns, habits, decisions, and boundaries *energetically*. Can you see every action, every thought and intention, as energy? Everything is composed of energy, including us. Holding a big-picture perspective and seeing your thoughts, words, and actions through a lens of neutral energy gives you a deeper clarity to see what would honestly bring you the most inner peace and joy. When emotions aren't dragging you down, you can see things clearly and take action on what would most excite you!

Name the Monster

Monsters live in the dark, so call them out! Name them. When you're aware of what you're doing and can name it—"boredom!" "fear!" "overwhelm!"—say it out loud. Over time, after you've become aware of the recurring emotions that creep over, you'll stop needing to label them. If you repress or ignore shadows and darker feelings, they'll creep up on you. Remember that darker emotions are only fear. When you witness that awareness of fear, it no longer controls you. Instead of running away and fearing negative emotions, dive in fully. After recognizing them, you can then detach. Visualize creating that space and separation.

Disidentify Yourself from Your Insecurities

We all have shadow aspects within us: fears, sore spots, old wounds, and repressed memories that haven't been fully healed. Guess what? There's no need to identify with your shadow. In fact, all it does is hinder you in your life experiences. Your soul and your ego's fears are two different things. Separate yourself from them—visualize them floating away while in meditation if you must! Your insecurities are not an aspect of your identity, so free yourself from them. They are only holding you back from soaring.

Cultivate Resilience

Nature teaches us the power in resilience. Take a look at spiders, for instance. Humans and the natural elements always seem to find a way to knock down a spider's web. Whether through rainfall, a gust of wind, a broom, or a vacuum, it seems like spiders can never catch a break. But notice how spiders always get back up and start weaving once again, almost immediately. They don't stop and contemplate whether starting again is worthwhile. They don't have an emotional breakdown or doubt their abilities. They display resilience. Spiders will continue to weave, even if it takes all afternoon to do it.

Let conflict be a lesson. Let enemies be teachers. *Let challenge lead to growth.* Sometimes a total collapse is necessary for epic transformation. Ruin is often needed before liberation. As Nelson

Mandala once said, "I never lose. I win or I learn." Find those hidden lessons. Make this a priority going forward! Don't let life dictate every emotional wave that washes over you; steer your ship and cultivate grit. Strengthen your resilience to bounce back when life tears down your creation. This is how we take control over our darkest thoughts.

Trust in Invisible Signs

There is something quite magical about feeling an interconnectedness with life. When you have faith that you are not alone in this journey, but rather supported in the unfolding of life itself, your energy radiates. This is a feeling of infinite trust. Perhaps we feel this interconnectedness when we're watching the sunset, seeing a dazzling rainbow sweep across the sky, holding our children, or falling in love. It's a feeling of unity and oneness. These feelings, when experienced, help us trust in the invisible nature of life that is always guiding, protecting, and supporting us. Start trusting in the invisible nature of this world. Have hope that answers will abound. Ask for what you wish out loud and regularly. Pour your heart out in a message, roll it up into a bottle, and send it out to sea. Ask for a message to be given to you in your dreams and trust that it will come. Answers never come in exactly the way we want. They may come later, in a different place, or from a different source than expected. But trust that the answer will come when you need it most. Our minds are so desperate to cling to something tangible. Our minds are so thirsty for certainty. Instead, try remaining observant, neutral, and curious. Trust that you'll be ready when it comes, and you'll take the necessary action to move forward.

Just Start

Sometimes the best way to get out of a negative spiral is to get moving. Just take the single first step. Put on some music, set a timer for twenty minutes, and just start. When fear bubbles forth, ask yourself, *What's the worst that can happen?* Sit in that and observe it. How does your body respond? Now ask yourself, *What's the best that can happen?* Quiet self-reflection is often where we receive our greatest insights. Listen to the pulse of your heart and allow your intuition to take you forward. Then, physicalize it. Don't think about it; *just start.*

Reframe Setbacks as Setups

Approach pivots and interruptions in your life as detours. Reframe your setbacks in life as setups for something new. Train your mind to see the possibilities. There are hidden gifts all around us. Did your appointment cancel? Look at it as a chance to have some needed leisure time. Did the job offer not come through? It's possible you dodged a bullet, and that job wouldn't have made you happy anyway. Maybe there's a potential for something better to come your way.

I've experienced many personal setbacks that turned out to be setups farther down the road. One of these setbacks led me to move to France, which in the big-picture scope of my life gave me infinitely more joy and fulfillment than my failed dreams ever would have. One of the personal setbacks I experienced was not getting a job offer after auditioning to be a princess character performer at Tokyo Disneyland. Since I was a teenager, I have dreamed of living and working in Japan as a Disney princess. I spent months leading up to the audition preparing my princess movements (each princess has a distinct wave and curtsey!), working out every day in the gym, and brushing up on my improv. When the day finally came to take the long bus ride to New York, I had my hair curled and my headshot and resume ready to go! I arrived at the audition at Pearl Studios and, within five minutes, all the girls were placed in a line as the casting director stared at our faces and profiles, determining who would stay and who would go. Within five minutes, I was cut and sent home. Incredibly disappointed at not having a chance at the dance or improv audition, I did leave with a tiny ounce of hope. My audition number was thirty-three (my favorite number), and I took it as a sign that something better would come to me. *Perhaps this just wasn't the right time.* Disappointed, I had no idea at the time that, several months later, my husband would get a job offer in France and we would begin the most joyful period of my life—one that gave me more wisdom and life experience than I ever could've gained working at Disneyland, one that offered us security and financial stability during the COVID-19 outbreak, and one that inspired me to become a filmmaker and ultimately get the chance to write this book.

That is what a setback turned setup looks like. Look at your missed opportunities as detours to something better. When we look back at the grand scheme of our lives, we'll always find moments when a missed opportunity led to a more aligned outcome. Sometimes a setback is a setup to something better, even if we can't see it yet. Every locked door is an open window leading somewhere else.

Lean into Discomfort

What if we learned to find appreciation in the contrast of life? What if contrast, or experiencing what we *don't* want, leads us to clarity? Contrast helps us refine our values, our preferences, and what we want. If we only experience good things, we will never know what we don't want. This contrast is crucial.

What if there was a way to find appreciation in the contrast? Or at least, *acceptance* in the unpreferable moments?

The hard reality is that living a joy-filled life is not only about appreciation. Living a life of inner peace and eternal joy is also about reflecting on that which you *don't* have. It's noting what is painful. In hard times, we need to lean into discomfort. There is a certain beauty in learning how to overcome, even *accept*, the challenges that are part of life. There is a peculiar elegance in letting go. It's bittersweet, but so is life. Life is not all sunshine, rainbows, and daffodils, as much as my fellow optimists and life enthusiasts like to think. Life is also filled with discomfort.

Without reflection, we repress our wide spectrum of human emotion. What would life be without growth? What would life be if we were all masters? A complete bore, a total snooze fest! So lean into it. Start to appreciate the contrast, for there is clarity to be found and preferences to be discovered.

Redirect Your Focus to Something New

One of the best ways to move forward in life is to try *new* things. Experience novelty. The best way to get over heartbreak is to start dating again. The easiest way to move on from a failed business venture is to pick up a new interest and throw all your new ideas on a blank canvas. The easiest way to deal with overwhelm is to slow down and limit your options. One of the best things you can do when you feel anxiety is to count down from a hundred in increments of three. The simple act of closing our eyes and counting can dramatically reduce feelings of stress and panic. This has gotten me through my own experiences of anxiety, and my family and friends have found it incredibly helpful as well. Obsessive, fearful thoughts can be redirected when we focus on something *new*.

Lean into Your Triggers

We all have specific triggers that set us off, and they are each quite unique to us. These triggers point to where we need healing. Certain triggers will repeat throughout our lives, in different situations, with different people. Be patient with yourself when these triggers arise. Look at every person in your life, not as an enemy, nor as a friend, but as a teacher. Make peace with having to go through similar hurts and triggers more than once. Look at every situation as a test, a lesson that wants to be learned, an experience that needs to be had. This is the evolution of *you!* Explore the nooks and crannies beneath each trigger until you find the core theme you're looking for. Write them down, and ponder on them: Where did this trigger originate? Where does this story *begin* for me? Become a detective; inquire about every dark thought, every fear, every insecurity. Discover each origin.

When we experience dark thoughts, we can either attach ourselves to them, or we can remain curious and learn from them. We can choose suffering, or we can choose neutrality. We can identify with our fears and worry ourselves to bits, or we can inquire and go deeper. Take a brave step forward and look it curiously in the eye.

Accepting Death

"When you learn how to die, you learn how to live."

—Morrie

One of the most peaceful ways to accept what is outside of your control in life is to remember that life will go on without you. When you feel afraid, it's helpful to meditate on what it means to be alive and what it means to die. Society is curiously perturbed by death. We are so afraid of it, we can't even talk about it.

As children, we learn to be afraid of graveyards and ghosts, and as adults, we fear the loss of potential, the ticking hands of time. We feel desperately called to leave behind a legacy that will outlive us. But when you're having fun, you don't worry about those ideas. When we contemplate the big picture of our lives on earth, we reconcile having very little time here. Our time is fleeting. Most of us will not be remembered in the grand scheme of it all. The majority of us will be forgotten pixie dust. Perhaps our grandchildren will remember us, maybe our great-grandchildren. Beyond that, we will be forgotten. To some, this sounds extremely dire. But does it not, in some small sense, make you heave a sigh of relief? *The pressure is off*. When you look death in the face, you no longer sweat the small stuff. You no longer care what anyone else thinks of you, or whether you're being impressive enough to your clients, your boss, or the guy you're dating. None of the stresses, at the end of your life, matter. What matters is how we spent the time we had, that we had fun and followed our excitements along the way.

It's critical that we harness the courage to live our lives the way we want to live them. It's *imperative* that we slow our lives down enough that we can drink in this beautiful opportunity of living, breathing existence. We must prioritize our desires, the inner callings of our hearts, and live fully according to our own value systems before attempting to change our lifestyles and dreams to suit someone else's. When you meditate on the concept of death, when you realize what it means to be fully alive, you realize the silliness in the drama of daily problems. At the end of the day, at the end of life, all that matters is that you had fun while you were here.

Don't speed through the journey of life; enjoy the adventure, the unfolding of all that is unknown. Those relationships in your life, the people around you—they aren't going to be there one day. Your job, the work you're engaged in right now, isn't going to be your job forever. I know we all *know* we're going to die, but I don't believe many of us have truly come to grips with it. When you experience a sudden death in your life, your life comes into focus. When you realize how fragile and fleeting a life is, you start to appreciate it more. You become grateful for what you have.

There's this practice in Buddhism where one meditates on an early death—the potentiality, the possibility, of it coming earlier than expected. In it, one meditates on bringing death into the middle of one's life. We live in a death-phobic society, where the idea of death and loss of potential is seen as terrible. This is rooted in our attachment, both to our own identity and to the cultivated identities of others. Thus, letting go of this attachment to the self, the identity, is so important.

What if we reframed our view of this inevitable unfolding? To fear death less, we need to first accept that early and sudden death is possible.

For those who have experienced the sudden death of a friend or loved one, you may feel death *wakes you up* to what it means to be fully alive. Perhaps you too are no longer shocked when others pass suddenly. This is acceptance—acceptance of what our mortal human agreement to life entails. While my dad's sudden passing inspired me to live my life more fully and courageously, ultimately never taking a single day for granted, I have still always been afraid of an early, premature death. The fear I have of losing time, of not fully experiencing all the magical opportunities this life has to offer, has greatly encouraged me to deepen my study in Buddhism, specifically the silent contemplation and meditation of accepting my own death. Through meditation, we learn to be accepting of the challenges that may arise. Developing a contemplative practice actually helps find peace in these harder topics. The more you confront your fears—actually sit with them and look them in the face—the less you will be afraid. The more you honor your fears by making space for them to be there, labeling them, and accepting them as they are, the smaller they become, and the more courageous you grow as a result. To accept death, at any time and any age, is the most courageous act of all.

We find peace by accepting life as it is. This comes in the form of surrendering to life's mysteries, practicing a nonjudgmental outlook on life, and acquiring a level of detachment from the outcomes of life over which you have no control. To believe we have full control of our lives is foolish. There is only so much preparation one can do; healthy habits and a positive mindset can only take one so far. Like driving, you can be the best, safest driver on the road, but there will always be reckless drivers out there. We have only so much control over the life we've been given. There is something mystical about timing, a poetic elegance in remembering the divineness in time. We are a single drop in the ocean, but a purposeful one. We chose to be here now, at this present time in life's history, and we chose to take part in this adventure. Take hold of the reins and have fun on the ride. Everything in this life is temporary, so appreciate today.

Life will move on without us. People will move on, people will forget. Whether it's dying or getting fired, being dumped or moving away, people will move on. You can, too. The only thing that matters in the end is love—love in ourselves, love in others, and love in life. Let love cradle and consume you. Time is the ultimate healer of wounds, but don't allow time to make you forget what really matters.

Living *fully* asks us to live openly, generously, and in total and complete trust. We must trust in life if we are to celebrate it.

Remember that you can't ever get this life wrong. No matter how many paths are presented to you, or however many directions you could take with your life, you will inevitably get to where you're meant to be. You can change your mind and head in the opposite direction from where you've been heading. You can take a sharp detour. You can carve out your own path, one that will take a little longer, maybe even one that'll present more challenges along the way. But you will always get to the spot where you are meant to arrive. *How freeing is that?*

So many of us are constantly worried about making a mistake, taking the wrong path in life, or tempting fate by taking a gamble. Sweet soul, have compassion for yourself. Nurture your tender heart and trust yourself. Your life is planned, for you, and *by* you. You cannot get this life wrong. What's for you will never go past you. Life will choose the how, the when, and the what. Your only job is to remain open to life's mysteries and take small, consistent actions every day that feel fun and inspiring. Trust in this life that has been so generously given to you. Please have patience for yourself when you feel worry or doubt. I am right here cheerin' you on.

Final Words

After living in the countryside and integrating a slower pace into my own life, I often wonder if I would ever survive living in a big city again. I wonder about daily life in fast-moving cities like Paris, London, and Tokyo. *Would I really be able to handle it?* Amidst the hustle and bustle, would I remember to live in a peaceful, slow way in a place where it isn't the norm? Would I stay true to myself by staying focused and present on my timelines, my own values, or would I get distracted and merge lanes with the big dreamers and goal-chasers who frequently flock to those cities?

While I believe we are powerful beings with the ability to choose our thoughts and emotions, I also believe that where we *choose* to live has a direct impact on our daily energy reserves. Our environment influences our emotions, but with patience, awareness, and self-discipline, we can all live slowly in even the most hectic of urban jungles. It just takes a bit more intention and self-reflection. It requires more focus and diligence in our daily habits—our morning and evening routines, upholding boundaries, remembering our big-picture priorities, and constant questioning ("Will this make me happy and bring me fulfillment?").

It is possible to live slowly anywhere. We are adaptable, conscious creators of our own realities. When the world moves fast, we can choose to live slow. When the people around us want more, we can be happy with less. That's the amazing thing about being human: We can *choose* to follow the rhythms and pace of our own hearts, bodies, and minds.

Today, when I venture to cities like Paris, New York, or Rome, I maintain my equilibrium. When your life is guided by your heart, and not the fear-based obsessions of "should," "FOMO," and doing "enough," you can find your center. In even the most chaotic and stressful environments, we can go back to our breath, our values, the big-picture perspective.

We can choose to go slow.

Selectivity is about being intentional about where we give and place our energy. You realize what is essential and the speed at which you need to move to thrive. You see the *energetics* in all aspects of life.

If there is only one thing you can take away from this book, it's to follow your inner voice. No one knows the best path or pace for you, more than you. You have all the answers. It requires stillness and being selective with what works for you and what doesn't. There is no need to look to a guru, guide, or person you admire to know the wisdom meant for you. You already have a compass: your intuition. Living slowly is one way to deepen that connection. When you live in total alignment with your core authentic self, in both rhythm and speed, and you further deepen that trust in yourself. *Honor your energy.* Honor your dreams.

Lastly, remember, that living a slow life isn't meant to look any certain way. My life is not perfect. It isn't glamorous or filled with an excess of abundance or pretty things. It is, however, one that feels free, present, and authentic to me. In living slowly, I've become free from the confines of societal pressures. I've released the restraints that control so many. I live with total peace and ease of mind, knowing I am supported by life, in all its unfoldings. I follow the flow of life and allow it to take me where I'm meant to be. This trusting nature developed when I started living slowly and intuitively. When I started honoring my inner voice and simplifying the excess in my life, through what I consume, what I buy, where I place my energy and attention. It was then that my world began to slow down.

In the beginning of this book, I mentioned that I have been living in France for four years and still don't know what there is to *do* here. I questioned whether that was enough. Is *not doing* enough? Is living and breathing enough of a reason to take up space?

The answer is a definite yes. Simply existing is enough. You, being here, breathing and living, are a miracle. Your worth is not in any of the things you do or the speed at which you move through life; it's in your miraculous existence on this divine planet.

We have purpose even in our not doing. We have *meaning* in our inaction. No matter the speed, no matter the dream, if you live authentically, you can't go wrong. I hope this book sharing what I've learned and ingrained on my own slow-living journey inspires you to experience a life that works for *you.*

Design a lifestyle that caters to your innermost callings.
Create a life that matches the speed of your soul.
Listen to your inner callings and flow with your natural, divine expression.
Dance on with life, sweet soul. Life is a ride, one meant to be enjoyed.

P.S.

Thank you so much for picking up this book and spending your sweet, precious time on earth with these words. I truly hope you took something away from it that revitalizes your soul and refreshes your life a little! In my experience, creators and writers desire to connect with their audience—and I am no exception! Human connection and sharing with one another is what we all desire on a deep core level. *I would love to connect with you.*

You have a standing invitation to share the lessons and stories you've been experiencing on your slow living journey on my Youtube community Discord or within the private "Simple Joys" Facebook group! It's a fun place for us all to connect and share our simple joys. I also happily welcome all reader feedback. If you like the book, please send me a note and let me know (helenawoodsblog@gmail.com), and please post a review on Amazon. Your review would really help get this book and message out to more kindred spirits who may resonate with it.

Thank you again for joining me on this slow (and magical!) journey. Enjoy the unfolding.

Acknowledgments

A huge thank you to Natasha, Julianna, and the team at Mango for helping make my dream of writing and publishing a book come true! Thank you for your warm encouragement, edits, and walking me through the process of book publishing.

I wouldn't have been able to have this dream happen without my sweet kindred spirits on YouTube. Thank you for your love and support over these years. I adore our community and how similar we all are in what we value and appreciate: life's simple joys.

I'd love to thank my darling love and husband, Alex. Thanks for teaming through life with me. I couldn't have finished this book without your motivation and steadfast belief in me.

And finally, to my mother, for always providing me with plenty of journals as a child. Thank you for always encouraging me to share my heart through the written word and to stand true in my sparkle.

About the Author

Helena Woods is a blogger, astrologer, world traveler, and filmmaker on YouTube. In March 2020, she launched her YouTube channel documenting her slow, simple life in France. Her work is focused on inspiring others to honor their inner voice, enjoy the present moment through slowing down, and notice the simple joys around us.

When she's not inspired by the natural world and her cultural experiences while living around the world, she's an astrocartographer, helping clients find the most supportive energies in the world to travel and relocate to. Helena is passionate about the sea, stars, and writing old-fashioned letters with a quill. In her free time, she's often gushing over cats or planning a Disney trip with her husband, Alex.

Mango Publishing, established in 2014, publishes an eclectic list of books by diverse authors—both new and established voices—on topics ranging from business, personal growth, women's empowerment, LGBTQ+ studies, health, and spirituality to history, popular culture, time management, decluttering, lifestyle, mental wellness, aging, and sustainable living. We were recently named 2019 *and* 2020's #1 fastest-growing independent publisher by *Publishers Weekly*. Our success is driven by our main goal, which is to publish high-quality books that will entertain readers as well as make a positive difference in their lives.

Our readers are our most important resource; we value your input, suggestions, and ideas. We'd love to hear from you—after all, we are publishing books for you!

Please stay in touch with us and follow us at:

Facebook: Mango Publishing
Twitter: @MangoPublishing
Instagram: @MangoPublishing
LinkedIn: Mango Publishing
Pinterest: Mango Publishing
Newsletter: mangopublishinggroup.com/newsletter

Join us on Mango's journey to reinvent publishing, one book at a time.